A VERY EXPENSIVE POISON

The Definitive Story of the Murder of Litvinenko and Russia's War with the West

LUKE HARDING

First published in 2016
by Guardian Books, Kings Place, 90 York Way, London N1 9GU
and Faber and Faber Ltd, Bloomsbury House,
74–77 Great Russell Street, London WC1B 3DA

A CIP record for this book is available from the British Library

ISBN 978-1-78335-0933

Typeset by seagulls.net

Printed and bound by CPI Group (UK) Ltd, Croydon, CR0 4YY

2 4 6 8 10 9 7 5 3 1

Contents

Dioxin: Any of three unsaturated heterocyclic compounds, two having the formula $C_4H_6O_2$ and the third $C_4H_4O_2$

Gelsemium: A colourless, inodorous, bitter alkaloidal substance obtained from the root of *G. sempervirens*

Polonium: A highly radioactive metallic element, discovered in 1898 by Professor and Marie Curie in pitchblende

Ricin: An extremely toxic lectin present in the seeds of the castor oil plant, *Ricinus communis.*

Thallium: The chemical element of atomic number 81, a soft silvery-white metal which occurs naturally in small amounts in iron pyrites, sphalerite and other ores. Its compounds are very poisonous (symbol: Tl)

Source: *Oxford English Dictionary*

Prologue:
The Men from Moscow

Passport control, Gatwick Airport, Sussex
16 October 2006

Two of the Russians arriving that morning stood out. What precisely made them suspicious was hard to identify. But in the mind of Spencer Scott – the detective constable on duty at London's Gatwick Airport – there was a curious sense of doubt. It was 16 October 2006. Passengers were disembarking from a Transaero flight from Moscow. They were collecting luggage. A stream of new arrivals queued up at passport control, and then proceeded for customs and excise checks.

The first Russian was of medium height, thirty-something, with blond Slavic hair. He was wearing a casual jacket and carrying an expensive-looking leather laptop case. He appeared prosperous. The second, with dark hair, receding slightly, and a yellowish complexion, was clearly his companion. They weren't behaving oddly as such. And yet there was something – a furtiveness that pricked Detective Constable Scott's attention.

'I though they were of interest and basically as they came through immigration controls I stopped them and questioned them,' he recalled. Scott hadn't been told to look out for them; he was acting on a hunch. He asked

[1]

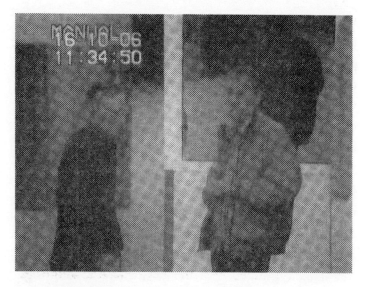

them their names. One man spoke English and identified himself as Andrei Lugovoi. His friend, he said, was Dmitry Kovtun. Kovtun said nothing. It appeared he spoke only Russian. Scott took a grainy low-res photo of them. Lugovoi was on the right. In it they look like dark ghostly smudges. It was 11.34 a.m.

Lugovoi and Kovtun's story seemed convincing enough: they had flown into London for a business meeting. Lugovoi said he owned a company called Global Project. Moreover, his friend was a member of the finance department at a respectable Moscow bank. Their travel agent had booked them in for two nights at the Best Western Hotel in Shaftesbury Avenue. The hotel wasn't cheap: £300 a night. Lugovoi handed over his reservation. It was genuine.

Still, there was something unsettling about their answers, Scott felt: 'They were very evasive as to why they were coming to the UK.' Normally, those subjected to a random stop would open up – about families, holiday plans, the lousy English weather. The two Russians, by contrast, were elusive. 'As I asked them questions, they weren't coming out with the answers that I wanted to hear or expected to hear. They were giving me very, very short answers,' Scott said. Their replies offered 'no information'.

Scott looked on the internet but couldn't find Global Project. The Russians told him that their business meeting was with 'Continental Petroleum Limited', a company based at 58 Grosvenor Street in London. Scott rang the firm's landline. A man answered, confirmed they were registered with the UK's financial authority. OK, then. The constable checked the police database. Nothing. Britain's intelligence agencies, MI5 and MI6, hadn't flagged Lugovoi and Kovtun either. Apparently, they weren't of interest.

A copper's nose was one thing; hard facts another. With no evidence to go on, Scott took soundings from his sergeant, who advised him to let both men 'go forward'. Britain's judicial and police system rests on a presumption of innocence – unlike in Russia, Lugovoi and Kovtun's homeland, where judges take informal guidance from above. After twenty minutes the Russians were told they were free to leave. They collected their luggage and headed for central London. Scott put their photo in a file. It was stamped: 'For intelligence purposes only.'

It was little more than a month later that Scotland Yard – faced with a situation of unprecedented international horror – realised Scott's instinct had been preternaturally correct. The two weren't businessmen. They were killers. Their cover story was just that. It had been painstakingly constructed over a period of months, possibly years. And it worked.

That morning, Lugovoi and Kovtun were bringing something into Britain that customs had failed to detect. Not drugs, or large sums of cash. Something so rare and strange and otherworldly, it had never been seen before in this form in Europe or America.

It was, as Kovtun put it, talking in confidence to a friend in Hamburg, 'a very expensive poison'. A toxin which had started its surreptitious journey to London from a secret nuclear complex in south-west Siberia. An invisible hi-tech murder weapon.

Lugovoi and Kovtun were to use it to kill a man named Alexander Litvinenko. Litvinenko was a Russian émigré who had fled to Britain six years previously. He'd become a persistent pain for the Russian government. He was a remorseless critic of Vladimir Putin, Russia's secret policeman turned president. By 2006, Litvinenko was increasingly anomalous: back in Russia many sources of opposition has been squashed.

There was a particular reason why Putin might want Litvinenko dead. Before escaping in 2000, Litvinenko had worked for the FSB, Russia's intelligence service, and the main successor agency to the KGB. Putin himself had been, briefly, his boss. But Litvinenko now had another employer: Britain's secret intelligence service, MI6.

Her Majesty's Government had given Litvinenko a fake British passport, an encrypted phone and a salary of £2,000 a month, paid anonymously into his HSBC account and appearing on his bank statement incongruously next to his groceries from Waitrose. He had an MI6 case officer, codenamed 'Martin'.

Litvinenko wasn't exactly James Bond. But he was passing to British intelligence sensitive information about the links between Russian mafia gangs active in Europe and powerful people at the very top of Russian power – including Putin. According to Litvinenko, Russian ministers and their mobster friends were, in effect, part of the same sprawling crime syndicate. A mafia state. It was his contention that a criminal code had replaced the defunct ideology of communism.

Litvinenko knew about this mafia's activities in Spain; he was, in the words of one friend, a walking encyclopedia on organised crime. So much so that MI6 loaned him out to colleagues from Spanish intelligence in Madrid.

All of this made Litvinenko a traitor, and the KGB's punishment for spies who betrayed their country was understood. From the very beginning of the Bolshevik revolution in 1917, Moscow had used poisons, bullets, bombs hidden in cakes and other lethal methods to snuff out its 'enemies', at home and abroad, from Leon Trotsky to Georgi Markov, the Bulgarian dissident and writer poisoned on Waterloo Bridge in 1978 with an ingenious ricin-tipped umbrella. As Stalin famously observed, 'No man, no problem.'

There was a spectrum. It went from killings that were demonstrative, to those where the KGB's fingerprints were nowhere to be found, however hard you looked.

Boris Yeltsin had stayed those methods in the post-communist 1990s; the KGB's poison factory seemingly mothballed; Russia's democrats briefly in the ascendant. Now, under Putin, such methods were back. The FSB was Russia's pre-eminent institution. It was all-powerful, beyond the law, and – like its Leninist predecessors – a purveyor of state terror.

In the glory days of the Soviet Union, the KGB dispatched professionals and undercover 'illegals' to carry out extra-judicial murders – known in the spy trade as 'wet jobs'. Lugovoi and Kovtun's mission to London was supposed to be exactly such an operation: ruthless, clinical, undetectable – an iron fist concealed in a velvet glove. It was to be done in the best traditions of the *Cheka*, the counter-revolutionary police force founded by Felix Dzerzhinsky, Lenin's friend. Dzerzhinsky's statuette with its cold, pinched features sat in Putin's office.

But, despite a resurgence under Putin, Russia's spy agencies had suffered the same degradation that had blighted all Russian institutions – the presidency, Russia's parliament or Duma, medicine, science and technology. Critics said the country, despite its great power pretensions, was slowly dying. Its modern assassins were a shambolic lot.

The idea was that nobody would notice the visiting Russians. Once they had poisoned their victim they would escape back to Moscow, leaving few ripples on the busy surface of London life. Their target, of course, would die horribly. But the Kremlin's hand would be hidden. The British would mark his death down as a baffling case of gastro-enteritis and those who carried out the murder would return to a life of shadowy anonymity. And, one imagines, reward. The payment for murder, Kovtun hinted, was a Moscow flat.

It didn't quite work out like that. Russia's poisoning project, when finally accomplished, would prompt a British public inquiry costing millions of pounds. One that examined the masses of evidence collected by the Metropolitan Police, from hotels, restaurants, car seats – even from a bronze phallus at a nightclub visited by the assassins in Soho. Scotland Yard was able to reconstruct minute by minute the events leading up to the murder. Its investigation – made public more than eight years later – was one of the most extensive in criminal history.

Yet despite this exposure there were soon to be other victims – opponents felled in murky circumstances abroad or, like the opposition leader Boris Nemtsov, killed outside the very gates of the Kremlin. Moscow would send tanks across borders, start a war in Europe, and annex a large chunk of neighbouring territory. Its proxies – or possibly Russian servicemen – would blow a civilian plane out of the sky.

The common theme here was contempt: a poisonous disregard for human life. For Vladimir Putin's critics have an uncanny habit of turning up dead.

1

Mafia State

Russia, 1988–1999

'You realise, of course, that you can be poisoned
here and we cannot really help you?'
UNKNOWN FSB OFFICER TO ALEXANDER LITVINENKO,
BUTYRKA PRISON, MOSCOW, 1999

In September 2006, in London, the exiled Litvinenko
put the finishing touches to a secret report. It was explosive stuff. The subject was Viktor Ivanov, one of Vladimir
Putin's closest friends and top advisers. Ivanov was a
career KGB officer, the head of Russia's powerful federal
anti-narcotics agency, and one of very few people who
had 'direct access' to the ear of the president.

Ivanov – so the report alleged – was also a vindictive, sociopathic 'monster', with long-standing links to
the St Petersburg mafia. This mafia in turn did business
with Colombian drug-smugglers. Putin, so the report
said, had connections with the same mafia gang in what
was Russia's most criminalised city. He even advised the
board of one of the mafia's front companies.

The report included colourful details about Ivanov's
biography. According to Litvinenko, he'd been a mediocre spy. While his colleagues were sent on important
overseas missions, Ivanov had been shuffled into the

human resources department of Leningrad's KGB office – 'a sort of dump place', as the report put it, and 'the dead and gloomy end of a professional career'. It continued: 'Other KGB men treated human resources people with contempt.'

In human resources, however, Ivanov made useful discoveries. He found himself well placed to collect compromising information on his KGB comrades. He could use this *kompromat* to destroy other people's careers. Ivanov also developed a set of personal operational rules that would allow him to thrive in the KGB. And to overleap his more able but less crafty co-workers. His two years serving in Afghanistan – invaded by the Soviet Union in 1979 – confirmed to Ivanov the efficacy of these insights.

Rule one: it was important never to come up with an initiative in the KGB. If you did you'd be asked to implement it and then punished for not doing it successfully. According to the report, Ivanov was silent in meetings. He transformed himself into 'a sort of professional Mr Nobody'. Rule two: he realised it was necessary to suck up to anybody more senior in the KGB's hierarchy – to recognise who had 'more rights in a bureaucratic sense'. The boss was always right.

Ivanov's rise coincided with the collapse of the Soviet Union, and followed a late-1980s order from the KGB's top brass to go into business. At the time, the only people who understood the free market were criminals. Ivanov established relations with the Tambovskaya crime gang and its leader Viktor Kumarin, a villain with a mop of dark hair and a neat moustache. Kumarin was then embroiled in a major turf war with his rival Alexander Malyshev, and Malyshev's gangster army.

The prize was control of St Petersburg's seaport. The port was a major trans-shipment facility for Colombian drugs, which arrived here before continuing their lucrative journey to Western Europe. According to Litvinenko, Ivanov helped Kumarin wipe out the competition. In return, he got a share of the seaport's business. The Tambovskaya group structured its criminal activities via a series of subsidiaries and daughter companies; Ivanov set up firms of his own, 'Block' and 'Basis'.

It was the early 1990s. Another KGB spy helped Ivanov. This was Vladimir Putin. Officially, he was no longer with the *kontora* – as the KGB styled itself. Instead, he was working for St Petersburg's new mayor, Anatoly Sobchak. As every recruit knew, though, hardly anybody ever quite leaves the KGB. The two spies, Ivanov and Putin, had something else in common: the KGB had marked them down as second-raters, mediocrities unfit for high office, something they must have resented.

Litvinenko's report said: 'Ironically, while Ivanov was cooperating with the gangsters, he was promoted to the operational department of [the] fight against smuggling and became its boss. His former subordinates described him as a monster boss – rude, authoritative and stubborn. It was a time when the line between the law enforcement officers and professional criminals was often very thin.'

The next paragraph reads: 'While Ivanov was cooperating with gangsters, he was protected by Vladimir Putin, who was responsible for foreign economic relations at the office of St Petersburg mayor Anatoly Sobchak.' It adds: 'Putin was himself not Mr Clean at that time.'

This was something of an understatement. Links between Putin and the criminal underworld turned up in all sorts of places. The report quoted leaked tape-recordings made in 2000 of Leonid Kuchma, Ukraine's then-president, who said his own spy agency had got hold of documents concerning a German company named SPAG that was a front for criminal activities. Its main job was 'laundering [the] money of a Colombian drug cartel by buying out real estate in St Petersburg'. Kumarin, the gangster, sat on the board of a SPAG daughter company. Putin, in the mayor's office, was SPAG's adviser.

Gangsters, cocaine, the KGB, spies, sleaze, millions of dollars in cash – all of it on Europe's doorstep, as Russia morphed in the late twentieth century from communist dictatorship to a new and murky form of hyper-capitalism. It was, as the report frankly put it, a 'weird time'. The masters of this changing universe were organised criminals and their upwardly mobile friends in Russian politics. What Ivanov and Putin were allegedly doing wasn't unusual for the standards of the time: taking a cut here, a bribe there. Everybody did that, given a chance.

What was unusual was that they would go on to rule the Russian Federation.

Litvinenko's 2006 report amounted to an eight-page hand grenade, tossed into the control room of Russian power. It was written for RISC management, a British security company based in London. RISC specialised in due diligence. This meant carrying out extensive checks on Russian firms and prominent individuals at the behest of western businesses. Such reports involved a mixture of official and more sensitive secret sources.

Litvinenko provided the detail on the St Petersburg mafia and its activities in the 1990s. Another exile actually wrote the report, a former KGB major called Yuri B. Shvets. Shvets was everything that Putin and Ivanov weren't. He was an intelligent and enterprising secret agent blessed with literary gifts. Tall, handsome, and with a sweeping mane of dark black hair, he looked every inch the romantic spy abroad. The KGB had recruited him in 1980, inviting him to join its prestigious external intelligence service, the First Chief Directorate.

Shvets had studied at the Patrice Lumumba People's Friendship University in Moscow. It was, he wrote, a surprisingly liberal institution by the standards of the late USSR, which attracted young men and women from ninety different countries. He described himself in his memoir as 'neither a convinced communist nor a dissident'. Not all of the university's students were so politically ambivalent: one of Shvets's predecessors was a Marxist-Leninist from Venezuela named Ilich Ramirez Sanchez. Sanchez, Shvets wrote later, was not your typical student, spending most of his time away and abroad. He would become better known as the terrorist Carlos the Jackal.

After graduation, Shvets spent two years at the Yuri Andropov Red Banner Intelligence Institute. The KGB training school was based in a pleasant forest in Yurlovo, not far from Moscow. There, he said, he was taught the secrets of the trade. He learned from legendary spymasters who had worked with the Cold War's most famous western defectors – the Rosenbergs, who stole the US's atomic secrets, and the upper-class Cambridge spy ring, Kim Philby, Guy Burgess and Donald Maclean.

Shvets also did a two-month training stint with a Spetsnaz or special forces unit. He parachuted from planes, learned how to handle a variety of weapons and to plant mines. He was taught how to blow up bridges and to interrogate enemy prisoners. He learned guerrilla tactics. He was instructed not to think or query the state. Shvets recalled how one wiry paratrooper colonel told him: 'Your duty is to execute, at any cost, any task assigned by our motherland.'

One of Shvets's classmates at the KGB academy was Putin. Putin had grown up in a working-class family in Leningrad; an older brother died during the Nazi siege of the city; his grandfather was Lenin's cook. As a teenager he learned judo to defend himself from neighbourhood toughs. From an early age he aspired to join the KGB, inspired – he later said – by the Soviet TV spy drama *The Shield and the Sword*. He studied law. The KGB recruited him in 1975 after he finished Leningrad University.

Putin's world view reflected the *a priori* thinking of the KGB. The agency was suspicious, paranoid and prone to conspiratorial reasoning. Putin was convinced that the US and the western world were engaged in an unsleeping plot against the Soviet Union.

Virtually all the graduates from the KGB institute got jobs afterwards in the first directorate and were sent to foreign 'residencies', as the KGB termed its covert offices abroad. For reasons which are mysterious, Putin didn't make the grade, Shvets believed. 'Putin belonged to the 1 per cent of losers. He was sent back to St Petersburg,' he said later. Others say Putin went back to his home city and was given the task of recruiting foreigners on Soviet soil. In 1984, Putin did eventually get a foreign assignment. After a second year-long stint at the institute he was moved to Dresden, in the GDR.

Between 1985 and 1987, Shvets found himself in the more glamorous setting of Washington, under journalistic cover at the Soviet embassy. He was a correspondent for TASS, the Russian news agency. He became disillusioned with the Soviet Union and, in particular, the KGB. By the 1980s, the KGB had virtually no sources in the west, he thought; instead, its operatives churned out a series of meaningless reports for incompetent and risk-averse bureaucrat-generals back at the 'centre' in Moscow.

Shvets quit the KGB in 1990 and sought political asylum in the US. From there he published a lively espionage memoir, *Washington Station: My Life as a KGB Spy In America*, which described his successful recruitment of an unnamed American agent, codenamed 'Socrates'. He began writing due-diligence reports for American corporations seeking to cash in on the new post-communist Russia.

One of the skills Shvets learned at KGB school was analysis: how to craft and present the perfect intelligence report. Often it would include a psychological pen-portrait of a target. The best of these telegrams were done with swift, compressed strokes.

The Litvinenko–Shvets dossier on Ivanov fitted this model. Under a heading titled 'personal characteristics', it described Ivanov as 'a very complex man with [a] difficult personality'. It went on to say: 'He is masterful at understanding the balance of forces around him, identifies the latent leaders (very important in the surreal world of Russian bureaucracy) and is highly capable of using his knowledge to his personal benefit.' If offended, Ivanov could become your 'worst enemy'. He had a 'vindictive' streak and would try to identify and then 'punish' anyone who leaked 'negative information' about him.

It ended: 'Many representatives of the new generation of the Russian leaders view Ivanov as a remnant of the past who fits more to Joseph Stalin times than to the modern environment. A source who worked with Ivanov told us that Ivanov apparently has a latent complex of inferiority. He apparently realises that he is not intellectually smart and compensates this by Byzantine-style intrigue, in which he feels himself on his turf.'

Litvinenko and Shvets were a good team. Shvets had a wide network of intelligence sources inside Russia who provided him with real information. Litvinenko, meanwhile, had worked for the FSB in the 1990s in the department tasked with fighting organised crime. He had direct knowledge of its operations. Litvinenko's English was poor, but Shvets, a long-term resident of the US, could write in fluent sentences. They worked together via email and phone calls from America to Britain.

On 19 September 2006, Litvinenko gave the eight-page report to RISC. Litvinenko also passed a copy of the report to another man, a Moscow-based business partner whom he had no reason to mistrust: one Andrei Lugovoi. Doing this was clearly dangerous, but Litvinenko had known the wealthy businessman for over ten years, had been working closely with him for the previous twelve months and believed him to be trustworthy. They had similar backgrounds: both were ex-KGB, moved in Berezovsky's circle and apparently shared grievances against the Russian state. Indeed, Litvinenko had previously commissioned Lugovoi to write his own version of a dossier on Viktor Ivanov. When it arrived from Moscow, this second Lugovoi report was 'trash', RISC felt – inferior to Shvets's classy document and a mere half-page of A4. Litvinenko handed Lugovoi Shvets's version while Lugovoi was on one of his frequent business trips to London to show him how it might be done.

Clearly, if the Litvinenko–Shvets report ever fell into the hands of the Kremlin it would provoke anger. Serious anger. Branding Ivanov a vindictive monster was one thing. But implicating Russia's president in shady deals with the St Petersburg mafia and Colombian drug smugglers was another. There were plenty of general reasons why the Kremlin might want Litvinenko dead. But this report on its own was certainly a strong enough motive to have him killed, British detectives were to conclude.

Shvets claims that Ivanov personally lost $10–15 million in kickbacks after the western company which commissioned the report read it with horror and pulled out of a major deal with Russia. The name of the company has not been revealed. Amongst his other business interests and his KGB role, Ivanov is chairman of Aeroflot, the Russian state carrier. (He denies wrongdoing.)

When Lugovoi flew back to Moscow, the FSB detained him at the airport. According to Shvets, they found Litvinenko's report. By accident or design? We don't know. Was this the moment that Lugovoi was recruited by the FSB, forced to do their dirty work in order to avoid punishment for his role in handling the report? Or – more likely, perhaps – was Lugovoi working for the FSB from the start and this was therefore a deliberate betrayal?

Either way, the contents of the report were passed back to the Kremlin. The nature of any subsequent conversation between Ivanov and Putin is unknown. But, weeks later, Lugovoi was on his way back to London with his partner Kovtun, this time in the role of assassin – on a mission to kill the author.

The origins of Litvinenko's own bitter personal feud with Putin go back to the 1990s, and to Litvinenko's career as an FSB officer. Those who knew him characterise Litvinenko as mercurial, dedicated and obsessive when on a case – a good sleuth or *operativnik* in an organisation riddled with wrong-doing.

Litvinenko had plenty of antecedents. Think Arkady Renko, the honest Soviet policeman who features in

Martin Cruz Smith's *Gorky Park*. Litvinenko's friend Alex Goldfarb would liken him to the eponymous hero of *Serpico*, the 1973 movie starring Al Pacino, in which a decent cop goes undercover to expose corruption inside his own force. Others would bend the rules, cheat, lie. Litvinenko refused. He would stick to the truth and the law.

Another friend and fellow exile, Viktor Suvorov, likened Litvinenko to a different literary character, from Alexandre Dumas's classic novel *The Three Muske-teers*. Like everyone who knew him, Suvorov referred to Litvinenko as Sasha. 'Sasha was pure D'Artagnan,' Suvorov said. 'He was tall, handsome, sporty and open.' He added: 'He met so many real criminals. He under-stood really bad people, how bad they were. And yet he was very optimistic. He still believed in humankind.'

Litvinenko was born on 12 December 1962 in the Russian city of Voronezh. He had something of a fractured childhood. His parents, Walter and Svetlana, divorced when he was a baby; he grew up with his grandparents in the city of Nalchik, in Russia's wild north Caucasus, close to the mountains. In between he had stints living with his mother in Moscow and an aunt in a town called Moro-zovsk. He went to secondary school in Nalchik.

His grandfather fought in the Great Patriotic War, as Russians call the Second World War. A month before he was due to be called up for national service at the age of seventeen, Litvinenko enlisted in the army. Between 1981 and 1985 he attended a Soviet military academy in Ordzhonikidze, now called Vladikavkaz. Vladikavkaz, in north Ossetia, is Russia's gateway to the Caucasus: a place of rugged beauty, hillside fortresses and heavy skies prone to mist and rain.

In 1988, Litvinenko got transferred to a special division of the ministry of internal affairs. Here, in Moscow, the KGB hired him. Litvinenko began work in military counter-intelligence. In 1991, he joined the department that combated organised crime, corruption and terrorism. With the end of the Soviet Union in December 1991 the KGB ceased to exist and Litvinenko's unit became part of the new FSK. In 1993 the FSK was renamed the FSB.

When still at military school and aged just twenty, Litvinenko married Natalia. He became the father of two small children, Sonya and Alexander. The relationship failed and by 1993 the couple were estranged. That summer – on 16 June – Litvinenko met his future second wife Marina, a ballroom dancing teacher. She had been married before too. It was her birthday party.

Marina was slim and attractive, with short blonde hair, boyishly cut, high cheekbones and clear blue eyes. She cut a gamine figure; her clothes smart and understated verging on conservative; earrings a single stud. I got to know her much later. What makes Marina extraordinary is her warm personality. She is someone of high emotional intelligence: concerned for others, friendly, affectionate, tactile. And – this came later too – courageous.

Before the party, two of Marina's close friends had been receiving threats from some former business partners over a ballroom dancing trip to Sri Lanka that had gone wrong. Frightened, the couple went to a police station. There they met Litvinenko – a senior FSB officer – who took the unusual step of offering them his personal protection. Marina's friends were impressed. Litvinenko struck them as professional and calm. They brought him along to Marina's birthday celebration.

Litvinenko was meant to be on holiday but he worked on the case flat-out. This was characteristic: once gripped by an assignment Litvinenko would often not sleep for three days. After rows with Natalia he moved out and lodged with his mother. That autumn he and Marina began living together. In summer 1994 they had a son, Anatoly; they married a few months later. It would be a happy partnership.

Three months later, in December 1994, Boris Yeltsin launched an attack on the rebel republic of Chechnya, in what was to become the First Chechen War. The goal was to wipe out Chechnya's bid for independence. The Kremlin anticipated quick, decisive victory. Instead, the invasion turned into a bloody disaster for Moscow, with the Russian tank force sent on New Year's Eve to re-take Chechnya's capital Grozny destroyed and the army humiliated.

Litvinenko had grown up in the Caucasus; he understood the mentality of southern Russia's majority Muslim population. In 1995, the FSB sent him back to Nalchik, to offer communications support to the forces fighting close by. At first Litvinenko supported Yeltsin's war. Gradually, however, he grew disillusioned – with the Russian army's brutal methods and with the president's political goals, seemingly driven by imperial pique.

In January 1996, the Chechen guerrilla leader Salman Raduyev raided the town of Kizlyar in Dagestan, near the Chechen border. His fighters seized the local hospital. They took 3,000 people hostage. After negotiations, Raduyev was allowed to return to Chechnya, with his fighters and 160 hostages. His convoy got as far as the last village before the border, Pervomaiskoye. A Russian helicopter gunship opened fire on the lead bus; the Chechens took cover in nearby cottages.

Litvinenko was sent with his FSB team into what was to become a hellish siege. Russian forces surrounded the village for five days – then bombarded it with tank fire and Grad missiles. On the ninth day of the crisis, the surviving rebels with their hostages broke out of the encirclement at night, fleeing across a field under heavy mortar and machine-gun fire. At least twenty-nine civilians and 200 combatants from both sides perished.

According to Marina, the slaughter had a profound affect on Litvinenko. The themes were familiar: the Russian state's indifference to civilian casualties, and the incompetence of its military command. He returned to Moscow in poor shape. 'He looked very bad, his hands and feet were frozen, and he needed a week to recover,' Marina said. His sympathy for Chechens and their struggle against the centre grew; it would later become a journalistic obsession and a future area of conflict with Putin.

During this same period, Litvinenko met and became friendly with a man named Boris Berezovsky. Berezovsky was a mathematician and academic who had gone into business as the Soviet Union collapsed. Like a determined object pushing at a tough membrane, he had penetrated Boris Yeltsin's inner circle. He published the president's memoirs and became friends with Yeltsin's influential daughter Tatyana Yumasheva.

Berezovsky was Jewish, clever, unscrupulous, self-promoting, ambitious, solipsistic, chameleon-like – a whirlwind of restless energy and speech. Asked years later what the appeal was of being with Berezovsky, Litvinenko's friend Alex Goldfarb – who worked for him – answered simply: 'It was fun.'

This was a moment in which Yeltsin, his poll ratings dismal ahead of Russia's 1996 presidential election, made a deal with a small group of businessmen. These were the oligarchs. They agreed to get Yeltsin re-elected. In return the president, in effect, sold them Russian state assets at crazily low prices. Berezovsky acquired an interest in a major oil firm, Sibneft, together with a young oil trader called Roman Abramovich.

As Berezovsky told it, his rise to power and influence made him enemies. Especially inside the former KGB. Russia's spy agencies were on the back foot following the KGB's failed coup in August 1991 against Mikhail Gorbachev. Berezovsky said he urged Yeltsin to rein in the new FSB, and to debar former KGB operatives from high office. Russia needed to go through the same 'lustration' process that east Germany and the new Czech Republic went through after the fall of communism, he said.

The FSB, however, had plans of its own. Its goal was to regain the KGB's lost supremacy. As Berezovsky later put it to British detectives: 'KGB never disappeared. They were shocked because of [democratic] revolution in Russia. Step by step they start[ed] to understand what happened and to get back control.' Yeltsin, he said, did 'strong damage' to them, but 'nevertheless they were trying all the time to organise'. The FSB 'didn't like' him, he said.

Berezovsky's nerve centre was the LogoVAZ Club, a hunting lodge in the centre of Moscow. In 1994, Berezovsky left this office, climbed into the back of his Mercedes, and sped off. A car bomb exploded, killing his driver and severely injuring his bodyguard. Berezovsky survived and spent two weeks in Switzerland recuperating. The FSB used this attempted assassination as an excuse to dispatch Litvinenko to investigate Berezovsky and keep an eye on his affairs.

This was the beginning of a relationship that would define Litvinenko's life. In March 1995, a gunman shot dead Vladimir Listyev, Russia's most popular TV anchor, in the stairwell of his Moscow apartment. Listyev was the head of ORT, Russia's first channel. Suspicion fell on Berezovsky, who had just taken over ORT together with a Georgian billionaire, Badri Patarkatsishvili. Berezovsky denied involvement; we don't know who was responsible but it would certainly have been unlike him to use those methods. He flew back to Moscow from London.

When Moscow police came to arrest Berezovsky, Litvinenko went to the scene. He realised that in custody Berezovsky's life was at risk: it was not unknown for the authorities to cause 'accidents' to happen behind closed doors. What happened next, Berezovsky told Scotland Yard, was 'very unusual': 'He [Litvinenko] took his gun and said [to the police] if you try and catch him now I'll kill you.' Litvinenko called the head of the FSB, who agreed to give an order to protect Berezovsky. The police retreated and left.

At the time, Berezovsky scarcely knew Litvinenko, the good Samaritan. Afterwards, he said, they became 'very close'. Marina Litvinenko said: 'Boris said many times Sasha [Alexander] saved his life, and he was very grateful.' Litvinenko was still working for the FSB but from then on became an informal part of Berezovsky's entourage.

Meanwhile, Litvinenko was growing disenchanted with the leadership of his own organisation. The FSB was riddled with corruption, he learned. In 1997, he was posted to the FSB's directorate for the investigation and prevention of organised crime, a covert unit known by the initials URPO. 'It was the most secret department. It was FSB within FSB,' Litvinenko said. His boss was Major General Evgeny Khokholkov. Unbeknown to General Khokholkov, Litvinenko had investigated him before. And been horrified at what he found.

Back in 1993, Litvinenko had investigated a group of bent FSB officers. He discovered that the officers – all members of the Uzbek KGB, transferred to Moscow – were taking bribes from an oil trader. The officers reported to Khokholkov. Khokholkov was also receiving protection money from Central Asian drug lords. Heroin was travelling from northern Afghanistan to Europe via Russia, with Khokholkov allegedly taking a cut.

The URPO special operations unit had its own secret office, away from the FSB's headquarters in the

Lubyanka building in central Moscow. URPO had been set up to perform 'special tasks' – including, if necessary, extra-judicial murder. Litvinenko, to his growing dismay, soon found himself expected to carry out unlawful activities as part of his new assignment. He received orders to detain and beat up a former FSB officer turned whistleblower called Mikhail Trepashkin. He was also instructed to kidnap a rich Moscow-based Chechen businessman, Umar Jabrailov. If necessary, Litvinenko was told to shoot Jabrailov's police body-guards. Litvinenko refused to obey.

But it was another order from a senior colleague that would provoke a political scandal and Litvinenko's dismissal from the FSB. Yeltsin had appointed Berezovsky deputy head of the security council. Berezovsky helped to negotiate a peace deal with the Chechen rebels. Hardliners viewed this agreement as treachery – and Berezovsky as its perfidious architect.

One day, Litvinenko's superior Alexander Kamish-nikov came up to him. According to Litvinenko, he began by saying: 'Look, we must be a true successor to the KGB, we must have continuity and you must defend the Motherland, you must discharge your duties prop-erly. We have fallen on hard times, difficult times, and we must be firm and strong.'

Litvinenko was uncertain what to make of this speech. Kamishnikov, however, then continued: 'Litvinenko, you know Berezvosky well, you must kill him.'

Litvinenko later told UK Home Office officials: 'I could hardly believe what he had said and asked him if he was serious. He moved closer and repeated: "You must kill Berezovsky. Russia has fallen on hard times and there are people who are very rich who have robbed our Motherland; they have corrupted authorities and they are buying everyone in authority.'" Kamishnikov said that a legal route would, of course, be preferable but in order to save the country it was necessary for Berezovsky 'to be destroyed'.

According to Marina Litvinenko, the conversation left her husband 'unhappy and nervous' for two months. In the best traditions of Soviet conspiracy, the order wasn't written down. Nonetheless, it was an order – one that Litvinenko viewed as tantamount to illegal terrorist activity.

Litvinenko tried to figure out what to do. It was New Year, and Berezovsky had gone to Switzerland for treatment after tumbling off his snowmobile. In March 1998, he finally tracked Berezovsky down to his dacha and told him about the conversation. Berezovsky refused to believe him. Litvinenko returned with several of his URPO colleagues – Andrei Ponkin, Konstantin Latyshonok and German Shcheglov. They persuaded Berezovsky the murder plot was genuine. Shocked, Berezovsky took the evidence to the deputy chief of Yeltsin's private office.

Litvinenko's action triggered turmoil inside Russia's power structures. The FSB ran its own 'investigation', carried out by the same people who had apparently ordered Berezovsky's liquidation. Privately, Khokholkov and Kamishnikov were furious. They wanted revenge. In April 1998, meanwhile, together with two URPO colleagues, Litvinenko recorded a video statement filmed at Berezovsky's Moscow office. It was for use in case he was jailed. Or worse, killed. They made a deposition to the military prosecutor.

Litvinenko was a punctilious officer, and over the coming months noted down the threats made against him. There were many. His phone was bugged; he noticed he was being followed. A well-known journalist with links to the security services, Alexander Khinstein, published Litvinenko's identity. Another article accused him of torture, extortion and muggings.

One day in May when he came into work, Lieutenant Colonel N. V. Yenin bawled him out in front of his colleagues. Yenin threatened to assault him, and said: 'You bastard, you traitor. You prevented honest Russian people from murdering this filthy Jew ... If you don't shut your trap we'll sort you out in our own way.'

Days later, Litvinenko was returning with his wife Marina from their dacha to their Moscow flat. A gang of young people attacked and beat him, kicking him in the face. Litvinenko got his gun out, said he was an FSB officer, and fired a warning shot in the air. He tried to arrest the youths. One of them told him: 'We know where you live. If you force us to go to the police we'll cut your wife's and your children's heads off.'

Khokholkov and his allies were determined to make Litvinenko suffer. In August he was suspended from his department and told to find another internal job. The FSB's human resources office made it clear that he had 'betrayed the system' by 'washing dirty linen in public'. There were further libels in the newspapers, including a claim that he'd failed to pay child support to his ex-wife Natalia.

Faced with a scandal, Nikolai Kovalyov, the FSB's director, had tried to get Litvinenko to drop his complaint. This didn't work. Berezovsky, meanwhile, was pulling all the strings he could at the Kremlin. Prosecutors began an investigation. After a few weeks URPO was dissolved; Khokholkov transferred; Kovalyov fired. It looked like victory for Berezovsky and Litvinenko.

President Yeltsin then appointed an unknown mid-ranking officer to replace Kovalyov as head of the FSB. This was Vladimir Putin.

Berezovsky had many flaws, but the greatest of them was surely his inability to distinguish friend from foe. He had known Putin since late 1991. He regarded him as a protégé. They'd been on holiday in France. 'He was my friend,' Berezovsky would tell Scotland Yard. At the time, Berezovsky viewed Putin as someone who would loyally serve his interests.

Berezovsky encouraged the suspended Litvinenko to go and see this new director, to introduce himself and to tell him everything he knew.

In his memoir, *The Uzbek File*, Litvinenko writes: 'Putin's appointment was a shock to everyone. Unlike Kovalyov, who rose through the ranks to a three-star general, Putin was a little-known colonel of the reserves working for the Kremlin administration. Everyone considered him a Berezovsky puppet. The consensus among the *operativniks* was that the new Director will not last long. He will be rejected by the system.'

Litvinenko continued:

One day Berezovsky called me.

'Alexander, could you go to Putin and tell him everything you have told me? And everything that you have not. He is a new man, you know, and would benefit from an insider's view.'

I was surprised. The Director of the FSB could surely find me if he wanted to see me. Nevertheless I called at his office.

'Litvinenko?' asked his secretary. 'We have been looking for you. They tell us there is no such officer.'

That was it, I thought, the system resists a new-comer.

'I am on suspension,' I said.

'Come tomorrow morning. The Director will see you.'

Litvinenko spent that night 'drawing up a scheme for Putin'. It contained everything he knew about organised crime and corruption, including the principal mob groups with their areas of activity. He drew arrows leading to their connections in government, with the FSB, the interior ministry and the tax service. He listed commercial companies used for money laundering. He included his Uzbek file, setting out the drugs trail from Afghanistan to Europe and America, the branches and contacts in Russia, and the 'protection ring' deep within the FSB.

The following morning, Litvinenko turned up with this impressive dossier. He brought along two colleagues, but Putin wanted to see him alone. Litvinenko recalled that he was unsure how to greet his new boss – should he address him as 'Comrade Colonel' or 'Comrade Director'? He felt sorry for Putin. 'We were of the same rank and I imagined myself in his shoes – a mid-level *operativnik* suddenly put in charge of some 100 senior generals with all their vested interests, connections and dirty secrets.'

In the end, Putin pre-empted Litvinenko, came up from his desk, and shook his hand. 'He seemed even shorter than on TV,' Litvinenko noticed.

It was to be their first and last substantial meeting. It was also unsuccessful. And rather surreal.

Litvinenko wrote:

From the first moment I felt he was not sincere. He avoided eye contact and behaved as if he was not the Director but an actor playing the Director's role on stage. He looked at my schematic, made some face movements as if he was studying it for a couple of minutes. Asked a couple of questions – 'What is this? What is that?' – pointing at random points in the scheme.

But he obviously could not grasp the details in that short while. 'Why is he doing this?' I thought. 'Is he trying to impress *me*?'

'Would you like to keep the scheme?' I asked.

'No, no, thank you. You keep it. It's your work.'

Litvinenko handed Putin a list of FSB officers whom he regarded as 'clean', and remarked that there were still 'honest people in the system'. He added that with Putin's backing they could fight the corruption that was rife in Russia and the security services. Together they could 'strike a blow' against organised crime. Litvinenko told Putin: 'If we decide to tackle the Russian mafia seriously it will be very dangerous.'

Putin nodded, feigning agreement. He took the list as well as the part of the dossier dealing with drugs. Putin wrote down Litvinenko's home phone number. He said he'd be in touch. He never called.

It was months later that Litvinenko discovered what happened as soon as he shut the door and left the director's office. Putin picked up the phone. He ordered the FSB's internal affairs unit to begin an immediate criminal investigation against Litvinenko, and to bug Litvinenko's telephone.

Putin's indifferent attitude at their meeting bewildered Litvinenko: why would he not want to investigate criminal wrongdoing at the top of his own service? Later, Litvinenko said that his contacts inside the FSB gave an explanation. Putin, Litvinenko alleged, had connections with Khokholkov's team from his time as deputy mayor for economic affairs in the St Petersburg administration of Anatoly Sobchak. Putin had 'common money' with Khokholkov and the Uzbeks. At the very least,

Litvinenko wrote, Putin was personally involved in 'a cover-up of organised criminal activities connected with drug traffic in Russia and Europe'.

The meeting with Putin lasted ten minutes. It took place in August 1998. From this moment on, Litvinenko's already tricky situation got worse. His weapon was confiscated and salary stopped. His friend Berezovsky, however, seemed oblivious to the worsening relations. In November, Berezovsky wrote an open letter to Putin, which began: 'Dear Vladimir Vladimirovich.' The *Kommersant* newspaper owned by Berezovsky published it. Berezovsky's tone was friendly – he still regarded Putin as an ally, and as an enemy of the communists, widely regarded as Yeltsin's chief political foe.

Berezovsky said he'd been 'inspired to write this letter by the pressing issues of national security'. He mentioned his 'good long-term relations' with the FSB chief, whom he commended for 'honesty and professionalism'. Berezovsky then explained how he had learned of the plot to kill him – and how Litvinenko and the four other whistleblowers had written up a report for the presidential administration. The investigation into the plot had gone nowhere, though, Berezovsky complained. He urged Putin to pursue the matter and to secure 'the constitutional order'.

Four days later, the stakes were elevated further when Litvinenko and his URPO colleagues staged an extraordinary press conference at the Interfax news agency in Moscow. They were to do something no FSB officers had done before: publicly to accuse their superiors of grievous crimes. Litvinenko, the main actor, sat in the middle. He did most of the talking. He made no attempt to hide his identity.

His companions were more bashful. One, Viktor Shebalin, wore a ski-mask; three others, Ponkin, Shcheglov and Latyshonok, put on dark shades. They looked like off-duty bank robbers. Only one other participant was unmasked: Trepashkin, the former FSB officer who had raised his own complaint against the agency. He was one of the men whom Litvinenko had been ordered to beat up.

Litvinenko told the journalists he was holding a press conference to draw the attention of Russia's leadership and parliament to abuses going on inside the FSB. He said that he and his subordinates had received illegal instructions to kill and kidnap people and to extort money. Instead of protecting the state, senior FSB officials were busy lining their pockets.

Asked if he was scared, Litvinenko said he perfectly understood there would be retribution. 'I know the habits of this organisation and therefore suspect that we shall all be strangled like blind puppies,' he replied, adding that 'as a citizen' he considered it his duty to act. He said the plot against Berezovsky demonstrated that there was 'anti-semitism' in Russia at the very top. It was clear, he said, he was being hounded for his opinion that 'nationalism is evil'.

The press conference was a sensation, massively reported on Russian TV and in print. Soon afterwards, in December, Putin gave an interview to the journalist Elena Tregubova at his office in the Lubyanka. Putin said he could understand why Berezovsky was alarmed – after all, Berezovsky had survived one assassination attempt. However, Putin took a dim view of Litvinenko's actions. He told Tregubova: 'FSB officers should not stage press conferences and should not expose internal scandals to the public.'

In January 1999, Putin fired Litvinenko, personally signing an order kicking him out. Putin also disbanded his unit. 'Sasha knew it [the press conference] was a very extraordinary event, that the FSB will not take it so easy,' Marina Litvinenko said. Her husband had told her, in darkly humorous tones, that one of two things would now happen to him.

'They will kill me or I will be arrested,' he predicted.

He was right: on 25 March 1999, Litvinenko was arrested. Four men dressed in civilian clothes grabbed him near Moscow's Rossiya hotel, shouting: 'FSB, you're under arrest!' They bundled him into the back of a van and started beating him with fists on his back.

After being interrogated by a military prosecutor, Litvinenko was hauled off to Lefortovo Prison. This is a drab, yellow three-storey Moscow building lined with spiraling razor wire. I would later visit it myself under unpropitious circumstances.

Lefortovo was the KGB's most notorious jail. Its former inmates included 'enemies of the state' during both the Stalinist and late Soviet periods. One was the writer Yevgenia Ginzburg, who was held there before being transported to Siberia. Another the Soviet dissenter Vladimir Bukovsky, who would become

Litvinenko's friend and guru. Alexander Solzhenitsyn, the Nobel Prize-winning novelist and dissident, wrote about Lefortovo in *The Gulag Archipelago*.

The FSB uses Lefortovo for its highest-profile cases. One wing serves as the FSB's investigative department. There are a series of upstairs suites – small, boxy rooms where FSB officers in olive-green uniforms interview suspects; downstairs a K-shaped prison. On arrival, Litvinenko was stripped, searched and dumped in a solitary cell. He immediately began a hunger strike. The prison governor persuaded him to abandon it. Litvinenko would spend the next eight months in Lefortovo, including thirty-six days in solitary confinement.

Litvinenko was charged with abusing his position and beating up a suspect. According to Marina Litvinenko, the military prosecutor in charge of his case, Vladimir Barsukov, told her that Litvinenko's real crime was to have gone public with his complaint against the FSB. Now he had to be punished. Barsukov added that if Litvinenko were acquitted, he would simply open another case against him. And, if necessary, 'another and another'. The goal was to lock Litvinenko away.

Barsukov was telling the truth. Litvinenko denied the charges against him and in November 1999 a judge at the Moscow garrison military court found him not guilty. Court officials removed his handcuffs. Immediately a group of masked FSB officers burst into the room and re-arrested him. It was an ambush. This time Litvinenko was transferred to Butyrka, a Moscow prison controlled and administered by the federal penitentiary service. He spent the next twenty-four hours in solitary, in a tiny shoe-box-like cell, without food, water or sanitation. The cell was so small he could only stand or sit.

Inside Butyrka a group of unknown people summoned Litvinenko twice. They asked what he knew about Putin, urged him to confess, and said frankly: 'You realise, of course, you can be poisoned here and we cannot really help you?'

Even by the standards of Russian justice, the new charge against him was ridiculous: he was accused of stealing from a vegetable warehouse. Litvinenko complained via his attorneys that the charge was fabricated, and in December he was released on bail. It was clear, though, that the FSB had no intention of giving up. In April 2000, military prosecutors dropped this charge and came up with another more serious one – stealing explosives and ammunition.

By this point, Litvinenko was running out of options. This new case would be heard in Yaroslavl, 170 miles (270 km) outside Moscow, and far away from public scrutiny. The hearing would be closed. A verdict had already been decided, Litvinenko was told – eight years at a labour camp in Nizhny Tagil, a city in the Urals.

The political situation had changed too. The previous week Russia had elected a new president, the country's second post-communist leader. Yeltsin was gone. A new era was beginning. There had been, in effect, only one candidate to succeed Yeltsin. This was Putin. He had been doing the job on an acting basis for the previous three months, since January.

If he stayed in Russia Litvinenko would go to jail for a very long time. Probably, he would never emerge. That left only one other possibility. Escape.

2

Journalist, Exile, Campaigner, Spy

London, 2000–2006

'Do you feel yourself safe, secure in Britain?
Come on! Remember Trotsky'
FSB OFFICER ANDREI PONKIN TO LITVINENKO, SPRING 2002

It was late September 2000 when the figure – sandy hair, sporting appearance, no obvious luggage – slipped out of his Moscow apartment. From here he travelled to Sheremetyevo Airport and boarded an internal flight. Was anyone tailing him? The plane flew south and landed two hours or so later in Sochi on the Black Sea. This was southern Russia: warm, subtropical, hedonistic.

Since Soviet times, Sochi has been a holiday destination, both for the Politburo and for the ordinary citizen. There is a pebbly beach; a botanical garden; pleasant cafés and hotels along a sinuous promenade. The sanatoria have beguiling names – Rainbow, Golden Sheaf, Zhemchuzhina (Pearl) – but are typically squat, communist-era rectangles. In the afternoons guests plough up and down azure pools; by evening prostitutes sit in the lobby.

This traveller had no time to linger. After arriving in Sochi he was on the move again. A steamer shuttled between the ports of the Black Sea, once part of a single empire, and now divided between Ukraine, Russia and

Georgia. The boat was heading to the Georgian town of Batumi. He got on last and handed his internal Russian passport to a customs officer. Plus a bribe of $10. In return, the officer agreed to glance away from a list of persons forbidden from leaving the Russian Federation.

The boat set off – Sochi, with its twisting green headland and brown-roofed hillside villas, diminishing in the distance. For Russians, Georgia is still the near abroad; only an internal passport is needed for entry. The figure disembarked at the port of Batumi and travelled directly to Tbilisi, Georgia's capital. The first part of Litvinenko's plan to escape had worked. But, as he knew, it was only a matter of time before the FSB noticed his disappearance, and – vengefully – came after him.

A week earlier, while in Moscow, Litvinenko had discussed his escape with his friend Yuri Felshtinsky. Felshtinsky, a successful historian and author, emigrated from the USSR in 1978 and settled in the US. He returned to Russia in 1998 to write Berezovsky's biography, at Berezovsky's request. The book never happened. The oligarch was an elusive subject. Felshtinsky may have failed to extract Berezovsky's life story from him but he did become a member of his informal team. They disagreed about Putin, however, who Berezovsky insisted was 'my friend'. (Felshtinsky predicted that future president Putin would toss Berezovsky in jail.)

During a state trip with Berezovsky to Baku, Felshtinsky and Litvinenko had shared a plane and a room. They got on. According to Felshtinsky, Litvinenko was a good storyteller who would talk for hours. As a

KGB and FSB officer, Litvinenko had been and was still forbidden from fraternising with foreigners; this was his first sustained encounter with anyone with experience of the west. By 2000 it was clear that Felshtinsky's forebodings about Putin were correct, and that Litvinenko's troubles were just beginning. Felshtinsky agreed to help his friend escape, with Berezovsky's considerable financial assistance.

Their plan went smoothly. Felshtinsky flew from Boston to Tbilisi and found Litvinenko alive and well. Litvinenko relayed a message to his wife instructing her to buy a new mobile phone. He called her on this number and told her to take a package holiday to somewhere in Western Europe. Two days later she flew out of Moscow with their son Anatoly. Their destination was Spain's Costa del Sol.

In Tbilisi, Litvinenko had no clear idea what to do next. He grew nervy and restless: instead of staying in his hotel room out of sight he wandered round the town, with its churches and old quarter. At one point the local militia almost arrested him, a suspicious Russian with no clear purpose in the city. Litvinenko's best option, he and Felshtinksy agreed, was to seek political asylum in the United States. But when Felshtinsky called in at the US embassy, desk officers showed no interest in his case.

To go further Litvinenko would need a full travel document: the FSB had stolen his international passport. Luckily, he had allies in high places. Berezovsky's business partner Patarkatsishvili was Georgian, extremely rich, and friends with Eduard Shevardnadze, Georgia's

then president. Patarkatsishvili arranged a Georgian passport for Litvinenko. The passport was genuine but the
details inside it were false. Litvinenko got a new name:
Mr Chernishev.

In Moscow, meanwhile, the FSB realised that its trou-
blesome former agent had escaped. One of Litvinenko's
ex-colleagues, Andrei Ponkin, called up Felshtinsky,
saying he was 'concerned' for Litvinenko's well-being.
Had he seen him? Felshtinsky claimed to be in Boston.
Ponkin kept calling. Berezovsky suggested they go to
Turkey and sent his private jet. The two men left Tbilisi
– Litvinenko going through passport control as Mr
Chernishev – and flew to Antalya on Turkey's Mediter-
ranean coast.

By now Litvinenko had realised that his exit from
Russia was irreversible. Returning home would mean
instant arrest. 'I analysed everything. It was clear my fate
was decided in Russia,' he said. He rang Marina in Spain
and laid out their options in stark terms. They could all
go back to Moscow. But from prison Litvinenko would
be unable to protect her and Anatoly. Marina believed
that after a stint in jail her husband would eventually get
out. Litvinenko demurred, telling her: 'I will never leave
prison. They will kill me.'

Marina agreed and flew to Turkey with Anatoly on
Berezovsky's plane. The Litvinenkos were reunited in
Antalya but their problem remained: where could they
go next? They knew no foreign languages, and practically nothing of the western world. Marina felt lonely
and disorientated. Litvinenko was nervous that the FSB

was closing in. His friends began to worry that he might do something outlandish.

Berezovsky called Alex Goldfarb, his long-time aide, in New York. It was 4 a.m. there. Goldfarb was a micro-biologist by training and US citizen who had emigrated from the Soviet Union in the seventies. He had worked as an academic, as a journalist, and for the philanthro-pist George Soros, administering a programme to award grants to hard-up Russian scientists. Goldfarb resem-bled a New York professor – round metal glasses, beard, corduroy jacket, slightly dishevelled appearance. He had a shining intelligence, easy manner, and superlative English. I would later get to know him well.

Goldfarb also possessed a cool head, invaluable in this moment of crisis. A couple of days after Berezovsky's summons, he arrived in Antalya. He rented a hire car and the four of them – Goldfarb, Litvinenko, his wife and son – drove to the Turkish capital Ankara, Goldfarb's wife Svetlana travelling by plane. Felshtinsky had returned to the States.

While in New York, Goldfarb had called a staffer at the US security council who dealt with Russia. He had told his contact he planned to bring a Russian defector to the US's Turkish embassy. The staffer was appalled and told him: 'Don't do this. You're not a pro. It's dangerous! Don't even think about it.'

Undeterred, the party turned up at the US mission in Ankara. The embassy had been pre-warned. A consular official checked their documents, took their cell phones and escorted them to a secure sound-proof glass room guarded by marines – the 'bubble'. Inside the bubble were two representatives of the CIA and a video-link with a Russian-speaker patched in from the United States.

The US agents interviewed Litvinenko on his own for three hours. He told them his story: his feud with Putin, the trumped-up charges, jail. The officials were non-committal. It was uncertain if the US would grant Litvinenko asylum. In the meantime he would have to wait. It was dark when Goldfarb collected Litvinenko and took him back to their hotel. The US embassy refused to provide security. At this point relations between Putin and the outgoing Clinton administration were warm. The White House viewed the Russian leader as fresh and dynamic – as an ally and a democrat. The Litvinenko case may have seemed like an ill-timed throwback to the Cold War.

By now, Litvinenko was convinced that the FSB was on his trail. Its next move, he thought, would be to kidnap him and to render him back to Moscow. That night, the Litvinenkos plus Goldfarb made a covert exit from their hotel, whizzing out of the underground car park. They drove in blackness to Istanbul. For security reasons they switched off their cell phones. The next afternoon Goldfarb found a message from the US embassy. He called back. There was an answer from Washington, which said sorry, we can't help you, good luck.

The situation was now desperate. Patarkatsishvili offered to send his yacht; he suggested the Litvinenkos could hole up on it for a couple of months, bobbing in the blue waters off Istanbul, while he arranged more fake passports. Berezovsky felt Litvinenko should go to ground in Turkey. Goldfarb explored flying to Barbados via the US – impossible, it turned out, without an American transit visa. But what about France? Or Britain? He looked on the internet. No transit visa was needed to go via London. Goldfarb booked tickets to Tbilisi via London's Heathrow Airport.

The next day, 1 November 2000, the four of them flew to the UK. Goldfarb knew London well but for the Litvinenko family it was *terra incognito*. They arrived at the transit section of Heathrow terminal three. Litvinenko and Goldfarb saw a uniformed policeman and approached him. The policemen stationed at the airport were used to all sorts of requests, including quite strange ones. The world in its many tongues and Technicolor guises flowed past. This sentence, though, stuck out.

Litvinenko said in English: 'I am KGB officer. I am asking for political asylum.'

Britain would become the Litvinenkos' new home. And – it appeared – a haven from enemies in Russia. Officials from the UK Home Office's Immigration and Nationality Directorate interviewed Litvinenko in a custody suite. The interview went on for eight hours. Marina called her shocked mother in Moscow. Little Anatoly roamed round the terminal building, munching on a packet of M&Ms; he recalls being bored and feeling sick.

Goldfarb had arranged for a London solicitor, George Menzies, to come to the airport. Alexander, Marina and Anatoly were temporarily allowed to enter the UK while Litvinenko's asylum application was considered.

The authorities took a dim view of Goldfarb's actions – people-smuggling. He asked if he might fly home to New York. They refused and deported him back to Turkey.

Over the next weeks, the family stayed in temporary accommodation paid for by Berezovsky. Litvinenko's escape had cost the oligarch around $130,000 – small change for a man whose expenditure averaged around £1 million a month. (His bills included lovers, yachts – two of them – the upkeep of his luxury properties including a chateau in the south of France, bodyguards, jewellery …)

Berezovsky himself went into self-exile soon afterwards. He left Moscow for his villa in Cap d'Antibes and then moved to London. His new office was in Mayfair, at 7 Down Street, a modern complex opposite a church and a vintner's. Down Street would become the hub for Berezovsky's last ambitious and tragically doomed project: to bring down the Putin regime.

During this early period of exile, Litvinenko was worried about his safety. Might the British send him back to Russia? Could the Kremlin dispatch its agents to the UK? Menzies suggested the family adopt new English names. The solicitor's office was in Carter Street, in south-east London. Carter sounded inconspicuous, middle-class, respectable.

Alexander's new official name gave no hint of his previous career in the KGB – Edwin Redwald Carter. Marina became Maria Anne Carter. Anatoly got the name Anthony. Anatoly was enrolled at an English-language international school in Baker Street; the family moved into a temporary flat in Lexham Gardens in South Kensington; Anatoly would later study at the private City of London boys' school. They began studying English, Alexander with the least success.

Days after arriving in London, Litvinenko got in touch with fellow émigré Vladimir Bukovsky. Bukovsky was a celebrated former political prisoner who had spent twelve years in a variety of Soviet labour camps, jails and psychiatric facilities. He revealed the political abuse of psychiatry in the Soviet Union – a practice that went on from the 1960s to the early 1980s, which saw thousands of dissidents tossed into mental hospitals for 'anti-Soviet' thinking.

In 1976, the USSR expelled Bukovsky. He settled in Cambridge, living alone in a suburban house on the city's outskirts. When I visited him there in 2012 it had an overgrown garden, antediluvian yellow-and-brown wallpaper and fittings, and a sink littered with unwashed tea cups and cigarette butts.

Bukovsky became Litvinenko's mentor and guru. According to Bukovsky, Litvinenko had a curious mind. He had missed out on university education and despite serving in the FSB knew practically nothing of the KGB. Bukovsky passed him documents that he had smuggled out of Moscow in 1991. They had come from the archives of the Central Committee of the Communist Party of the Soviet Union.

The files detailed the USSR's long history of involvement in sponsoring international terrorism. The KGB supported liberation movements in Central and South

America, Palestine and the Middle East. It supplied terrorist groups with explosives, weapons and cover documents. They blew up innocent people.

Litvinenko was appalled by what he read. He called Bukovsky, a night-owl, at four in the morning. The calls continued – sometimes as many as twenty or thirty a day. 'He [Litvinenko] was totally shocked and said: "Listen, it looks like the KGB was always a terrorist organisation,"' Bukovsky recalled. 'I started laughing because I had known that since the age of sixteen. I said: "Well, Sasha, who do you think killed thirty or forty million of our citizens? It's them."' Bukovsky was referring to Stalin's 1930s purges, administered by the NKVD secret police.

The more Litvinenko read, the more he discovered the system was evil, Bukovsky said. When the communist regime collapsed, the regime continued in milder form. 'More or less the same bureaucrats were sitting in the same cabinet, in the same offices, and old habits die hard, as you know,' Bukovsky said. As an operative, Litvinenko found that many criminal threads led back to his own FSB building, and to neighbouring offices. The KGB, he discovered, had patronised organised crime too.

Marina Litvinenko said her husband's tutorials with Bukovsky transformed him. 'He was reborn. He became a dissident,' she said.

Litvinenko began work as Berezovsky's security adviser. According to Bukovsky, the billionaire's carelessness amazed them both. Litvinenko found Russian intelligence had compromised Berezovsky's inner circle and put moles inside his office. Berezovsky refused to fire them. 'He was an incredibly naïve person,' Bukovsky said. 'When we first explained that Putin is going to kill him if he has a chance, he didn't believe us.' Berezovsky muttered that Putin had attended his wife's birthday party, 'so it couldn't be true'.

In addition to working for Berezovsky, Litvinenko also embarked on a career as a journalist and writer. There was an obvious subject for him to explore. Prior to his escape, he had become interested in the infamous bombing of some Russian apartment blocks, which had occurred the previous year. In September 1999, nearly 300 people were killed when four multi-storey apartment blocks were destroyed in the cities of Buynaksk, Moscow and Volgodonsk. Putin, then prime minister, blamed the explosions on Chechen terrorists. He used the bombings – and the prevailing national mood of fear and anger – to persuade Yeltsin to launch a military attack on Chechnya and its rebel leadership: the second Chechen war.

Something about the bombings was strange, though. In Ryazan, locals spotted three people – two men and a woman – unloading sacks from the back of a white Zhiguli car with Moscow licence plates. They put them in the basement of a suburban apartment block. A resident, Alexei Kartofelnikov, rang the police. Officers found three sacks containing the explosive hexogen and a homemade detonating device. The block was evacuated, the bomb made safe, and a major hunt launched for the suspects. They turned out to be agents of the FSB.

Nikolai Patrushev, the FSB's director, later claimed that the sacks merely contained sugar, and that they had been left in the basement as a 'training exercise'. The Duma's communist opposition queried this. Now, Litvinenko, together with his friend Yuri Felshtinsky in the US, launched his own investigation. The pair concluded the FSB was responsible for the bombings. And that Putin covertly sanctioned the operation – involving the mass slaughter of men, women and children – to provide a *casus belli* for his pre-planned attack on Chechnya.

Their findings became a controversial book, *Blowing Up Russia*. It argued that the apartment bombings were the foundational act in Putin's rise to power, a plot akin to the 1933 burning of the German Reichstag. The war in Chechnya boosted Putin's public profile and catapulted him into the Kremlin. The Soviet Union's collapse had put Russia's spy agencies on the back foot. With Putin's ascent to the presidency the KGB achieved its ultimate goal: 'absolute power'. The FSB, Litvinenko argued, is a thoroughly criminalised entity and part of a government–mafia state.

Sometimes the agency makes use of organised criminals; sometimes it eliminates or jails them. Litvinenko gives a gruesome account of the FSB's special operations in the 1990s – contract killings, shootings, ambushes, abductions, with victims burned alive and their eyes gouged out. The 'agencies of coercion' are involved in all sorts of crimes. They include bribe-taking, money-laundering and protection rackets. Their agents are untouchable. They have official ID.

Litvinenko's knowledge of criminal structures was formidable. In the introduction, Felshtinsky warns the

reader that *Blowing Up Russia* isn't 'superficial journalism' but 'something between an analytical memoir
and a historical monograph'. Dense as it sometimes is,
it's a compelling piece of research. And an empirical one,
flowing directly from Litvinenko's personal knowledge
of investigations.

Much of what Litvinenko wrote turned out to be
correct. He was the first person to predict what would
happen if Putin came to power. According to Felshtinsky,
Litvinenko warned in early 2000 that people would be
killed and arrested, and Putin's opponents purged: 'I can
feel this. He will kill all of us as well. Trust me. I know what
I'm saying.' The book was published in 2001. The Moscow
newspaper *Novaya Gazeta* ran extracts, and a documentary
film – *Assassination of Russia* – followed in 2002.

Claims that the FSB was behind the apartment bombings gained traction. Litvinenko was invited to give
video evidence from London to a parliamentary commission which launched its own investigation. Its deputy
chairman was a Duma member, Sergei Yushenkov. He
recruited a prominent Soviet dissident, Sergei Kovalyov,
as chairman. The commission included journalists,
lawyers and Tatiana Morozova, the daughter of a woman
killed in the explosions. It asked the FSB and prosecutor
general for documents, especially in relation to Ryazan.

The FSB's apparent reply was characteristic. In
August 2002, Vladimir Golovlyov, a Duma deputy who
had helped to distribute the film, was shot dead. Then,
in April 2003, Yushenkov was assassinated outside his
Moscow home. Two months later, Yuri Shchekochikhin,

a member of the *Novaya Gazeta* team and a senior Russian MP, was mysteriously poisoned and died in agony.

Felshtinsky had given Shchekochikhin a manuscript copy of *Blowing Up Russia* for publication. As well as working for the newspaper that serialised the book, Shchekochikhin was also a member of Kovalyov's commission and had separately investigated FSB corruption. His symptoms – blistering on the skin, dramatic organ failure, coma – suggest he was the victim of a deadly toxin, most probably dioxin. The authorities refused to give Shchekochikhin's family his medical records. These were classified as a state secret.

The commission's legal counsel, Mikhail Trepashkin, was arrested. Trepashkin was Litvinenko's close friend and had taken part in the 1998 press conference; sacked from the FSB, he became a lawyer. The charges against him were absurd. Road police placed a handgun in his car and then accused him of illegally possessing a firearm. He was further charged with espionage.

An initial print-run of Litvinenko's book was successfully smuggled into Russia. In 2003, the FSB seized a second shipment and impounded 5,000 copies, on the grounds that it revealed state secrets. This was the first time a book had been banned in Russia since Solzhenitsyn. Nonetheless, it prevailed: in 2002 a poll suggested that 40 per cent of Russians doubted the official version of events. The Kremlin remains twitchy about *Blowing Up Russia*. In 2015 it was placed on a federal list of so-called 'extremist' literature.

*

In 2001, the Home Office granted Litvinenko indefinite permission to remain in the UK. This made his position more secure, at least on paper. In fact, there were continuous threats emanating from Moscow. Bukovsky recalls how Litvinenko and Anatoly, then eight, visited him in Cambridge:

'It was springtime. We were walking in Cambridge, beautiful sight, the birds are singing and suddenly there was a call on his phone, so he answered it and became rather gloomy. By his replies, I understood that it's some kind of threat. I asked him after the phone call was over: what was it?

'Litvinenko said: "Some former colleagues from Lubyanka, the headquarters of the KGB. They said to me: 'Do you feel yourself safe, secure in Britain? Come on! Remember Trotsky.'"'

Trotsky's ice-pick murder in Mexico in 1940 was probably the most spectacular extra-territorial assassination of the communist era. Stalin had personally ordered it; the NKVD carried it out. Asked if Litvinenko understood the threat, Bukovsky replied: 'Oh, definitely.'

The person who called Litvinenko in Cambridge was Ponkin, his old associate, now apparently back informing for the FSB. Ponkin told him that Russia's prosecutor general was making up a case against him. According to Litvinenko, the prosecutor's message was unambiguous.

Litvinenko said Ponkin told him that he should return alone to his own country as soon as possible, and then nothing would happen to him. 'And if you do not return yourself then you will either be brought back in a body bag, or you will be pushed under a train,' he reported his saying. Litvinenko interpreted the call as an attempt at negotiation. He told Ponkin: 'This is a very nice offer but I refuse it.' Ponkin relayed that Marina 'wouldn't be touched'.

The warnings continued via different channels. Russian spies traced Litvinenko's home address in London – at the behest, Litvinenko believed, of FSB chief Patrushev. FSB agents shadowed him in Britain. In March 2002, a diplomat from the Russian embassy, Viktor Kirov, turned up at the family's flat. He rang the doorbell, demanded to speak to Litvinenko, and said he wanted to give him 'a package'. Marina refused to let him in. He came back the next morning.

Litvinenko went to his local police station and complained. He told them Kirov was the deputy *rezident*, that is, the number two in the UK bureau of the SVR, Moscow's foreign intelligence service. Litvinenko's solicitor George Menzies wrote to the Home Office asking it to 'take whatever steps are in your power' to stop the embassy from harassing the family. The Home Office said there was nothing it could do.

That autumn, Trepashkin emailed from Moscow with gloomy news. He had met Colonel Viktor Shebalin, another former FSB colleague, and a man with vast contacts among serving officers. Trepashkin wrote that Litvinenko's publication of *Blowing Up Russia* had sealed his fate:

'In the course of the conversation, he [Shebalin] said that "you have been sentenced to extrajudicial elimination", i.e. after the publication of this book, you will definitely be killed. Saying this, he asked me to stress that he would not be involved in this killing. He repeated several times about his non-involvement in the murder. Who specifically was going to eliminate you, Shebalin did not name, but he hinted that such people do exist (so you better write your will in advance).'

Litvinenko gave the email to Bukovsky, who translated it. It was passed to the Metropolitan Police. According to Goldfarb, Litvinenko was fatalistic about this and other threats. Menzies also sent the email to the Home and Foreign and Commonwealth Offices. In retrospect his letter seems poignant. Menzies wrote:

'Our client [Litvinenko] does not consider that there is likely to be any substance behind this threat. That is to say, he considers that whilst he stays in the UK it is extremely unlikely the "sentence" as described would be carried out. However, given the nature of the threat, we felt it proper to draw this matter to your attention and to invite you to remind the Russian Embassy in London of the attitude of Her Majesty's Government to the contemplation, let alone the carrying out, of such actions.'

The Home Office came back to Menzies with a polite brush-off: 'We have no remit to intervene with the Russian Embassy in such matters.'

Tony Blair's government, it appeared, was unwilling to make a fuss on Litvinenko's behalf. And it's doubtful that an official British complaint would have caused the intelligence officers serving at the Russian embassy in Kensington, west London, to break into a sweat. In any case, with UK officials seemingly unbothered, secret operations against Litvinenko continued.

Next, Ponkin flew to London with a Russian businessman. Litvinenko agreed to meet them at the Piccadilly branch of Wagamama, a Japanese noodle bar. Ponkin had a suggestion: Litvinenko should assassinate Putin! Ponkin said he had a friend in the Federal Protection Service, General Yuri Kalugin, who could provide details of Putin's movements two weeks in advance. All Litvinenko needed to do was to get hold of some Chechens to do the hit …

The offer was a classic FSB 'provocation', and not a very good one. Its apparent goal was to add to the mountain of 'evidence' being gathered against Litvinenko in Moscow. This eventually resulted in Litvinenko being convicted *in absentia* of treason. Ponkin, meanwhile, delivered another message: 'Don't discredit our president. Stop writing articles.' This was, Litvinenko said, one of the many hints that he should cease his critical journalism and shut up.

Litvinenko did the opposite. He wrote a second book, *The Gang from the Lubyanka*. It is based on extended interviews with Litvinenko, conducted by a Moscow journalist, Akram Murtazaev, and edited by Goldfarb. Litvinenko was one of the first writers to allege links between Putin and his associates and organised crime groups.

His thesis – at the time novel – was that Russia's police and intelligence agencies had been perverted. They had started to make money from the very activity they were supposed to investigate, disrupt and prevent. There were other damaging allegations. Litvinenko claimed Putin was a KGB informant at university. And that he'd been on an undercover mission to penetrate Yeltsin's inner circle of advisers, his long-term goal being to preserve the power of the FSB and Russia's security agencies.

Litvinenko and Felshtinsky also continued to pursue the apartment bombings. They flew to Georgia to seek out Achemez Gochiyaev, a Chechen accused of planting one of the bombs. Gochiyaev was hiding in the Pankisi Gorge, a hideout used by Islamist rebels. They had been in contact with Gochiyaev via third parties. They failed to meet him and were forced to leave Georgia in a hurry after they received a message from Berezovsky, warning them he had heard they were in danger. Immediately after they left, their driver, who was working for the Georgian security services, was murdered.

There were further ominous warnings. In 2004, the Litvinenkos heard a noise outside their home in London – and the smell of fire. It was just before midnight. Marina rang the police. The blaze turned out to be small. It emerged that two Chechens had firebombed their house, as well as the neighbouring property of Litvinenko's new friend, the Chechen separatist leader Akhmed Zakayev.

Handsome, groomed and with an immaculately trimmed white beard, Zakayev had begun his career as an actor playing Shakespearean roles in Grozny's theatre. He fought in the first Chechen war and became foreign minister of Chechnya's breakaway government. In 2000, after a car accident, he sought treatment in Western Europe, moving to Britain two years later.

Zakayev was the main emissary abroad of the Chechen republic of Ichkeria. By this point Ichkeria no longer existed: Russian troops had recaptured Grozny. Like Litvinenko, Zakayev was a noxious figure for the Russian government, which accused him of terrorism. By the end of the decade most of Chechnya's independent leaders had been wiped out; Zakayev was the last man standing.

As well as Zakayev, Litvinenko became friends with a curious Italian called Mario Scaramella. Scaramella was the secretary to an Italian parliamentary commission that investigated links between Italian politicians and the KGB. Set up in 2002, the Mitrokhin Commission was politically motivated – an attempt by Silvio Berlusconi's centre-right government to smear its enemies, in particular the former and future centre-left prime minister Romano Prodi.

Scaramella claimed that Prodi was a KGB operative. To support this controversial thesis he fed fake documents to Litvinenko in London. Litvinenko certified them as genuine. Whether he did this because he believed them or simply because he was paid to do so, we don't know. Perhaps it was a combination of both factors. In fact, the Mitrokhin archive itself – based on notes made by a KGB defector – was more damning about other Italian officials at the Moscow embassy, who came out of the investigation far worse. (There was no evidence Prodi was ever KGB, but plenty showing Italian diplomats in Moscow falling into honeytraps and scrapes.)

This was a murky business indeed. Litvinenko was apparently trading in compromising material, for which there is always a ready market in Russia, known as *kompromat*.

Some of Litvinenko's campaign work struck his friends as a little loopy. He blamed the 7/7 bombings – a series of coordinated bomb attacks in central London, carried out in 2005 by four British Islamist men – on the FSB. He also wrote in an article for the *Chechenpress* website that Putin was a paedophile. The incident that inspired it was certainly somewhat bizarre: the president, encountering a group of tourists in the Kremlin, pulled up the shirt of a small boy and kissed him on the tummy. Still, as Goldfarb observed: 'Putin is probably not a paedophile.' To Litvinenko's critics the article was further proof of his sheer public wildness.

Asked later if Litvinenko was a bit of a conspiracy theorist, Goldfarb added: 'Well, at the time I thought so, but with what has happened since, I have become a conspiracy theorist myself, so it's very hard to judge.'

In July 2006, the Duma rushed through two new laws that seemed to have a direct bearing on Litvinenko. The new legislation allowed Russia's spy agencies to eliminate 'extremists' anywhere abroad, including in the UK. The definition of 'extremism' was also expanded. It now included 'libellous' statements about Putin's administration.

Bukovsky and Oleg Gordievsky – the former KGB colonel turned high-profile MI6 informant – understood perfectly what these changes meant: that state murder in western countries now had official cover. In a letter to *The Times*, they wrote: 'Thus, the stage is set for any critic of

Putin's regime here, especially those campaigning against Russian genocide in Chechnya, to have an appointment with a poison-tipped umbrella. According to a statement by the Russian defence minister Sergei Ivanov, the black-list of potential targets is already compiled.'

Russia was about to host the G8 summit in St Peters-burg. Western leaders should be prepared 'to share responsibility for these murders' or not go, Bukovsky and Gordievsky wrote. Needless to say, there was no boycott.

Litvinenko's activities in exile were multifarious: campaigner, journalist, security consultant, investigator. In London he gave interviews and attended public meet-ings. The common thread that linked these personas was Litvinenko's hatred of Putin, the man who had put him in jail, and of the FSB. He was the Russian president's most persistent and ebullient critic.

One important activity, however, remained hidden.

The bank entries speak of middle-class normality. Shop-ping trips to Waitrose and Sainsbury's, direct debits for Sky Digital, and London's congestion charge. The account is with HSBC. Its holders are 'Mr Edwin Redwald Carter & Mrs Maria Anna Carter'. The balance in 2006 fluctu-ates between £969.02 and £8,076.36. The Carters don't appear to be especially well-off. Nor are they broke.

In fact, Litvinenko's bank statements tell us a lot. They give a picture of a typical, health-conscious family (purchases from The Natural Choice), with one child and a car. The Litvinenkos were living at 140 Osier Crescent, a terraced house of yellow brick with a small balcony and a parking spot. The modern estate is in Muswell Hill, in the north London borough of Haringey.

The bank statements root the Litvinenkos in their area. There are debits of £5.40 from Transport for London in East Finchley and Highgate – Litvinenko's regular off-peak travel-card. Visits too to The Children's Bookshop in Muswell Hill. And Japanese food: Yo! Sushi at Gatwick Airport and Itsu, Litvinenko's favourite restaurant in Piccadilly Circus. The odd small sum of money comes in from time to time – a £75 payment from the David Lloyd centre, where Marina taught a kids' class in ballroom dancing.

One regular credit entry is unusual, though.

On the 26th of each month, Litvinenko received an anonymous payment. It appears on the statement simply as 'Transfer', from an unnamed bank account. The account ends with the digits '3698'. The sum in sterling is always the same: '2000.00'. The paying organisation appears – one might think – to be rather bashful.

The sum of £2,000 found in among the groceries and trips to Tesco came from the British Secret Intelligence Service (SIS), also known as MI6.

British intelligence didn't recruit Litvinenko in Moscow. Nor was he ever a spy in Russia: his career in the KGB and FSB involved detective work against criminals, not intelligence. When he arrived in the UK at the end of 2000 seeking political asylum, Litvinenko told Home Office officials truthfully: 'I didn't work in intelligence and I didn't work against England.' He added: 'I have as yet had nothing to do with British intelligence.'

Duplicate Statement of Account

Account Name	Sortcode	Account Number	Sheet Number
Mr Edwin Redwald Carter &		9391	182
Mrs Maria Anna Carter			

Your Bank Account details

Date	Payment Type and Details	Paid Out	In	Balance
21MAR06	SUB BALANCE BROUGHT FORWARD			4220.93
21MAR06	MAE ITSU LTD			
	LONDN W1J 00S	11.13		
21MAR06	MAE CONGESTION CHARGE			
	0645 9001234	8.00		4201.80
22MAR06	CHQ 100157	5.00		
22MAR06	ATM CASH HSBC MAR22			
	LU PICC CIRC@13:11	50.00		4146.80
23MAR06	DD ORANGE	40.00		
23MAR06	MAE TESCO STORE 2296			
	COLNEY HATCH	29.66		
23MAR06	MAE POST OFFICE LTD			
	CAMDEN HIGH S	170.00		
23MAR06	MAE THE NATURAL CHOICE			
	LONDON	22.38		
23MAR06	MAE BY APPOINTMENT KEN			
	LONDON	39.50		
23MAR06	MAE VIRGIN MEGASTORE			
	LONDON W1J B	28.98		
23MAR06	ATM CASH BARCLAY MAR23			
	BRENT CROSS @15:48	60.00		3756.28
24MAR06	CR NET INTEREST			
	TO 23MAR2006		0.37	
24MAR06	MAE Wellington S/Stn			
	Highgate	28.16		
24MAR06	MAE VICTORIA HEALTH-MU			
	LONDON	18.50		
24MAR06	MAE FAGINS TOYS LTD			
	LONDON	28.26		
24MAR06	MAE EARLY CLOTHING,			
	LONDON N1C	32.00		
24MAR06	ATM CASH RB SCOT MAR24			
	TESCO COLNEY@20:36	50.00		3599.73
26MAR06	ATM CASH HSBC MAR26			
	MUSWELL HILL@13:27	100.00		3499.73
27MAR06	DD ADT COLLECTIONS	24.95		
27MAR06	TFR TRANSFER			
	3698		2000.00	
27MAR06	MAE TESCO STORE 2296			
	COLNEY HATCH	51.08		
27MAR06	MAE CONGESTION CHARGE			
	0845 9001234	8.00		5415.70
27MAR06	BALANCE CARRIED FORWARD			5415.70

According to Marina Litvinenko and Alex Goldfarb, Litvinenko began working for MI6 in 2003, some two years after he fled to London. The secret service agency put him on its payroll the next year. In Britain, he was never a full-time agent.

Instead, Litvinenko worked for the agency as an expert adviser. MI6 consulted him on Russian organised crime in Europe, with Litvinenko travelling to various European countries, especially Spain, but also to the Baltic states, Italy and Georgia, assisting their law-enforcement efforts. He spent more time away on 'business trips'. He continued his journalistic work but kept a lower profile.

In line with its long-standing policy, the British government has neither confirmed nor denied that Litvinenko was an MI6 employee. Its file on Litvinenko hasn't been made public. We don't know who hired him. Or if Sir John Scarlett – MI6's prickly then chief, known by the initial 'C' – ever perused Litvinenko's personnel record.

Scarlett knew about Moscow agents. He had been involved in the operation to recruit Gordievsky, the UK's most prized defector. Scarlett was fluent in Russian and lived in Moscow in the 1970s. In 1994, Scarlett, by this point Moscow station chief, was expelled from Russia in a political row.

Marina Litvinenko says she knew of her husband's undercover job. After all, she says, how else might Alexander explain the mysterious £2,000-a-month payments? She didn't know details. She was uncertain if Litvinenko worked for MI5 or MI6, the numbers a source of confusion.

MI6 gave Litvinenko the tools of the trade. He got a British passport for trips abroad – not in his name, of course, but under an as-yet-unrevealed pseudonym. MI6 also assigned him a handler, codename 'Martin', and he was given a dedicated encrypted phone for calling him. Since Litvinenko's English was spotty, 'Martin' was almost certainly a Russian-speaker.

The pair would typically meet in coffee shops in London's West End, including in the basement of the Waterstone's bookshop in Piccadilly – an inconspicuous spot for a rendezvous, with a backdrop of novels and historical biographies. 'Martin' drank coffee; Litvinenko ate pastries. A Russian oligarch, Alexander Mamut, later bought the Waterstone's chain and launched a dedicated Russian-language section upstairs.

According to Goldfarb, MI6 spies were nice guys – a procession of well-bred Johns and Tims. Goldfarb, an expert microbiologist, says MI6 contacted him in 2003. The agency wanted to know if Iraq's Saddam Hussein had biological weapons. He didn't know. He met the spooks in a Piccadilly branch of Caffè Nero.

What did Litvinenko do for MI6? Litvinenko had spent ten years investigating the Russian mafia and its links with Kremlin officials, including Putin. He knew names, faces, backstories. Goldfarb says Litvinenko asked him to translate the 'Uzbek File', which features as a chapter in his book *The Gang from the Lubyanka*.

The Blair government's take on Russia was increasingly negative, but framed through the prism of Putin's rollback of civil society and democracy. This was something new – apparent evidence of how crime lords and politicians conspired to send Afghan drugs to European capitals via St Petersburg. One of those allegedly involved, directly and indirectly, was Putin. Litvinenko writes: 'As an operative officer I have well-founded suspicions regarding Mr Putin – that he is a member of this gang.'

Like all foreign spy agencies, MI6 has a network of agents in the field. It also relies on electronic intelligence, supplied by the UK government's monitoring station, GCHQ, in Cheltenham, and passed to government 'customers'. In addition, the UK is part of Five Eyes, a spying alliance encompassing the US and its National Security Agency (NSA), Canada, Australia and New Zealand. It's probable that Litvinenko reviewed intercept material gleaned from eavesdropping operations against mafia targets. Marina Litvinenko says her husband identified individuals who featured in surveillance photographs.

In Moscow, former FSB colleagues claimed Litvinenko revealed the names of Russian 'sleeper agents' in the UK to MI6 – another act, from the Kremlin's viewpoint, of treason. This seems fantastical. Litvinenko never worked in Russian intelligence. So it's unlikely he would have known the identities of undeclared Russian spies, living long-term in Britain, the US and elsewhere.

Litvinenko's attitude towards spying appears pragmatic rather than romantic. The tradecraft didn't interest him much. He was also very discreet. Litvinenko was frequently in contact with Scaramella, the Italian, while helping the Mitrokhin Commission in Rome. Scaramella asked Litvinenko repeatedly if he was a British agent.

Litvinenko told Scotland Yard later: 'During all our initial meetings he always, insistently, importunately, asked every day whether I was working for MI5 and MI6. He was the only person who asked me so often about it. I told him, Mario, what difference does it make for you? I said, you know, if I say yes you'll think I'm an idiot because such things like this are not spoken about. And if I say no, you won't believe me.'

Litvinenko denied he was working for British intelligence, telling Scaramella: 'I have played spies in my life up to here. And the main thing is, I write books, why would they need me? Think yourself.'

Litvinenko's consultancy work for Her Majesty's Government threw up two important questions. Neither has been properly answered.

One, did the Kremlin discover that Litvinenko worked for MI6?

Two, did MI6 consider Litvinenko to be at risk from Moscow's assassins? If not, why?

In addition to his work for MI6, Litvinenko began in 2005 to provide regular information to Spain's intelligence services. In fact it was British intelligence that introduced Litvinenko to its Spanish counterpart. The Spanish security service assigned Litvinenko a Russian-speaking handler named 'Jorge'. The £2,000-a-month retainer paid by MI6 also covered Litvinenko's work with Spanish spooks and Spanish prosecutors. With increasing frequency, Litvinenko began flying to Madrid and Barcelona. Marina said her husband would return from his trips to Spain with presents – a Real Madrid T-shirt, porcelain souvenirs. As an undercover spy he flew business class, on one occasion even managing to get the autograph of David Beckham, a fellow passenger, for his son Anatoly. But his reason for being in Spain was far from frivolous.

The Spanish authorities were at the time grappling with a serious and chronic problem. From the mid-1990s onwards, *vory v zákone* – in Russian, thieves in law – began to enter Spain. *Vor v zakone* was the highest rank in Russian organised crime. Spain provided a useful haven for Russian mafia bosses, as a base for operations, and a territory safer than Russia itself. Their influence grew. Their activities in Russia included contract killings, kidnappings, drug-running, prostitution and arms-smuggling. Profits in Russia, including from illegal casinos, were laundered in Spain and invested in real estate.

In 2004, Spanish prosecutors created a formal strategy to 'behead' the Russian mafia.

The biggest group active in Spain was the Tambov gang, the same St Petersburg outfit that Litvinenko investigated in the 1990s as an FSB officer. It also included Alexander Malyshev, once the Tambov's competitor, and now its Spain-based criminal partner. The authorities began extensive investigations. They discovered the mafia had no known jobs or sources of income but were living in lavish mansions. The cash clearly came from money-laundering. The challenge was to prove this.

According to the Spanish daily *El País*, Litvinenko provided information on top mafia figures. They were Vitaly Izguilov, Zakhar Kalashov and Tariel Oniani. In the early 1990s, Litvinenko's FSB department had investigated Oniani, a Georgian-born Russian citizen, in connection with a string of kidnappings. One of its victims was the chairman of the Bank of Russia. The case against Oniani was dropped after Litvinenko got a call from above ordering him not to touch him. Kalashov was a hit man. He, too, enjoyed protection from official Russian structures.

Spanish security officials launched two major operations against the Russian mafia, codenamed Avispa (2005–7) and Troika (2008–9). The first phase of Avispa in 2005 saw the arrest of twenty-eight people, twenty-two of them alleged thieves in law. Litvinenko provided the Spanish with details of locations, roles and activities of gang members. The Spanish hailed the operation as the biggest ever undertaken against a global mafia network.

In reality, the results were somewhat mixed. The biggest targets – Kalashov and Oniani – both managed to escape the country on the eve of the raids following a tip-off, most probably from the Russian security services or a corrupt Spanish official. Kalashov was arrested in Dubai in 2006 and extradited to Spain. His fortune, according to court documents, was €200 million.

A secret diplomatic cable, leaked in 2010, and sent from the US embassy in Madrid, suggests that Litvinenko was key to these Spanish operations. His main contribution was to untangle the intimate links between the Russian mafia, senior political figures and the FSB. They were, in effect, a single criminal entity.

In January 2010, Jose Grinda Gonzalez, a special prosecutor for corruption and organised crime, met with US officials in Madrid. In a 'detailed, frank' briefing to a new US–Spain counter-terrorism group, Grinda said that the mafia exercised tremendous sway over the global economy. He said that Russia, Belarus and Chechnya had become 'virtual "mafia states"' and predicted that Ukraine – under its new Kremlin-backed president Viktor Yanukovych – was 'going to be one'.

The special prosecutor said it was an 'unanswered question' whether Putin was personally implicated in the Russian mafia and whether he controls its actions.

The leaked cable reads: 'Grinda cited a "thesis" by Alexander Litvinenko … that the Russian intelligence and security services – Grinda cites the Federal Security Service (FSB), the Foreign Intelligence Service (SVR), and military intelligence (GRU) – control organised crime in Russia. Grinda stated that he believes this thesis to be accurate.'

There was evidence that certain Russian political parties operate 'hand in hand' with the mafia, the prosecutor said. This evidence came from the intelligence services, witnesses and phone taps. He said that the KGB and its successors created the ultra-nationalist Liberal Democratic Party (LDPR), which is home 'to many serious criminals'. He also claimed there were ties between politicians, organised crime and arms trafficking.

According to Grinda, organised criminals in Russia 'complement state structures', with Moscow employing the mafia to do whatever the 'government of Russia cannot acceptably do as a government'. He said that Russian military intelligence, for example, used Kalashov to sell arms to the Kurds, with the aim of destabilising Turkey.

Grinda added: 'The FSB is absorbing the Russian mafia but they can also eliminate them in two ways: by killing organised crime leaders who do not do what the security services want them to do, or by putting them behind bars to eliminate them as a competitor for influence. The crime lords can also be put in jail for their own protection.'

The evidence collected by Spanish investigators would lead to the arrest in 2008 of Gennady Petrov, the Tambov gang's alleged boss; his number two, Alexander Malyshev; and Izguilov. Leaks to the Spanish press talked of the 'hair-raising' contents of wire-tapped conversations. In them, senior mafia figures boasted of their connections with Russian government ministers to 'assure partners that their illicit deals would proceed as planned'.

It wasn't until 2015 that the names of some of these ministers were revealed. Grinda, together with a colleague Juan Carrau, presented a 488-page complaint to Spain's Central Court. The petition brought together ten years of investigative work against the Russian mafia.

According to the news agency Bloomberg, which got hold of the petition, Petrov had his own top-level government network in Moscow. It features many of Putin's allies. They include Viktor Zubkov, Russia's prime minister between 2007 and 2008 and the chairman of Gazprom, the natural gas extractor and one of the world's largest companies. Zubkov's son-in-law Anatoly Serdyukov, Russia's former defence minister, also features.

Other officials mentioned as being 'directly related' to the alleged gang leader are deputy prime minister Dmitry Kozak and Alexander Bastrykin, who studied law with Putin in Leningrad. Bastrykin is the head of Russia's investigative committee that opens (and shuts) major criminal cases. It was Petrov who allegedly secured Bastrykin's appointment. One other name is Leonid Reiman, a former communications minister.

Putin appears three times, including in a 2007 conversation between two Tambov operatives. (They are discussing a house in the Alicante region – and say that Putin owns a neighbouring property in nearby Torrevieja. Dmitry Peskov, Putin's press spokesman, describes this as 'nonsense'.)

The most intriguing name is that of Nikolai Aulov. Aulov is deputy chief at Russia's Federal Narcotics Service. His boss is none other than Viktor Ivanov, the politician and former KGB officer who had the ear of Putin and who was the subject of Litvinenko's 2006 report. The dossier logs seventy-eight phone calls between Aulov and Petrov and describes Aulov as 'one of the most important persons for Petrov'. In 2008, the petition says, Petrov asked an associate to get Aulov to put pressure on Russia's new customs chief. The mafia boss wanted to facilitate port shipments for his group.

The court document seeks to charge twenty-seven people, including Vladimir Reznik, a deputy in Putin's ruling United Russia party and chair of the Duma's financial markets committee. Petrov was spotted on the island of Mallorca with Reznik. Spanish police raided Reznik's Mallorca mansion, allegedly a gift from the gangmaster.

It was an extraordinary picture – mobsters and ministers; money-washing and gun-running; the Kremlin not so much a government as a well-entrenched international crime group with truly big ambitions.

The accused Russian politicians deny wrongdoing. Reznik told Bloomberg his relationship with Petrov is 'purely social'. Meanwhile, Spain's prosecution of Russian mafia suspects ran into various legal snafus. The suspects would hire Spain's best lawyers; often they got bail. The strategy to behead them, though, was working.

All of this was thanks to Litvinenko. He made clear to 'Jorge' that he was willing to testify in court against Putin and Ivanov, spilling everything he knew about Putin's alleged links with the Tambov gang.

This would be some court case. And enough reason for powerful people in Moscow to want Litvinenko silenced.

3

First Deployment

25 Grosvenor Street, Mayfair, London,
Summer–Autumn 2006

'Are you guys from the KGB?'
AUSTRALIAN HOTEL GUEST TO LUGOVOI AND KOVTUN,
17 OCTOBER 2006

There is something surreal about Mayfair. It is London's
wealthiest district, a dark-blue square on the Monopoly
board and home to successive influxes of the international super-rich. Arabs rich from oil, Greek shipping
tycoons, African dictators – all find a home here, washed
in by a global tide of credit crises, coups and recessions.

In Mayfair's Hanover Square, boys and girls in red
uniforms play games at the end of the school day, among
plane trees and an exotic palm from the Canary Islands. It's
all rather English pastoral. The girls sport straw boaters.
Around the square are boutiques, florists, a library and
pigeons; nannies chatting in Russian sit on park benches.

North of the square you find Grosvenor Street and a
row of fashionable eighteenth-century Georgian town-
houses. This was once the abode of earls, lords, admirals
and the odd poet. Now there are the understated brass
plaques of commerce. It's not entirely clear what many
of the businesses based here do. Hedge funds? Corporate

PR? Wealth management? The location radiates prestige, reliability, trustworthiness.

And a little mystery. If London is the spy capital of the world, Mayfair is its centre. It is the traditional home of private intelligence companies. There are casinos, luxury car showrooms and exclusive nightclubs. Nearby is Pall Mall. Here, in gentlemen's clubs, the establishment comes together. Defence officials, spooks and ministers meet to do deals and exchange gossip. The Houses of Parliament are down the road.

Most of those who work in private intelligence have at some point been on the other side. They include ex-spies, army officers and former Scotland Yard detectives – sometimes ones prepared to bend the law.

Their work includes providing business intelligence, investigating employee fraud and supplying personal protection. Another lucrative market is due diligence. Companies looking to expand internationally need information on prospective partners, especially in jurisdictions with lousy records of governance, like Africa, the Middle East and the ex-Soviet Union.

Litvinenko visited Grosvenor Street often. He would arrive here on foot, walking past the Bentleys, Porsches and Ferraris, before disappearing into an entrance with an ornate classical portico and heavy oak front door. This was 25 Grosvenor Street. On the fourth floor were two companies, Titon and Erinys. Both were bespoke intelligence firms. They operated in the commercial market but also had links – never quite defined – with the world of British spying.

When Litvinenko first fled to Britain, Berezovsky was paying him a salary of $6,000 a month. The money came from Berezovsky's New York-based International Civil Liberties Foundation. It was reduced in 2003 and again in 2006. Berezovsky told police there was nothing malicious about these cuts. They were done by mutual agreement, he said, as Litvinenko became more 'independent', and started working for British and Spanish intelligence.

Litvinenko was understandably upset as his income fell. And, according to Goldfarb, 'a little bit worried' about his financial future. He was forced to seek other sources of income. He'd hoped that MI6 might give him a full-time job. It didn't.

The agency did, though, introduce Litvinenko to Dean Attew, Titon's director. It asked Attew if he might help Litvinenko to develop a commercial footprint. Litvinenko would conduct investigations into Russians who were of interest to clients. In return he'd get a fee.

Litvinenko knew about the Russian mafia and therefore had something to offer Titon. He also had one good source in Moscow. This was the investigative journalist and prominent Putin critic Anna Politkovskaya. Politkovskaya visited the UK often – her sister lives in London. She would bring Litvinenko news of the latest Kremlin intrigues. Some of Litvinenko's other contacts were in jail (like former FSB-officer-turned-lawyer Trepashkin) or out of date.

What he needed was a Russian partner. In 2005, Litvinenko had what appeared to be a piece of luck. Andrei

Lugovoi – at that time a successful Moscow-based businessman – rang him up. They had first met in 1995, when both had loosely been members of Berezovsky's circle.

On 21 October 2005, Litvinenko had dinner with Lugovoi in a Chinese restaurant in Soho. Lugovoi said he had flown in for a match between Chelsea and Spartak Moscow. He brought someone with him: a pensioned-off Russian intelligence officer. The officer was a technical expert whose job was to place special microphones in foreign embassies and official buildings. His name remains unknown.

Recalling their conversation, Litvinenko said that forty minutes into the meal Lugovoi made him an interesting offer: 'Alexander, if you like to work with me we can earn money together.'

Litvinenko could take orders from London-based companies seeking to do business in Russia, Lugovoi said. Back in Moscow, Lugovoi would collect sensitive information. They would be a team, a sort of mini-version of the New York-based corporate investigations and risk consultancy firm Kroll. They would make money. Litvinenko said: 'Thank you, thank you.'

Litvinenko's first foray into this industry with his new partner was with a company called RISC Management, run by a former Scotland Yard detective called Keith Hunter. It offered 'security investigations and services'. Hunter specialised in Russian clients, one of them Berezovsky. Litvinenko was asked to investigate Russia's deputy agriculture minister on behalf of a vodka company. Was the minister corrupt?

The money wasn't huge, but Litvinenko found these corporate assignments interesting; his new colleagues good people. Increasingly, Lugovoi flew to London. The intelligence product he brought with him, as his part of the arrangement, was uninspiring. His work on the vodka assignment appeared to have been culled from the Russian internet.

Still, RISC paid $7,500 to Lugovoi's Cyprus bank account. Lugovoi was ex-KGB, which meant a lot in Putin's Russia. Maybe Lugovoi was the key that would prise open the door to Gazprom and other state giants.

In January 2006, Litvinenko, his Chechen friend and neighbour Zakayev, and their wives, were guests at Berezovsky's sixtieth birthday party. It was a lavish black-tie affair held at Blenheim Palace, the ancestral home of the Duke of Marlborough near Woodstock in Oxfordshire. Lugovoi flew in from Moscow. They

shared a table and posed together for a photo in front of the palace's entrance of classical columns. Lugovoi, standing on the left of the picture, is an ingenuous presence, his smile as ever disarming. It was the only time that Marina Litvinenko met Lugovoi.

Lugovoi flew back to the UK in March, April (twice) and May (twice) and June. He was a man of means who stayed in the best hotels – in Knightsbridge, Mayfair, Piccadilly. The trips were so frequent they aroused mild suspicion. A British consular official in Moscow noted on his visa application: 'Speak to applicant and ask why he has used his last visa eight times and why he was in the UK and what he was doing?'

Another embassy official noted Lugovoi's reply: 'The applicant says he has travelled to the UK purely for holidays because he has friends there (Alexander Litvinenko) and he likes the UK. He travelled either alone or with his wife.' Lugovoi's passport is a galaxy of Russian exit and UK entry stamps – Stansted Airport, 22 January 2006, Gatwick, 5 April 2006.

Meanwhile, Litvinenko's dealings with Berezovsky were cooling. The dispute was over money. There was no terminal quarrel. Berezovsky continued to pay Anatoly's private school fees, and said of Litvinenko: 'We continued good relations.'

Litvinenko's relationship with Lugovoi, however, continued to grow – what had started as a business alliance apparently developing into friendship. Over the summer, Lugovoi and his wife Svetlana visited Litvinenko at his home in Muswell Hill. On the walls Lugovoi saw photos

Date: 26/5/56

**British Embassy
Moscow**

Consular and Visa Section
10 Smolenskaya Naberezhna
Moscow 121099

Telephone: (007) 095 956 72
Facsimile: (007) 095 956 74

Email: Visa.Enquiries2@fco.g
Web Page: www.britaininruss

DOCUMENT VERIFICATION REPORT

Applicant's name – Lugovoy

Reference Number – MOS/ 819490

Date of Application – 26/5/56

Document:	Result of Check:
1. Speak to applicant and ask why he has used his last visa 8 times and why he was in the UK and what he was doing? 2.	The applicant says he has travelled to the UK purely for holidays because he has friends there (Alekandr Litvinenko) and he likes the UK. He travelled either alone or with his wife.

Check undertaken by: MARINA I   (Signature) ....

Time and date of check: 10:10 26.05.06

ECO's Conclusion: I am satisfied, to a high degree of probability, that the document(s) is/are false.

I can draw no conclusion from the information contained above.

(delete as appropriate)

ECO: CW.

of Litvinenko with Bukovsky and Oleg Gordievsky, the former KGB colonel and station chief in London who famously defected to Britain in 1985. All three were prominent Putin enemies.

Litvinenko introduced Lugovoi to his circle of contacts, including Titon's director Attew. The meeting took place at Heathrow Airport's terminal one, while Lugovoi was on his way back from Canada to Moscow. Attew disliked him intensely: 'Seven years of watching people around gaming tables and reading body language left me feeling extremely uncomfortable when I sat with Lugovoi. I didn't enjoy the experience and was very pleased to be leaving there.'

Attew's own status was a matter of sensitivity. Lugovoi would later claim that Attew was Litvinenko's handler and an MI6 agent. And that Attew had tried – unsuccessfully – to recruit him as an asset for British intelligence. MI6 have not, of course, confirmed or denied this but it would not be unlikely that Attew was a former spook and he was certainly well connected in that world.

Soon after the Heathrow meeting, something very odd happened at 25 Grosvenor Street. In the early hours of the morning intruders broke down the black oak front door. They ignored the immediate offices and went to the fourth floor, taking out the entire door-frame to the Titon vestibule. They spent four or five minutes inside. Seemingly they stole nothing.

The next day Attew made a thorough search. No clues. 'In my business, that's a reconnaissance,' he said. 'That's a recce.' At the time Attew didn't connect it with Litvinenko. Later the break-in made gruesome sense.

The job was done by professional agents. This was the FSB, almost certainly, scoping the ground for a future operation. Litvinenko had always warned Berezovsky that he was most at risk from people who'd featured in his past. In his keenness to make money, and to provide for his family, Litvinenko had forgotten his own rule.

It was a warm autumn day when the two Russian visitors arrived in Grosvenor Street. That morning, 16 October 2006, their undercover mission had almost met with failure when DC Scott, the customs officer, stopped them at Gatwick Airport. But their cover story had held up. Most importantly, the costly poison they had been given back in Russia was intact. This was polonium, a rare and highly radioactive substance. It is probably the most toxic substance known to man when swallowed or inhaled – more than 100 billion times more deadly than hydrogen cyanide.

The next task was to deploy it. They had come to poison Litvinenko.

Scotland Yard would never establish how Lugovoi and Kovtun carried the polonium into Britain. The amounts involved were very small and easy to disguise. There were several possibilities: a container with the poison administered by a pipette-style dropper. Or an aerosol-like spray. Even a modified fountain pen would do the trick. Within its container the polonium was safe. Out of it it was highly dangerous. Ingested, you were dead.

Lugovoi and Kovtun, it would become apparent, had no idea what they were carrying. Their behaviour in Britain was idiotic verging on suicidal. Nobody in Moscow appears to have told them Po-210 had intensely radioactive properties. Or that it left a trace – placing them in specific locations and indicating, via telltale alpha radiation markings, who sat where. It was possible to identify anything and everything they touched: door handles, telephones, wash basins.

These clueless assassins left numerous trails. The most vivid was radiation: subsequently tested by forensic experts, and turned by experts from the Metropolitan Police into colourful three-dimensional graphics. Another was financial: a series of clues whenever Lugovoi paid a bill with his Bank Metropol Mastercard. One other was cellular. Phone records, retrieved by detectives, showed who called whom, for how long, and when.

And of course there were witnesses. They told a remarkable story: of two killers who, in addition to the business of murder, indulged in sight-seeing, shopping, boozing, fine dining – and flirting. During their trips to London they tried to pick up women. Without success. Surely, the KGB was better at seduction in its heyday?

Earlier that morning – at 11.49 – Lugovoi had called Litvinenko from Gatwick Airport. He confirmed they were meeting that afternoon at the intelligence firm Erinys, Titon's sister company at 25 Grosvenor Street. They would be discussing a potentially lucrative new line of business regarding the energy giant Gazprom. Lugovoi and Kovtun travelled by train to central London. They checked into the Best Western Hotel on Shaftesbury Avenue, in the heart of Soho.

The first rule of spycraft is not to draw attention to yourself. In Lugovoi and Kovtun's case the reality was comically, even ludicrously, different. From the moment they stepped onto UK soil, Lugovoi and Kovtun attracted attention wherever they went. It wasn't just that they were assassins: the problem was they *looked* like assassins, a pair of stage villains from FSB Casting.

The two Russians walked through the main entrance of the Best Western Hotel. Its Yugoslav-born manager, Goran Krgo, was on duty. Lugovoi did the talking, he recalled. Their rooms weren't ready until 2 p.m, so he suggested they go and have lunch in a café nearby. The two guests didn't have much luggage, which was unusual, he said.

When they came back, Lugovoi's room – 107 – was ready. Lugovoi and Kovtun went upstairs. They emerged twenty minutes later, having swapped their casual clothes for 'business' attire. Their appearance prompted hotel staff to chuckle. Kovtun was wearing a silvery metallic polyester-type suit and Lugovoi was kitted out in checks. They had matched their shiny outfits with colourful shirts and ties. They wore chunky jewellery.

According to Krgo, the two men resembled stereo-typical Eastern European gangsters. 'I remember these guests quite vividly. We were laughing. The girl who worked behind the desk was amused by the dress code … and making general comments.' Krgo added: 'The colours didn't match, the suits were either too big or too small, they just didn't look like people who are used to wearing suits. They looked like – I think the expression is like a donkey with a saddle.'

At 3 p.m. Litvinenko met Lugovoi and Kovtun in Grosvenor Street. It was the first time Litvinenko had ever met Kovtun. Lugovoi introduced him as an old childhood friend with whom he was now in business. Kovtun said little. Litvinenko didn't warm to him particularly, but nonetheless Kovtun must have seemed as if he might be another useful Russian contact he could tap for information. After all, if he was Lugovoi's friend, he could trust him, surely?

The three Russians entered number 25 together – through its grand entrance with two white Doric columns – and took the lift to the fourth floor. Waiting for them there was Tim Reilly, the Russian-speaking head of Erinys; he shook their hands and led them inside.

Erinys and Titon International shared a boardroom. It wasn't exactly sumptuous but had a few old-school establishment touches: an oak dining table covered in a green baize cloth; leather-upholstered chairs; a map of the world (nodding to Erinys's ambitions). Tea and coffee sat on the sideboard. A bay window looked out onto the street.

Attew had previously introduced Litvinenko to Reilly as someone who might be useful to Russian-facing clients. Reilly warmed to Litvinenko. He thought him gregarious, dynamic and full of energy, but also prone to flash off in too many different directions. (Reilly attributed Litvinenko's 'lack of mental discipline' to his background in the Soviet Union, where contacts were everything and analytical detail irrelevant. He said also that Litvinenko was learning and adapting to life in the west.)

For Reilly, the meeting was about a possible security contract with Gazprom. He shook hands with the Russians and showed them into the boardroom. Lugovoi arrived with shopping bags. The meeting began in typically English style, with talk of the sunny weather. Then Lugovoi steered the conversation round to tea. He suggested they all drink some, joking that the English had cups of tea all the time. Reilly declined and told them he'd just drunk water from the cooler. Lugovoi was weirdly persistent.

'They kept on saying to me – don't you want any [tea], won't you have any?' Reilly recalled.

Reilly served cups of tea to his three guests. He sat to the right of Litvinenko, who was at the head of the table with his back facing the bay window; immediately across the table from Reilly was Lugovoi. Kovtun sat to Lugovoi's left. He said nothing. Lugovoi had visited Erinys two or three times before. 'He was professional enough, smartly dressed, quite keen to impress, quite self-assured,' Reilly said – a classic *Novy Russky*, or new Russian on the make, in his view.

'We would call it nouveau riche, so they would have all the accoutrements of the western world and then there would be an odd, you know, shiny tie or something like that,' he added. 'It was quite funny. It sounds awful, but you could spot this straightaway. He was capable, he was reasonably intelligent.'

After making tea, Reilly – fortuitously for the would-be assassins – disappeared off to the loo.

We don't know how the polonium was deployed. The forensic evidence suggests that either Lugovoi or Kovtun slipped it into Litvinenko's cup of tea or water. Litvinenko failed to notice, or was otherwise distracted. For the next thirty minutes, the tea or glass of water sat in front of him, a little to his left – an invisible nuclear murder weapon.

The conversation was of Gazprom. Lugovoi and Kovtun must have been barely listening: for them, the only question was, would Litvinenko drink?

Litvinenko didn't drink. The plan – pre-mediated, for sure, but possibly improvised in its execution – failed. One can only imagine what must have been going through Lugovoi's and Kovtun's minds when the meeting broke up, his drink untouched.

When nuclear scientists examined the Erinys table they found it was 'heaving' with radioactive contamination, in Reilly's damning words. It appeared there had been substantial spillage. Reilly wondered whether he too had been an intended target. One spot in front of where Litvinenko had been sitting showed 'full-scale deflection'. This meant an off-the-scale reading of more than 10,000 counts per second. Other parts of the baize had readings of 2,300 counts per second. One chair – where either Lugovoi or Kovtun had been sitting – registered at 7,000 counts per second.

The Russians would later claim that it was Litvinenko who had got hold of the radioactive polonium. They claimed that he had poisoned them, during this, their first significant encounter in Mayfair. All subsequent traces, they said, could be explained by this initial radioactive contact. It was a version they would repeat to Russian state media, which transmitted it as true.

This was a whopping lie, and easily disproved. Scotland Yard reconstructed Litvinenko's journey from his home to Green Park using his Oyster Card. He had travelled on the number 43 bus, getting on at Friern Barnet, then taking the tube into central London from Highgate Station. The bus – vehicle registration LRO2 BCX – was found and tested for contamination. There wasn't any.

Lugovoi and Kovtun, by contrast, left a lurid nuclear stain wherever they went, including in their hotel rooms, well before their first meeting with Litvinenko. After leaving Erinys, Litvinenko took the pair to his favourite branch of Itsu in Piccadilly Circus, close to the Ritz Hotel. They sat downstairs. Polonium was found here too. The visitors farewelled Litvinenko and returned to the Best Western Hotel.

Phone records show that at 19.55 Lugovoi made a phone call. He rang a woman identified only as 'female A'. Lugovoi's intentions were amorous. He had met female A on a previous visit, detectives established, and was keen to meet her again. Despite his best efforts, she turned him down.

Rebuffed, Lugovoi went out for dinner with Kovtun. At 8.30 p.m. they met Alexander Shadrin, the boss of Continental Petroleum Limited, which had formally invited them to London. CPL had won exploration licences to two oil fields in western Siberia. The firm had sought Lugovoi's help after a gang tried to grab the oilfields – a ubiquitous criminal practice in Russia involving corrupt judges and bureaucrats, and known as 'raiding'.

Improbably, Lugovoi had helped to secure rulings from provincial Siberian courts in CPL's favour. For a far-away foreign investor to win victory over local crooks was a miracle. Apparently, Lugovoi had powerful friends. The judgment appeared to have more to do with Lugovoi's elaborate cover story than with justice. The FSB may have arranged the ruling in order to help Lugovoi and Kovtun secure British visas for their many trips to London.

CPL's office was at 58 Grosvenor Street, immediately across the road from Erinys and Titon, in a Georgian townhouse. The company was respectable. It even had aristocratic connections. Chairman of the board was the Honourable Charles Balfour, an old Etonian. It was Balfour who had written a letter to the British embassy in Moscow supporting Kovtun's visa application.

Viewed with hindsight, this was not Balfour's finest moment. He listed his interests in *Debrett's*, the British toffs' handbook, as 'gardening, shooting, fishing, and bee-keeping'. He is descended from the Conservative prime minister and foreign secretary Arthur Balfour; his brother is the current earl.

The Russians had dinner with Shadrin at Pescatori, a family-run Italian fish restaurant in Dover Street. Lugovoi enjoyed the finer things in life. The bill shows the party ordered oysters, a grilled lobster, two tuna steaks (very rare), with grappa and espresso to finish. According to Shadrin, Lugovoi talked of his bottling plant in Russia. He insisted on picking up the £214.20 bill. He told Shadrin that since he was 'pitching for business', he would get the tab. Radiation was found here too: at their table, on cushions, in the gents'.

Afterwards, Lugovoi claimed that he and Kovtun strolled around Soho for one and a half hours. They dropped into a bar, Dar Marrakesh in the Trocadero Centre, where Lugovoi smoked a £9 shisha pipe on the terrace. It was 11 p.m., a balmy night. Scotland Yard later retrieved Lugovoi's pipe. It was easy to spot: the handle gave off a ghostly alpha radiation glow.

Back at home in Muswell Hill, Litvinenko felt mildly unwell. He threw up, just once. His vomiting spasm was due to exposure to radiation – just from being *near* the poison. Litvinenko thought little of this episode. He had unwittingly survived his first encounter with polonium and an attempt to kill him.

At 1 a.m. the would-be killers returned to the Best Western Hotel. At some point that day or the next Lugovoi handled polonium in the privacy of his room, 107. He appears to have transferred it here from one container to another. And to have disposed of it down the bathroom sink.

We know this because Lugovoi's plughole showed exceptionally high alpha radiation readings of 1,500 counts per second. There are lower readings elsewhere in the bathroom, and in the bedroom next door. Kovtun's room, 306, is also heavily contaminated. There are 1,500 cps on a chair and coat-hanger, with lower readings from a radiator and phone directory.

The two Russians had booked into the Best Western for two nights, with Lugovoi paying in advance. The next day, 17 October, they abruptly checked out and took a taxi to the Parkes Hotel in Beaufort Gardens, Knightsbridge. Lugovoi explained the switch by saying he 'didn't like the condition of the rooms'. The real reason, most probably, was to distance himself from the poison, which he had efficiently tipped down the bathroom u-bend.

The Parkes Hotel was the scene of two encounters, both blackly comic. Front office manager Giuliana Rondini was on duty that afternoon. At 2 p.m. two guests walked in: Lugovoi, wearing a beige or brown casual-type jacket with a zip at the front, and Kovtun, in a grey jacket and black round-necked T-shirt. They told her they had moved hotels because their previous one was 'overbooked'. Rondini checked them into the hotel's last available rooms, 23 and 25.

The Russians returned to the lobby ten minutes later. Lugovoi asked Rondini where she was from. When she replied Sardinia he said he'd been there, to the capital Cagliari. They chatted. She asked if they needed a restaurant for the evening. Lugovoi then made a request. Was there was somewhere fun for later where he and Kovtun 'might meet some girls'?

Rondini was used to dealing tactfully with these kinds of delicate enquiries from lonesome international travellers. She recommended a place just across the street –

1 Beaufort Gardens. 'It was well known with girls. It was a brothel,' Rondini said.

Failing that, she suggested an Italian restaurant, Pizza Pomodoro, in Beauchamp Place. Rondini said: 'It was a place where you could go and have a pizza but also have fun and pick up girls. Pizza with extras, I would say.'

Meanwhile, a regular Australian guest staying at the hotel spotted Kovtun and Lugovoi in the lift. She told Andrea Furlani, who worked at reception, that they had struck her as strange.

She asked them: 'Where are you from?'

Lugovoi replied in English: 'Russia.'

She then said in tones of ice-breaking amusement: 'Are you guys from the KGB?'

The two Russians started backwards. They looked horror-struck. Neither of them responded. The lift continued its descent in awkward silence. Later that day the Australian saw Kovtun and Lugovoi again in the hotel lobby and said a friendly hello. They ignored her. The pair must have been confused. Was this an uncomfortable coincidence? Was the Australian a spy? A British agent? Fuck!

At 6 p.m. Lugovoi and Kovtun met Litvinenko again outside the Oxford Street branch of Nike. They visited the offices of RISC Management. Daniel Quirke, one of RISC's investigators, took them into the fifth-floor boardroom.

According to Litvinenko, Kovtun produced a small minidisc. Quirke fetched his laptop. There was a beep. Kovtun inserted the disc and typed in a four-digit access code. This program, apparently, enabled Kovtun to pick a telephone number in Russia and to listen in. He played two audio files. The room was filled with the sound of Russian voices; the quality was crisp and clean.

Quirke was surprised. It appeared Lugovoi and Kovtun were keen to monetise information collected by eavesdropping, by selling it potentially to British clients. The legal dimension didn't feature. 'When he [Quirke] saw it, his eyes started out of his head,' Litvinenko said. Kovtun, it appeared, had good technical skills.' He took out his own computer and demonstrated it himself. Andrei [Lugovoi] doesn't know how to use this kind of stuff,' Litvinenko added.

Afterwards, the three Russians took a taxi to Chinatown and went for dinner. Nothing happened to Litvinenko's tea. Lugovoi paid the bill on his card and they went on to a pub.

Recollecting their conversation, Litvinenko said: 'They found a place in a corner, ordered some beer and started to order for me. But I said, no, guys, I can't stay in such dirty places like that.' Litvinenko told the police he didn't like the noise or 'the prostitutes'. He took the 134 bus home.

About 11.30 p.m. Lugovoi rang Litvinenko to say that he was missing out on fun times. He said that he and Kovtun had hired a rickshaw and that they were going on an hour-long joyride through central London – two off-duty assassins enjoying themselves amid the bright lights of Soho. They trundled past red double-decker buses, crowded bars, West End theatreland. Their rick-shaw driver was Polish. He spoke 'not bad' Russian. It appears they asked again about girls. The driver recommended a private members' place in Jermyn Street popular with big-spending Russians.

This was Hey Jo's, an erotic club founded in 2005 by a former fruit-and-veg stall owner from Essex called Dave West. It featured mirrored walls, frilly pink cubicles, waitresses dressed as naughty nurses, and a bronze phallus. There was a dance-floor and a Russian-themed restaurant, Abracadabra, with silver tables. The bordello theme extended to the bathrooms, where water spouted from penis-shaped gold taps.

Lugovoi and Kovtun spent two hours at Hey Jo's, leaving at 3 a.m. Detectives were able to piece together where they'd been. They found traces of radiation in cubicle nine – on the backrest and cushions. There were low levels on a bench, a table in the restaurant, and on a door in the gents'. No polonium was found on the phallus, also tested. The floor was clean. Apparently the men from the KGB didn't dance.

Even in these promising surroundings, their side-mission to pick up women was unfruitful. The next morning, checking out of the Parkes Hotel for the flight back to Moscow, Rondini asked Lugovoi how they had got on.

His reply was uncharacteristically honest. 'We were not lucky that night,' he told her.

Lugovoi's conversations back in Moscow following his first unsuccessful attempt to poison Litvinenko can only be imagined. In short, he had failed. 'Probably the chief yelled at them and said they weren't good enough. It meant they had to go back and get another vial [of polonium],' Goldfarb suggested.

The upshot was that within days Lugovoi returned to the UK, this time alone, taking with him another container of radioactive poison. He flew on 25 October from Moscow to London, on British Airways flight 875. He sat in business class, seat 6K. He arrived shortly after midnight at the Sheraton Park Lane, a grandly positioned hotel overlooking Piccadilly, with a frontage of black classical pillars. Inside, the hotel was rather worn. Lugovoi stayed in room 848, on the eighth floor.

After six years in Britain, Litvinenko was careful about security. He was *akkuratny* – a Russian word meaning neat, careful, punctual, exact, thorough. As a former FSB officer he practised good operational security. He didn't discuss sensitive matters on the telephone. He told Quirke that he was concerned about London, describing it as such an open city and a place where people from Russia can come and do anything they want.

Despite these precautions and the litany of death threats in the past, Litvinenko trusted Lugovoi, who had now returned for a second time to kill him. Why?

For one thing, there was a sense of shared history. Both were ex-KGB. Both, seemingly, had spent time in Russian jails on false charges, victims of state injustice. In 2001, Lugovoi served eighteen months behind bars after apparently trying to free Berezovsky's friend Nikolai Glushkov from jail. Glushkov was later released and fled to the UK in 2005. The Russian authorities had accused him and Berezovsky of embezzling funds from Aeroflot.

Glushkov was never convinced that Lugovoi actually went to prison. It's an open question when precisely he began cooperating with the FSB. Some believe it was as early as 2001 at the time of his dubious 'jailing', and that the spy agency gave him a long-term mission to penetrate enemy circles in London. Others think that Lugovoi was forced to turn assassin after the Kremlin got hold of Litvinenko's Ivanov report in the autumn of 2006.

Certainly other compatriots trusted Lugovoi. The morning after his return to London, Lugovoi set off in a chauffeur-driven Mercedes to an estate near Leatherhead, Surrey. His driver, Bruno Bonnetti, remembers him sitting on the back seat, talking in Russian on his mobile. They pulled up outside a palatial home; an iron security gate swung open. A tall man with a white moustache wearing a jogging suit, and in his early fifties, appeared. The man embraced Lugovoi. This was Badri Patarkatsishvili, the Georgian billionaire and associate of Berezovsky who had assisted in Litvinenko's escape. Nearby, another chauffeur was washing the oligarch's Maybach car.

Patarkatsishvili had hired Lugovoi in the 1990s to be head of security at his ORT TV channel. According to his friend Yuli Dubov, the Georgian later loaned Lugovoi $7 million. Generally speaking, the tycoon thought that ex-FSB officers made bad businessmen. Nonetheless, Patarkatsishvili told police that Lugovoi was a nice bloke, hard-working, a good employee. Lugovoi and Patarkatsishvili talked for some hours, sitting at the bottom of the garden in the gazebo. Lugovoi tried to persuade

Patarkatsishvili to come in as an investor in a new water business. He declined.

'Badri never liked slaves,' Dubov said, reflecting on Lugovoi's charm. 'Lugovoi was a very good guy, nice-looking and nice-talking. He gave the impression of being absolutely on the level, straightforward, one of us.'

Undoubtedly, Patarkatsishvili thought more favourably of Lugovoi than he did of Litvinenko – someone, in his view, 'who had crazy ideas about Russian politics' and who was 'obsessed by the FSB', as a result of his unhappy career. The police later impounded Lugovoi's radioactive Mercedes.

On his return from Surrey, Lugovoi met Litvinenko in his hotel. They sat in the ground-floor Palm Court, an afternoon tea room furnished in high art deco style, with Chinese screen paintings, vases and lamps. Litvinenko produced two Orange SIM cards so that he and Lugovoi had a secure way of communicating. As ever, Litvinenko drank tea, from a silver teapot. Lugovoi ordered three glasses of red wine and a Cuban cigar.

According to Lugovoi, Litvinenko revealed here that he worked for Spanish intelligence. He suggested that Lugovoi accompany him the next month on a joint trip to Spain. In Madrid they'd meet Litvinenko's Russian-speaking Spanish handler, Jorge. It's unclear if Litvinenko was acting under MI6's direction here or simply wanted to present Lugovoi to his Spanish contacts as a useful Moscow-based source.

Litvinenko also had another important appointment. He was due on 8 November to meet Grinda, the Spanish public prosecutor. It would be their first encounter. All Litvinenko's previous dealings had been with the Spanish secret service, which fed evidence to his prosecutors.

For Litvinenko, this was a serious escalation in his war with the Kremlin. It meant he was willing to testify in open court about the activities of the Russian mafia – and its friends in government. It's unclear when Lugovoi learned of the planned meeting. According to Goldfarb, it may have triggered Moscow's frantic efforts to kill Litvinenko, and to silence him as a witness. 'That gives you a motive,' Goldfarb said. Grinda was more circumspect, later saying he didn't believe it was the cause.

Either way, this was the moment for Lugovoi to poison Litvinenko again. For unknown reasons, Lugovoi failed to deploy the latest vial of polonium he had brought. One possible explanation is that the Palm Court bar had video cameras, which Lugovoi would have seen. Or perhaps he suspected he was being watched. Did the British have him under counter-surveillance? (The answer – no.) It's possible he had got fresh orders from Moscow. Either way, Lugovoi decided to abort the operation.

This left him with a problem: what to do with the poison?

Lugovoi's solution was simple. In his hotel room he tipped the polonium away down the bathroom sink again, this time mopping it up with a couple of towels. He left the towels for the cleaner. And he appeared to have dumped the container in the white pedal bin next to the lavatory.

When scientists later tested Lugovoi's hotel room on the eighth floor they walked into a scene from an atomic horror story. The door to Lugovoi's room was highly contaminated. It showed full-scale deflection and a reading of more than 30,000 counts per second. Inside, there was further contamination – on the carpet, guest directory, and telephone book in a cupboard.

The situation in the bathroom, white-painted and with a tiled floor, was even worse. The inside of the pedal bin registered another full-scale deflection, with 30,000-plus. There was radiation everywhere: on the wall under the sink, the floor and bath, plus another massive reading from the bathroom door.

The two scientists wearing protective gear gazed at their instruments incredulously. They asked to be withdrawn from the room. The team was stood down on safety grounds.

Amazingly, two months later, detectives located the towels that Lugovoi had chucked away. They had ended up stuck in a laundry chute in the hotel's basement. A three-foot-by-three-foot metal service tube ran the full height of the building. At its bottom was a mountain of unwashed sheets and towels.

Lugovoi's bath towel was found in a green laundry bag on a shelf. His hand towel was discovered at the base of the chute.

The levels of radiation were so alarming that the towels were sent to the Atomic Weapons Establishment at Aldermaston, the UK government nuclear facility. The contamination was massive. The bath towel gave a reading of 6,000 counts per second, or 130,000 becquerels per square centimetre. (The unit of radioactivity is named after Henri Becquerel, the French physicist who shared a Nobel prize with Marie and Pierre Curie.)

The most extreme object, though, was Lugovoi's white hand towel. The initial reading came in as full-scale deflection, greater than 10,000 counts per second. Retested at Aldermaston, it yielded an astonishing result: in excess of 17 million becquerels per square centimetre. To give an idea of context, the equivalent of 10–30 million becquerels absorbed into an adult male's blood would be likely to be fatal within one month.

The towel was the single most radioactive object recovered by Scotland Yard during its decade-long inquiry. Probably the most radioactive towel in history.

4

The German Waiter

Hamburg, Germany, 1996–2006

'I have a very expensive poison'
DMITRY KOVTUN TO HIS FRIEND D3 IN HAMBURG,
30 OCTOBER 2006

Dmitry Kovtun had big dreams. Dreams of a better life in the west, of a well-paying job, of a successful career. One day the fantasy took the shape of a vodka factory. Kovtun would be the owner. The factory would be based in Moscow. It would produce vodka with a new and revolutionary type of seal! Another dream was rather more saucy. Kovtun would star in movies. Not just any old movies: specifically, porn movies, with Kovtun playing the role of the stud. Or soft-core magazines. The sex industry would bring him cash, lots of it, maybe fame as well.

Somehow, though, reality never quite matched up to Kovtun's expectations of it. For him, at least, it was a disappointment. The glamorous career never quite materialised. He didn't get the breaks. The same could not be said for his silver-tongued friend Andrei Lugovoi. Everything Lugovoi touched turned to gold. But perhaps some of Lugovoi's good fortune might rub off on him?

Kovtun first met Lugovoi in 1978 or 1979. The boys grew up in the same building where his family and

Lugovoi's family had been granted flats at the same time. 'Our fathers were friends and worked together at the army general HQ of the USSR armed forces,' Kovtun said. 'We were pupils at different schools – I am one year older than Lugovoi – but we spent a great deal of time together as children, visited each other, exchanged books.'

The two families had a shared military story. Kovtun's father Vadim was a high-ranking officer. (His mother, who lives in Moscow, is a vet.) Lugovoi's family had a record stretching back to the 1905 Russo-Japanese war. Lugovoi's father was a colonel in the Soviet army; his grandfather fought with the Red Army against the Nazis in the battle for Berlin in 1945. A brother worked on Russian nuclear submarines. Lugovoi would make much of this patriotic tradition.

It was inevitable that Kovtun and Lugovoi would don uniforms too. In 1982, Kovtun joined an elite Soviet military command academy in Moscow; Lugovoi followed the next year. 'We saw each other regularly and associated on friendly terms while studying there,' Kovtun said. He was trained as an engineer for wheeled and tracked vehicles; a practical course took him to Murmansk *oblast* in Russia's frozen north; a few old snaps show him there in the sub-arctic.

In 1986, Kovtun graduated as second lieutenant. He was sent to Czechoslovakia and then to Parchim, a town with a large Soviet airfield surrounded by the countryside and forests of Mecklenburg-Vorpommern, in East Germany. Times were changing, though. Back home, Mikhail Gorbachev was trying to reform a tottering

USSR. Lugovoi had stayed in Moscow and got a job as a Kremlin bodyguard with the KGB's ninth directorate. As ever, his assignment was starrier than Kovtun's.

When the Berlin Wall came down Kovtun was stuck in Parchim, seemingly on the wrong side of history as the communist bloc fell apart. In 1990, he began dating a Russian girl from home, Inne Hohne; they'd met at a Moscow hotel while he was back on leave. In 1991, they married in Russia. Inne, together with her young daughter from a previous relationship, moved with Kovtun to East Germany.

Two months later, Kovtun's unit received bad news. He and his comrades were being transferred back to Russia's Caucasus. The north Caucasus was the most explosive corner of what was now the new Russian Federation: the scene of wars and skirmishes between Russian troops and a restive Muslim population since the time of the young Tolstoy and the early years of the nineteenth century. (Three years later, in 1994, Boris Yeltsin pulled the trigger on what would become the first Chechen War.)

Inne told her husband she wasn't going to Chechnya. She wanted to stay in Germany. Kovtun didn't fancy fighting either. They came up with a plan. He would desert! They would escape together to West Germany and claim political asylum there. They would start a new life.

Escaping the Russian base turned out to be simple. According to Inne: 'We packed our things one night and crept out of the barracks, through the fence.' They took a taxi to Hamburg, driving through the dark. They spent the night at a police station. The next morning they were

taken to the aliens' department. About twenty-five officers from the same Soviet military group also ran away
from military camp, though at different times.

Back in Russia, the authorities started criminal
proceedings against Kovtun for desertion.

The Germans accepted Kovtun's asylum claim and
placed him temporarily on a boat in Hamburg. Germany's
second biggest city was a temple of post-war prosperity,
with a port, a proud mercantilist tradition and a laid-
back and cosmopolitan sensibility more British than
German. It was in Hamburg that John le Carré – then a
British intelligence officer – wrote the novel that made
him famous, *The Spy Who Came in from the Cold*. Kovtun
and his wife found themselves living in an asylum seekers'
hostel in Blankenese, an affluent district in the west of
the city, with large villas, some of them overlooking the
right bank of the Elbe.

The hostel was in Björnsonweg, a quiet suburban
street named after Norway's national bard, Bjørnstjerne
Bjørnson. It passes an old municipal waterworks – there's
a sign in art deco letters – and ends in a small forest.
According to neighbours there were two hostels here,
one home to Africans, the other to asylum seekers from
the Middle East and elsewhere. (The street was well-
named: as well as being a poet and playwright, Bjørnson
was a public intellectual involved in the struggle for
freedom of expression and against racism.)

Kovtun had made it to the west but his marriage didn't
survive the transition. According to Inne, Dmitry was a
feckless husband. He had, she said, a major drink problem.

Contacted by German police in 2006 out of the blue, a decade and a half after severing all ties with Kovtun, Inne Hohne paints a singularly unflattering picture of her first husband. Their marriage was brief, she said, and something of a disaster. At the beginning of 1992, they split because of what she called his 'escalating drunkenness'.

She told detectives: 'He drank a lot, which was eventually the reason for our separation, and in addition he hung about in Hamburg and on the Reeperbahn.' In addition: 'Dmitry wanted to be a porn star.'

The Reeperbahn where Kovtun spent his days was the city's red-light district. The area in St Pauli had grown up to serve the needs of sailors visiting the port. In the pre-internet 1990s it was a street of peep shows, live sex acts and cinema booths, where you could toss a Deutschmark into a slot and view a minute of porn. The unknown Beatles played their first gigs here. Today, the Reeperbahn is more of a cuddly tourist destination than a house of sin. The last live sex theatre has closed; the sex shops are mostly gone; Andrew Lloyd Webber's tame *Cats* was a fixture in its musical theatre.

Hohne was stupefied by the suggestion that her former husband would be involved in espionage or covert Russian intelligence work. 'No, I cannot imagine that,' she told police. He was, she said, temperamentally unsuited to complex projects of any kind. 'He is not really the type for this, not the sort of person who does big deals or is suited in any way to this.'

Inne would characterise Kovtun as a dandy and one of life's serial failures. 'Dmitry is not particularly down to earth, more a man about town,' Inna would tell the police. 'He had all sorts of dreams and plans, none of which he realised, however.' Kovtun was 'not a particularly reliable type of person', she recalled.

In 1994, Kovtun began seeing a Russian-German woman, Marina Wall. She had moved after the Soviet collapse with her family from Siberia to Germany. They married in 1996. Wall had affluent connections; this may have been part of the attraction. Marina's doctor mother Eleanora works in Hamburg as a psychotherapist in an upmarket clinic. Eleanora and her wealthy partner Hartmut Kohnke own a string of rental properties in the city, divided into small flats and let mainly to students. Kovtun was named as 'main tenant' in one of the properties owned by Kohnke's firm, Garant.

Despite having rich German in-laws, Kovtun failed to become prosperous himself. According to Litvinenko, he complained bitterly about how stingy they were. Kovtun told Litvinenko: 'I am interested in money and money alone in this life. Nothing else.' Kovtun said that his tight-fisted in-laws owned a 'super expensive clinic in the centre of Hamburg and over 200 items of property'. They had bought nothing for him, he moaned, apart from a couple of package tours with his wife Marina. Kovtun told Litvinenko he 'lived like a pauper'.

This was largely true. Kovtun's mother-in-law, who retained a soft spot for Dmitry even after he became embroiled in scandal, confirmed: 'Money and he didn't go together.' The shiny position Kovtun had been hoping for didn't present itself. For a period Kovtun was on the dole, broke, and relying on German welfare handouts. Sometimes he picked up odd jobs. He worked as a refuse collector. He washed dishes in various Hamburg restaurants.

One of them was Il Porto. Il Porto was an Italian fish restaurant in Grosse Elbstrasse, in the heart of Hamburg's waterfront tourist area, overlooking the Elbe and the city's busy port. Opposite were the giant cranes of the German shipbuilder Blohm + Voss; from Il Porto's pavement tables you could watch ships coming into harbour. Further west along the cobbled Elbstrasse is the Haifisch or Shark Bar, several old merchants' houses and Hamburg's 1960s-built commercial fish market. The restaurant occupied the ground floor of a renovated Jugendstil building. It had balconies and a mansard flat in the roof.

Kovtun worked at Il Porto between 1996 and 2001. The restaurant's gregarious Italian owner Franco Schiavone employed him as assistant waiter. He wasn't especially competent, but Shiavone liked him and kept him on. Kovtun's German was poor. His main job was to collect the dirty plates.

Later Schiavone was a man with two stories – one he wanted to tell, and one he didn't. Of Kovtun, he merely said: 'I want to forget Dmitry.' Schiavone was far happier talking about his own life and colourful career. As a young man in the swinging sixties he worked at La Dolce Vita restaurant in Soho, London, as well as in Swansea. He was a waiter in Paris and in Cannes, where a friend would smuggle him into press conferences with Hollywood stars. In 1978 he moved to Hamburg and later did a stint on a cruise liner. 'My philosophy is, in life you have to keep moving,' he told me.

Schiavone's staff were international. His assistant waiter Kovtun was a Russian; his chef an Albanian. During this period Kovtun became friends with the Italian manager, who in the subsequent inquiry was referred to by the codename D3 in order to keep his anonymity. He would play a crucial role later in his story. D3 had hired Kovtun in 1996 when he turned up at Il Porto asking for a job. They played chess, and sometimes went for a beer after work. They kept in touch sporadically after D3 left Il Porto and moved on. 'We talked about a lot of things,' D3 said. Once, Kovtun gave D3 a present. It was a book on Niccolò Machiavelli, the Italian political philosopher. A sign of Kovtun's intellectual interests? Or a fitting choice from a future assassin?

Il Porto was a business success. But in 2001 Hamburg city gave permission for a large and charmless office block to be constructed directly in front of the harbour. It blocked the restaurant's 'Elbblick' – its picturesque view of the Elbe – killing off his custom. Schiavone shut Il Porto. 'I practically gave it away,' he said. He opened up another establishment, La Vela, down the road.

Out of a job, Kovtun harboured dreams of running his own business. In 2002, he and Marina Wall came up with the idea of a consultancy firm, advising Russians or Russian companies looking to set up in Germany. According to Wall, however: 'The business did not materialise.' By this point Wall and Kovtun were drifting in opposite directions. At the end of the year they separated;

Kovtun stayed in her flat for a while, sleeping in a second bedroom. Wall met a new partner, a Pole, and became pregnant with their first child.

'Dmitry could not sort himself out here. He did not find any work, he had been a high-ranking officer in Russia and could not prove himself here,' Wall said. In 2003, after twelve years living in Germany, Kovtun decided to go back to Russia. During his absence the Kremlin had amnestied army deserters. His father had died in 1995; he moved back in with his mother. He was thirty-eight.

After the split, Kovtun remained on good terms with Marina, and with his German ex-mother-in-law, who lived with her partner in Haselau, a village 21 miles (35 km) north-west of Hamburg in Schleswig-Holstein. From time to time he would visit them. 'Every woman finds Dmitry charming. It is just that he does not fancy working and he is not a family man,' Wall said. 'He is more a man about town. That is why we were not suited.'

And then suddenly, in 2005, as if by magic, Kovtun's luck changed. He was back in touch with Lugovoi, his old friend from military school days. They were going into business together! While Kovtun had been scrubbing pots, Lugovoi had been accruing influence. And money. Lugovoi owned a security firm, Ninth Wave. He was providing bodyguards to VIPs. He had acquired a drinks factory too. Kovtun told Wall he was spending most of his time in Voronezh, doing vodka production with Lugovoi. They went cycling together, puffing up the slopes of Dombay, a mountain resort in southern Russia.

Was this rekindled friendship with Lugovoi only about business? Or something else?

In July 2006, Kovtun called Wall and said he would be visiting Hamburg. She and Kovtun were getting divorced; Kovtun was due to attend a hearing on 9 August. In the end, he didn't make it. He told her his new Russian passport wasn't ready. He would come soon, he said – in the autumn.

The ostensible purpose of Kovtun's trip to Hamburg at the end of October 2006 was to tidy up his affairs. Every six months he flew to Germany to get a stamp. Wall had made him an appointment at the city council's aliens' department in Hamburg's Platz der Republik. This was a large rectangular neo-classical building, not far from where Il Porto used to be, with an equine statue of the German emperor William I in front of the entrance. Here Kovtun would get a German resident's permit inserted into his new Russian Federation passport.

The real purpose of the trip was different. From Hamburg, Kovtun intended to travel back to London again, a city he had visited for the first time two weeks previously. There he had a job to finish: to poison Alexander Litvinenko. It sounded easy. But Kovtun and Lugovoi's previous attempt of 16 October in the offices of Erinys hadn't worked and Lugovoi's second effort, on 26 October, had misfired too, with the polonium ending up on a bathroom hand towel. Litvinenko was still alive.

Kovtun flew into Hamburg at midday on 28 October 2006, on an Aeroflot flight from Moscow. Marina, her new partner and children met Kovtun at the airport. They drove him in her BMW to their home at Erzbergerstrasse 4 in the centre of town. Wall's flat was in a late-nineteenth-century building belonging to her mother and her partner; sepia paintings of Hamburg-Altona's old town hall and St Michael's Church decorated the entrance lobby. Most of Wall's neighbours in the five-storey property were students. The area, Ottensen, is central and congenial, with an S-bahn station nearby, as well as cafés and shops.

Kovtun said he was going to London to watch a foot-ball match. Since he didn't have a credit card, Wall's partner booked him a plane ticket on the internet. Kovtun gave him €70 in cash.

Subsequently, Kovtun's movements in Germany were easy to reconstruct. As in London, the police found a trail. He had brought with him from Moscow radioac-tive polonium-210, the unique substance with which he intended to kill Litvinenko.

Like Lugovoi before him, Kovtun, seemingly, knew little or nothing about its properties. For example, that it left a ghostly signature wherever he went. Kovtun was, it seems, the classic dupe, tricked by whoever gave him the poison in Moscow. And – though it didn't turn out that way – expendable.

From the moment he arrived, Kovtun contaminated everything he came into contact with. German detectives found polonium in Wall's car, on the front passenger seat where he'd sat. And at her home. Radioactive traces were discovered in the living room and bedroom where he'd spent the night in Erzbergerstrasse. Traces too in a cupboard, on pillows – even on a teddy bear and a child's jacket hanging on the coat rack.

Kovtun moved; so did the trail; it followed him like a spectre. The next day, 29 October, Wall's mother Eleanora drove Kovtun to her house in Haselau, where Kovtun stayed the night. They spent a jolly evening. In the kitchen Kovtun unpacked gifts from Moscow – a bottle of vodka, chocolate-coated marshmallows and two glass jars containing pickled mushrooms, a present from Kovtun's mother. Kovtun was wearing his black polo-neck pullover and dark-blue jeans. 'He's a very soft person. He isn't a businessman, he's a philosopher,' Eleanora told German police.

Despite her fond view of Kovtun, polonium was found in Eleanora's house too. The following morning, 30 October, Kovtun visited the aliens' department. One faint trace of radiation was discovered – under Kovtun's new passport photo.

The trail of polonium was itself remarkable, but the German police discovered other significant evidence as well. They found witnesses, including one to whom Kovtun confided about his real motive for going to London.

Usually, when he visited Hamburg, Kovtun would meet with D3, his restaurant manager friend from Il Porto. On 30 October, Kovtun called D3, told him he was in town and said he would like to see him. This was normal: generally Kovtun would make contact out of the blue.

At about 7 p.m., D3 was having dinner with another friend from his Il Porto days, codenamed D5. The pair were eating in the Tarantella restaurant, a newly opened bistro in the city centre next to Stephansplatz. Kovtun arrived by S-bahn and phoned to say he didn't know where to go. D3 found him on the opposite side of the street. He invited him to join them. As usual, Kovtun was broke. Kovtun said he didn't want to eat. According to D3, he and D5 ended up sharing some of their meal with Kovtun. Kovtun asked his former colleagues to order some red wine for him, which they did, a quarter of a litre.

So far, so unremarkable. All three left the restaurant, with D5 strolling on ahead to buy cigarettes. Their destination was a slot machine arcade in Steindamm, twenty minutes away on foot. At the time Steindamm was a sort of mini-Reeperbahn, a sleazy area of Hamburg known for its drugs, porn shops and street walkers.

As they walked along, Kovtun revealed something extraordinary. 'It happened when Dmitry and I were now alone and he told me this tale,' D3 said. Kovtun had mentioned he was flying to London on business. Now, he said, he was actually going there to commit a murder. What's more, he needed D3's help.

The conversation, recounted by D3 to German police, went like this:

KOVTUN: Do you know someone called Litvinenko? Have you heard of him?
D3: No.

KOVTUN: Litvinenko is a traitor! There is blood on
his hands! He does deals with Chechnya!

The conversation was a weird one. D3 hadn't the faintest
clue who Litvinenko was; why should he? Nor did he
know anything of Litvinenko's alleged treachery.

The conversation got weirder.

KOVTUN: Do you know a cook who is working in
London?

D3: Yeah, that guy who was with us at Il Porto.

Though he had lost touch with him, D3 mentioned a
young Albanian chef who'd been their colleague back in
the nineties and early noughties. Since then he'd moved
to the UK. D3 didn't know details. Then:

KOVTUN: I have a very expensive poison. I need
this cook so he can put the poison in Litvinenko's
food or drink.

D3: You're crazy! The cook is married, has kids.
[Jokingly] Wouldn't it be much easier to shoot
this Litvinenko instead?

KOVTUN: It's meant to set an example. Litvinenko
is well protected in London. I intend to lure him
out with an interview. And then to poison him.

D3: Look, stop all this nonsense. Why don't you
get a proper job? Why are you telling me, of all
people, this crap?

KOVTUN: You mustn't tell anybody.

D3: Who the hell am I supposed to tell?

KOVTUN: I'll soon have my own flat in Moscow.

D3: [Conciliatory] That's nice. I could come and
visit you there.

Asked by police if Kovtun had put a figure on the cost
of the poison, D3 said he couldn't remember. He said:
'Dmitry mentioned a sum which was incredibly high.'
It was clear that Kovtun's own reward for his role in the
operation was real estate in the Russian capital. Who
would be paying for it wasn't clear.

At the time, D3 thought that Kovtun's fantastical tale
was 'rubbish', the ramblings of a man who had watched
too many TV spy dramas. The story sounded crazy, nuts.
It confirmed his belief that Kovtun was a dreamer. Did
he ask how Kovtun obtained such an expensive poison?
'No. I didn't believe him and therefore I didn't ask,' D3
replied to police.

The story seemed even less plausible because during
the same conversation Kovtun mentioned his latest
money-making idea. Even by Kovtun's dismal standards,
it was a daft one. Kovtun said that he and his ex-wife
might pose naked in *Praline*, a popular soft-porn magazine. *Praline* was sold at every station kiosk. They would
make 'loads of money', he told D3.

Outside the casino, D3 asked Kovtun where he
intended to sleep. Kovtun said he would kip at D3's
place. Back at D3's flat they had another glass of wine.
Kovtun shared D3's large bed, leaving early the next
morning. D3 croaked that he should take a couple of

bottles of wine with him, one for Marina and one for her mother.

D3 didn't believe Kovtun's bizarre tale but nonetheless decided to help. He called Il Porto colleagues who were still in touch with the Albanian cook. They found the Albanian's UK number. The Albanian agreed to talk to Kovtun, whom he had barely known when they were at the Hamburg restaurant. They passed the mobile number to Kovtun.

On the night before his flight to London Kovtun couldn't sleep. He set the alarm on his mobile for early the next morning. He was – we can only assume – preoccupied with his looming mission. Would this latest assassination attempt end in embarrassment and mishap? Would those in Moscow tolerate another failure? At 6.30 a.m. Kovtun boarded a Germanwings flight from Hamburg to London's Gatwick Airport. He arrived at 7.25 a.m. local time. He went through passport control. No one stopped him. Kovtun continued straight to the heart of London, and to a four-star hotel just east of Park Lane.

5

Murder in Mayfair

Millennium Hotel, 44 Grosvenor Square,
Mayfair, London, November 2006

'There is still some tea left here.
If you want to you can have some'
ANDREI LUGOVOI TO LITVINENKO, 1 NOVEMBER 2006

The Millennium Hotel is an unusual spot for a murder. It overlooks busy Grosvenor Square: an enclave of grass and plane trees. It's practically next door to the heavily guarded US embassy. Rumour has it that the CIA has its station on the fourth floor. A statue of Franklin D. Roosevelt – wearing a large cape and holding a stick – dominates the north corner of the square. In 2011 another statue would appear, that of the late US president Ronald Reagan. An inscription hails Reagan's contribution to world history in the twentieth century and his 'determined intervention to end the Cold War'. A friendly tribute from Mikhail Gorbachev reads: 'With President Reagan, we travelled the world from confrontation to cooperation.'

The quotes would seem mordantly ironic in the light of events that took place just round the corner, and amid Putin's apparent attempt to turn the clock back to 1982, when the former KGB boss Yuri Andropov – the secret policeman's secret policeman – was in charge of a doomed empire called the Soviet Union. Next to the inscriptions is a sandy-coloured chunk of masonry. It's a piece of the Berlin Wall, retrieved from the east side. Reagan, the monument says, defeated communism. This was an enduring triumph for the west, democratic values, and for free societies everywhere ...

Grosvenor Street – home to Erinys, and the scene of Lugovoi and Kovtun's earlier murder attempt – was 500 metres away.

Like most upmarket London hotels, the Millennium Hotel has CCTV. Its multiplex system can run up to forty-eight cameras; on 1 November 2006, forty-one of them were operational. The cameras work on a time-lapse system. They take an image every two seconds; the video is retained for thirty-one days. This footage has a jerky quality, a little like the early days of cinema – images jump; people appear and vanish; life ebbs and flows. And yet it's an honest record. A time stamp – days, hours, minutes – fixes everyone. The stills offer a miraculous time machine, a journey into verisimilitude.

But even modern CCTV has its limitations. Some parts of the Millennium Hotel weren't covered by it – as Lugovoi, an expert in surveillance, and a former VIP bodyguard, would have noticed. One camera was fixed above the reception desk. It shows the check-in counter; a bank of three computer screens; uniformed hotel staff. In the left of the picture is a part-view of the foyer. There are two white leather sofas and a chair. Another camera – you wouldn't notice it, unless you were looking – records the steps leading up to the lavatories. Opposite the ladies' and gents' is a business centre and a bank of pay-phones.

The hotel has two ground-floor bars accessed from the foyer. There is a large restaurant and café. And a smaller Pine Bar immediately on the left as you enter through a revolving door from the street. The bar is a cosy wood-panelled affair, furnished at the time in traditional English style with equine pictures on the wall. Three bay windows look out onto the square. In CCTV terms the Pine Bar is a security black hole. It has no cameras, its protean guests invisible.

The evening before Kovtun flew into London, camera 14 recorded this: at 20.04 a man dressed in a black leather jacket and mustard-yellow jumper approaches the front desk. On either side of him are two young women. They have long, groomed blonde hair: his daughters. Another figure wanders up from the sofas. He's a strikingly tall, chunky-looking bloke wearing a padded black jacket and what resembles a hand-knitted Harry Potter scarf. The scarf is red and blue, the colours of Moscow's CSKA football club.

The video captures the moment the Lugovois checked in on 31 October – on this, his third frantic trip to London in three weeks, Andrei Lugovoi arrived with his entire family. He came from Moscow with his wife Svet-lana, daughter Galina, eight-year-old son Igor, and friend Vyacheslav Sokolenko – the guy with the scarf. At the hotel Lugovoi met his other daughter Tatiana. She had arrived from Moscow a day earlier with her boyfriend Maxim Bejak. The family party was due later the following evening to watch CSKA Moscow play Arsenal in the Champions League at the Emirates Stadium in north London.

Like Lugovoi, Sokolenko was ex-KGB. But Sokolenko wasn't, detectives would conclude, a murderer.

Camera 14 records the Lugovoi party at the front counter. Tatiana shared room 101 with her sister Galina; Lugovoi, Svetlana and Igor were in 311. Sokolenko and Kovtun – who was to check in the following morning – occupied room 382. It was found to be riddled with polonium; the biggest readings came from objects Kovtun touched – phone, heat-control panel, sink. CCTV records Kovtun arriving at the Millennium at 08.32 on 1 November – a diminutive figure carrying a black bag over one shoulder. He's wearing a black zip-up top and drainpipe jeans with turn-ups; before flying out from Hamburg Kovtun had bought trousers from the Massimo Dutti store.

Kovtun makes calls on his mobile. (The number is never discovered.) Around 10 a.m. the Russians leave the hotel and walk north to Marble Arch. Lugovoi buys a ticket for his family, plus Sokolenko, on a Big Bus sight-seeing tour of London.

The events of the next few hours were to become infamous – with Litvinenko the fated victim, the Russian state an avenging god, the media a sort of over-excited Greek chorus. What actually took place was another piece of improvisation that might easily have misfired. Lugovoi and Kovtun had decided to lure Litvinenko to a further meeting. But the evidence suggests they still hadn't figured out how exactly they were going to kill him.

At 11.33 a.m. Kovtun borrowed Lugovoi's mobile phone and called up the Albanian cook – the man who might help with putting 'the very expensive poison' in Litvinenko's food or drink.

The cook – identified as C2 – was in an Albanian coffee shop in Stratford, east London. He was tied up with helping a customer. The conversation, such as it was, went like this:

KOVTUN: Hello? I'm Dmitry. I want to meet you. I'm in London.

C2: I'm busy. When I have time I will call you back.

The cook spoke languages other than Albanian: Italian, English and German. Kovtun, by contrast, was never much of a linguist. 'His English wasn't as good as my English,' the Albanian said. 'He could only speak Russian.' At Il Porto they couldn't have become friends, the cook explained, because Kovtun never really learned German properly, which is why he got the job of clearing tables.

The cook plot had clearly fallen through. Another approach was required.

At 11.41 a.m. – eight minutes after the unsuccessful conversation with C2 – Lugovoi called Litvinenko up on his mobile. He suggested a meeting. Why didn't Litvinenko join him later that day at the Millennium Hotel? Litvinenko said yes; the plot was back on.

Scotland Yard would later precisely fix Litvinenko's movements on the afternoon of 1 November: a bus from his home in Muswell Hill, the tube to Oxford Circus, a 3 p.m. lunch with his Italian associate Mario Scaramella in the Itsu sushi restaurant in Piccadilly. In between he fielded several calls from Lugovoi, who was becoming increasingly importunate. Lugovoi called Litvinenko again at 3.40 p.m. He told Litvinenko to 'hurry up'. He had, he said, to leave imminently to watch the football.

Lugovoi would tell British detectives that he arrived at the Millennium Hotel at 4 p.m. The CCTV shows that he was lying: half an hour earlier, at 3.32 p.m., Lugovoi appears at the front desk and asks for directions to the gents'. Another camera, camera 4, records him walking up the stairs from the foyer. The image is striking. Lugovoi seems preoccupied. He's unusually pale, grim, grey-visaged. His left hand is concealed in a jacket pocket. Two minutes later he emerges. The camera offers an unflattering close-up of his retreating bald spot.

And then at 3.45 p.m. Kovtun repeats the same procedure, asking for directions, vanishing into the gents' toilets, reappearing three minutes later. He's a slight figure. What were the pair doing there? Washing their hands having set the polonium trap? Or preparing the crime, a heinous one, in the sanctuary of one of the cubicles?

Radiation tests were to show massive alpha radiation contamination in the second cubicle on the left – 2,600 counts per second on the door, 200 on the flush handle. Further sources of polonium were found on and below the gents' hand-dryer, at over 5,000 counts per second. There was full-scale deflection in two sinks.

The multiplex system records someone else arriving at 15.59 and 41 seconds – a fit-looking individual, wearing a blue denim jacket with a fawn collar. He's on his cellphone. This is Litvinenko at the blurred edge of the picture; he calls Lugovoi from the hotel lobby to tell him he's arrived. The CCTV tells us little beyond this. Apart from one important detail. Litvinenko never visits the hotel bathroom. He's not the source of the polonium: it's his Russian companions-turned-executioners who bring it with them to London, in this, their second poisoning attempt.

Earlier that week I had flown to Moscow with my wife Phoebe. I was there on a recce – my newspaper, the *Guardian*, was posting me to Russia as its new Moscow bureau chief. It was a moment of excitement and trepidation. There were logistical issues. Where would our children – Tilly, eight, and Ruskin, six, go to school? And how in this churning metropolis of 12 million people – amid traffic, Soviet tower blocks and eight-lane boulevards – might we find a space to call home?

We flew to Moscow with British Airways, flight 875. Our borrowed flat overlooked Novy Arbat in central Moscow. There were meetings with property agents and tours round a succession of rather dismal, low-ceilinged flats. Visits, too, to the British and American schools. On the second day it snowed: heavy flakes tumbling from a grey sky onto a shuffling procession of vehicles.

My previous postings had been in Delhi and Berlin. We considered ourselves adaptable, good at languages, cosmopolitan. But Moscow looked like a challenge. Our move was scheduled for January and the depths of a Russian winter.

On 30 October we flew back to the UK, on BA 875. The plane was full. Most passengers were Russian football fans on their way to London for the CSKA match. They were a drunken bunch. A few had been swigging from bottles of duty-free. They refused to sit down. Someone smoked in the loo. And then a sozzled Russian travelling with his teenage children punched a steward in the face. The pilot was given priority landing. At Heathrow, armed police boarded the plane and dragged him away. They found a bottle of cognac – two-thirds empty – rolling under his seat. His daughter was crying.

It was a memorable flight, the atmosphere of revelry ending up sour. Memorable for several reasons, it turned out. Lugovoi had flown on the same BA plane during his second October trip to London, days before. Though we didn't know it, the plane was contaminated with polonium.

We had been sitting just a few rows away from Lugovoi's radioactive seat, we later discovered. It was a prescient coincidence. The hidden events unfolding in Moscow and London would dominate my professional life in Russia and beyond, for the next four years, and cast a dark shadow over our family life, too.

Meanwhile, the large number of Russians visiting London for the football was the perfect cover for Lugovoi and Kovtun. Amid this influx, with thousands of Russian passport holders coming through Heathrow, who would spot a couple of assassins, carrying with them an invisible weapon?

While serving with the FSB in Russia, Litvinenko perfected his observation skills. It was part of his basic training. How to describe the bad guys: their height, build, hair colour and distinguishing features. What they were wearing. Any jewellery. How old. Smoker or non-smoker. And of course their conversation – from the major stuff such as admissions of guilt down to trivial details. For example, who offered whom a cup of tea?

When detectives later interviewed Litvinenko he gave them a full and – in the circumstances – remarkable account of his meeting with Lugovoi and Kovtun in the Pine Bar. He made one small error: he said the teapot on their table was silver. In fact it was white and ceramic. Litvinenko confused it with the silver teapots in the Park Lane Sheraton Hotel, where he'd met Lugovoi the previous week, the rather crumbling institution on Piccadilly with the China-themed Palm Court restaurant. He also forgot Kovtun's first name; after all, he had only met him on one previous occasion.

Otherwise, his recall was perfect.

Litvinenko said that Andrei approached him in the foyer from the left side and said: 'Let's go, we are sitting there at the bar.' He followed Lugovoi into the bar; Lugovoi had already ordered drinks. 'He sat down in the corner and I sat. There were two tables pulled close together, sort of like a single one.' Lugovoi sat with his back to the wall; Litvinenko was diagonally across from him on a chair. There were glasses sitting on the table but no bottles. And 'mugs and a teapot'.

Litvinenko's account of the conversation is that Lugovoi explained he could only stay for ten or fifteen minutes. 'Straightaway a waiter came up to us,' Litvinenko told Detective Inspector Brent Hyatt. It was a waiter with 'grey hair', wearing a white shirt and black bow tie. This was Norberto Andrade, the hotel's veteran head barman.

As Lugovoi knew, Litvinenko didn't drink alcohol. Moreover he was hard up and reluctant to spend any money of his own in a fancy establishment. Andrade approached Litvinenko from behind, and asked him: 'Are you going to have anything?' Lugovoi repeated the question and said: 'Would you like anything?' Litvinenko said he didn't want anything.

And then: 'He [Lugovoi] said, "OK, well we're going to leave now anyway, so there is still some tea left here, if you want to you can have some." And then the waiter went away, or I think Andrei asked for a clean cup and he brought it. He left and, when there was a cup, I poured some tea out of the teapot, although there was only a little left in the bottom and it made just half a cup. Maybe about 50 grams.

'I swallowed several times but it was a green tea with no sugar and it was already cold by the way. I didn't like it for some reason, well, almost cold tea with no sugar, and I didn't drink it any more. Maybe in total I swallowed three or four times.' Litvinenko said he didn't finish the cup.

And then:

DI HYATT: The pot with the tea in it was already there?

LITVINENKO: Yes.

DI HYATT: How many mugs were on the table when you came in?

LITVINENKO: I think three or four cups.

DI HYATT: And did Andrei drink any more from the pot in your presence?

LITVINENKO: No.

DI HYATT: OK, and what happened next?

LITVINENKO: Then he said Vadim [Kovtun] is coming here now … either Vadim or Volodia, I can't remember. I saw him for the second time in my life.

DI HYATT: What happened next?

LITVINENKO: Next Volodia took a place at the table on my side, across from Andrei.

The three men discussed their meeting scheduled for the following day at the private security firm Global Risk. The bar was crowded, with 'lots of people', Litvinenko said. He felt a strong antipathy towards Kovtun. It was just their second encounter. There was something strange about him, Litvinenko thought – as if he were in the midst of some personal torment.

LITVINENKO: Volodia was – seemed to be – very depressed, as if he was very much hungover. He apologised. He said that he hadn't slept for the whole night, that he had just flown in from

Hamburg and he wanted to sleep very much and he couldn't stand it any more. But I think he is either an alcoholic or a drug addict. He is a very unpleasant type.

DI HYATT: Volodia [Kovtun], how did he know to come to the table? Did Andrei contact him and ask him to come and join you, or was there already an arrangement for him to join you?

LITVINENKO: No … he [Kovtun], I think he knew in advance. Even possibly they had been sitting before this and maybe he went up to his room.

DI HYATT: Just going back to when you had some tea, you didn't ask the waiter for a drink. It was mentioned that there was some tea left. How insistent was Andrei that you have a drink, or was he indifferent? Was he saying, 'Go on, go on, have some'? Or didn't he care?

LITVINENKO: He said it like that, you know, 'If you would like something, order something for yourself, but we're going to be leaving soon. If, if you want some tea, then there is some left here, you can have some of this …' I could have ordered a drink myself, but he kind of presented in such a way that it's not really need to order. I don't like when people pay for me but in such an expensive hotel, forgive me, I don't have enough money to pay for that.

DI HYATT: Did you drink any of the tea in the presence of Volodia [Kovtun]?

LITVINENKO: No, I drank the tea only when Andrei was sitting opposite me. In Volodia's presence, I wasn't drinking it … I didn't like that tea.

DI HYATT: And after you drank from that pot, did Andrei or Volodia drink anything from that pot?

LITVINENKO: No, definitely. Later on, when I left the hotel, I was thinking there was something strange. I had been feeling all the time, I knew that they wanted to kill me.

There is no evidence to say whether it was Kovtun – the former waiter, good at mixing drinks – or Lugovoi who put radioactive polonium in the teapot. From Litvinenko's testimony, it's clear this was a joint criminal enterprise. Lugovoi would subsequently explain that he couldn't recall what drinks he'd ordered in the Pine Bar. And that Litvinenko had insisted upon their meeting, to which he'd reluctantly assented.

Subsequently, police tracked down Lugovoi's Pine Bar till receipt. Lugovoi was a man who murdered with a certain breezy style.

The order was:

3 Teas
3 Gordon's gin
3 Tonics
1 Champagne cocktail
1 Romeo and Julieta cigar, no 1
1 Gordon's gin

The tea came to £11.25; the total bill £70.60. Lugovoi paid on his credit card.

Andrade, the man who brought the tea, was from Brentwood in Essex. He'd worked at the Pine Bar since 1981, and was in his late sixties by 2006; his slicked-back grey hair recalled an earlier, more glamorous era. He would retire two years later. Over the years he had served many celebrities. They included the actor Sean Connery, probably the greatest James Bond, and the man who owned the 007 spy franchise, film producer Cubby Broccoli, whose second Bond movie starring Connery was *From Russia With Love*.

It was a Wednesday. Andrade was working his regular 11 a.m.–7.30 p.m. shift. The bar was extremely busy, he said; there was a property auction going on in the ballroom. Several Russian clients had come to the hotel that week for the football. He was serving drinks, while his 'very professional' younger colleague Jacob worked from behind the bar. Lugovoi walked in. He asked for a Havana cigar, and said he would be 'coming in shortly for drinks', Andrade said. The barman said he'd add Lugovoi's cigar to his bill.

Half an hour later, Lugovoi returned, took a seat at table one, strategically positioned in the corner with a clear view of the entrance, and ordered three green teas with fresh lemon and honey. Jacob took a teapot and cups from a stack next to the bar's Giga coffee machine. Andrade said he delivered the tea to the table but didn't pour – customers generally preferred to pour themselves, he explained.

Almost immediately, Lugovoi called him back and demanded more honey. Over the next half an hour Norberto said he was shuttling 'very rapidly back and forth' between the bar and table one – the Russians were a demanding party and called him back for gin, then 'a couple of minutes later' asked for champagne.

At the time, his impression of the men from Moscow was favourable: 'They were extremely well-behaved and well-dressed gentlemen.' Andrade said he didn't notice Litvinenko join Lugovoi at the table. But he did recognise Lugovoi and Kovtun. He said he'd seen them in the bar on a previous occasion.

By this point, Lugovoi and Kovtun must have concluded that their poisoning operation had worked. Litvinenko had drunk the green tea. Not much, admittedly. But, he had drunk. Surely, enough?

Later, in fact, it was found that Litvinenko had an astonishing 26.5 micrograms of polonium in his bloodstream. Less than one microgram would have been enough to kill him (estimates suggest that one gram alone could kill 50 million and sicken another 50 million). His exposure to radiation in this dose was approximately 175,000 times greater than that given off in an X-ray.

The meeting lasted twenty minutes. Then, Litvinenko told police, a tall Russian in a dark cardigan materialised at the bar. It was Sokolenko. Sokolenko 'said something' to Lugovoi, who replied: 'Yes, yes, all right' and 'Go on, I will speak to you later.'

Lugovoi gazed at his watch. He said he was expecting his wife, Svetlana. Mrs Lugovaya (Russian surnames have different feminine versions) appeared in the foyer and, as if on cue, waved her hand, and mouthed: 'Let's go, let's go.' Lugovoi got up to greet her, and left Litvinenko and Kovtun sitting together at the table.

There was one final, scarcely believable scene. According to Litvinenko, Lugovoi came back to the Pine Bar accompanied by his eight-year-old son Igor. Another guest, Duncan Cunningham, noticed Igor in the hotel, holding a bag from the Hamley's toy store in London, and looking uninterested, fed up and bored by dull adult company.

Lugovoi introduced his small son to Litvinenko. He said to Igor: 'This is Uncle Sasha, shake his hand.'

Igor was a good boy. He obediently shook Litvinenko's hand, the same hand that by now was pulsing with radiation. When police examined Litivnenko's denim jacket they found massive contamination on the sleeve – Litvinenko had picked up and drunk the tea with his right hand. The party plus Litvinenko exited the bar. The Lugovoi family and Sokolenko went off to the match. Kovtun declined to go, declaring: 'I'm very tired, I want to sleep.'

Forensic experts would test the entire bar area, the tables, dishwasher and crockery. They examined 100 teapots, as well as cups, spoons, saucers, milk jugs. Litvinenko's teapot wasn't difficult to discover – it gave off readings of 100,000 becquerels per centimetre squared, a satanically high number. The highest reading came from the spout. (The teapot was put in the dishwasher afterwards and unknowingly reused for subsequent customers.) The table where they sat registered 20,000 becquerels.

Polonium was a miasma, a strange creeping fog. It was found inside the dishwasher, on the floor, till, the handle of a coffee strainer. There were traces on bottles of Martini and Tia Maria behind the bar, the ice cream scoop, a chopping board. It turned up on chairs – with large alpha radiation readings from where the three Russians sat – and the piano stool. Whoever sent Lugovoi and Kovtun to London must have known of the risks to others. Apparently they didn't care.

The most crucial piece of evidence was discovered several floors above the Pine Bar. It was found in Kovtun's room, number 382. When police forensic teams took apart Kovtun's bathroom sink they found a mangled clump of debris. The debris was stuck in the sediment trap of the sink's waste pipe. Tests on the clump showed it contained 390,000 becquerels of polonium. The levels were so high that they could only have come from primary contamination – from polonium itself.

After putting the poison in Litvinenko's teapot, Kovtun went back upstairs to his room. There in the bathroom he poured the rest of the liquid polonium solution down the sink. No one else – other than Lugovoi and Sokolenko – had access to the room. Police concluded that Kovtun had knowingly handled the murder weapon, and afterwards got rid of it. It was an intentional act of disposal.

The science was objective, conclusive and utterly damning. As an inquiry into Litvinenko's poisoning would later hear, it had the simplicity of undeniable fact.

Kovtun would claim innocence. He was never able to explain away this pivotal piece of evidence.

The Russian operation to murder Litvinenko would have had a codename – so far unknown. It could finally be marked down as a success. It was the sixth anniversary of Litvinenko's arrival in Britain, on 1 November 2000. He didn't know it yet, but he was dying. The agent used to kill him had been chosen in order to leave no trace of how death was brought about. It was working. From this point on nothing – not even the most gifted medical team, not even a miracle from the heavens – could save him.

6

A Bit of a Puzzle

Critical care unit, University College Hospital,
London, November 2006

'This case is not political. This case is criminal'
LITVINENKO TO DETECTIVE INSPECTOR BRENT HYATT,
20 NOVEMBER 2006

That evening Alexander Litvinenko began to feel violently
unwell. Earlier, Marina had cooked him a light dinner.

The meal was something of a celebration. Six years
previously, on 1 November 2000, the Litvinenkos had
escaped Russia and arrived in the UK. The years had
been good ones. Litvinenko had found work. He was a
self-employed writer and a part-time British spy. Marina
had made friends, learned English. Anatoly, now twelve,
was studying at an elite London boys' school.

Russia wasn't forgotten, of course: Anatoly remembered the fierce winters, sledging in the snow, the
Moscow metro with its grandiose ceilings and art deco
lamps. There was no prospect of going back there, and
in the meantime Britain had become home. Litvinenko
viewed his newly acquired British citizenship – it came
through three weeks previously – as a kind of marvellous
protective shield. In the past his enemies had hounded
him in London: there had been menacing phone calls,

firebombs tossed outside his Muswell Hill home. But surely these ghosts were gone?

After dinner, Litvinenko sorted out his files, sat at his computer and watched the news. A journalist contact called him from the US. At about 11 p.m. he and Marina turned in.

Then, ten minutes later, Litvinenko was retching and vomiting. 'I started to feel nauseous,' he told police. 'Gradually, Marina said: "Maybe it will pass," and I said: "No, I don't think it will pass." And then I started vomiting. I managed to run as far as the toilet bowl in our room and that's it. About twenty minutes later I vomited again.'

Marina said: 'Suddenly, he started to feel unwell. He said he felt sick. It was very sudden. Of course, he couldn't say anything. He just vomited.' When it stopped, Litvinenko said that the feeling was similar to that he'd had on 16 October, after his meeting with Lugovoi and Kovtun. Later that evening he'd thrown up once and afterwards recovered.

Marina assumed that this new episode would also pass. First, Litvinenko threw up his dinner. He vomited again. This time his sick looked like water, Marina noticed, and was 'a very strange colour'. Marina prepared a common Russian remedy for stomach problems: a little magnesia added into water. Her husband drank it. Still he didn't feel any better.

After an hour, Litvinenko moved into the study, so as not to disturb his wife and son, who had school the next day. He passed a wretched night. 'Every twenty or thirty minutes I had to run to the toilet and I was vomiting, vomiting, vomiting,' he said. The manganese hadn't worked – the foam was coming out of his mouth.

At 6 a.m. Marina woke and peered inside. Litvinenko was awake, looked terrible, and told her: 'I can't stop vomiting.' He said that the stomach contractions kept coming, even though there was nothing to throw up. Additionally, Litvinenko complained he couldn't breathe properly. He said: 'I need more oxygen.' It was a cold day outside; she threw open the windows. Something was very wrong. Litvinenko said later: 'I was feeling really bad.' The strong pains in his stomach grew. He said to his wife: 'Marina, I think I have been poisoned.'

That morning Marina dropped Anatoly off at East Finchley tube station as usual, and called a Russian doctor, Yuri Prikazchikov, who advised her to buy mineral salts. She visited the chemist's. Litvinenko drank the salts. He threw them up immediately. He was increasingly exhausted, unable to eat or drink.

Litvinenko was forty-three years old, and in extremely good physical shape. Every week while Anatoly was at a taekwondo class, Litvinenko would run 10 miles (15 km). Afterwards, he swam vigorously up and down the East Finchley leisure centre pool. In central London he walked everywhere. He was never ill. Except now he was.

Marina suggested calling an ambulance. 'It was a very strange feeling. We didn't know what to do,' she said. Her husband said no. Then, in the early hours of 3 November, at 2 a.m., Litvinenko relented, and said: 'Please Marina, we should call.' She dialled 999 and the ambulance arrived within five minutes; two women paramedics checked his blood pressure and pulse; they concluded he probably had some kind of bacterial infection. They advised water and painkillers and departed.

The pain got worse. Litvinenko was also suffering from diarrhoea; he noticed he was passing blood. Marina rang Dr Prikazchikov again. At 2 p.m. he arrived at the Litvinenkos' home in Osier Crescent; the doctor took one look at Litvinenko and, without examining him further, took a step backwards, wide-eyed. The doctor told him: 'I don't know what illness it is, but it looks very much like typhoid fever but it is not typhoid fever.' Prikazchikov said he needed immediate hospitalisation. An ambulance came and took him to Barnet and Chase Farm Hospital in north London.

For doctors at Barnet Hospital, Litvinenko was one of numerous admissions – another patient tossed their way during a hectic winter season, punctuated by flus, super-bugs and a spike in elderly visitors.

That Litvinenko was in poor shape was obvious. His symptoms were abdominal pain, diarrhoea and vomiting. Medical staff diagnosed gastro-enteritis with mild dehydration. They prescribed ciprofloxacin, a broad-spectrum antibiotic. As a precaution, to prevent possible infection spreading, they put him in a side-room. He was admitted as Edwin Redwald Carter, his British pseudonym. The hospital's assumption was that Mr Carter would start to recover in a few days.

At first, this seemed to happen. 'He did feel a little bit better when he was hospitalised,' Marina said. The antibiotics stopped the vomiting; Litvinenko felt less exhausted.

Nevertheless, there were two issues of concern. One was medical: tests showed that Litvinenko's white blood-cell count was unusually low. In fact his white blood-cell and platelet count was steadily sinking. This didn't really fit with a diagnosis of gastro-enteritis. It might be a side effect of the fairly powerful antibiotics he was taking, doctors thought.

The other was scarcely believable, from the realm of spy thrillers and John le Carré rather than real life. On 7 November, Mrs Carter – as medical notes reference her – first raised the possibility that her husband may have been poisoned. He had, she said, worked for the Soviet KGB. And knew 'dangerous people'. Was it possible that someone might have put something in his food or drink?

The story made little sense. Doctors reassured her that this was 'unlikely', though they did record on Edwin Carter's file: 'Patient and wife concerned about intentional infection of patient, query poison?'

Litvinenko and his wife were increasingly convinced that his ever more painful symptoms were not the result of contaminated food or bad sushi. They suspected foul play. Was this some kind of reckoning? Litvinenko gave an interview to the BBC Russian Service, explaining that he'd narrowly survived a poisoning attempt and was now recovering in a London hospital. He mentioned his lunch with the Italian Mario Scaramella, but kept quiet about his meeting with Lugovoi and Kovtun.

The poisoning claim was sensational indeed. But was it true? *Chechenpress*, the Chechen website for which Litvinenko worked, picked up the story, as did the independent opposition radio station *Echo of Moscow*.

Alex Goldfarb got a call from one of its journalists. Goldfarb was in Paris. He perused the internet – where the story was starting to bubble – but was disinclined to take it terribly seriously. He rang his friend Alexander, who confirmed he thought he'd been poisoned. An incredulous Goldfarb told him: 'But come on, who would poison you? It's too much. Probably you have some sort of stomach ailment.'

Others were similarly sceptical. From his hospital bed, Litvinenko called his friend and fellow exile Viktor Suvorov and told him: 'I'm poisoned.' (Suvorov had previously advised Litvinenko to be careful, and suggested he might do well to move out of London, as he had, to a quieter part of the country.)

Suvorov replied: 'Sash, come on! It's rubbish.'

Litvinenko persisted: 'No, really. I'm poisoned. I'm calling you from hospital.'

It was proving equally difficult to persuade hospital staff to take his theory seriously.

Then on 11 November, a week after he was admitted, something terrible and strange happened.

Litvinenko's hair began to fall out. At first, in small clumps. Marina was visiting her husband in hospital every day; sometimes Anatoly went too. She saw him on Sunday, 12 November; he complained of pain in his throat. When she returned the next morning Litvinenko looked much worse: a spectral figure, weak, pathetic and 'completely different'. Marina stroked her husband's head, a calming gesture. She looked at her hand in horror: his hair was on her glove. It was on his shoulder and pillow too – everywhere. Marina was distraught. And, uncharacteristically, angry. She railed at medical staff: 'What's this? Can anyone tell me what's happened to my husband?'

With Marina was Valentina Michena, a Russian ex-nurse in her late fifties whom Marina had befriended. Michena had arrived in the UK from Russia in 2000. She knew nobody, was lonely, and began chatting to Marina in a shop. 'Marina is a lovely, lovely person,' she said. Michena became a surrogate granny to Anatoly. When Litvinenko fell ill she moved into the family's Muswell Hill home. She offered to cut Litvinenko's hair, what was left of it. The doctors agreed. They asked Michena to collect the hair in a plastic bag, so they could test it.

Litvinenko was unperturbed by his dramatic hair loss. He was a good-looking man but had never been vain or preening. Michena tugged at the hair from the front; the hair at the back yielded less readily. 'My appearance does not bother me at the moment,' he told her. She finished the job with clippers. He was bald.

'During those five days while I was visiting, his hair was falling down easily,' Michena said. 'It was like you would blow a dandelion.'

By this point Litvinenko was convinced he'd been the victim of a serious poisoning. He even knew who he thought had done it. In his BBC interview, he'd pointed to Scaramella, his Italian contact. In fact, he was certain that it was the two Russians – the known Lugovoi and the unknown Kovtun – who were to blame. Litvinenko was by nature an optimist, and remained confident he would beat his illness. By concealing Lugovoi and Kovtun's role, he was hoping to draw them back from Moscow to the UK, where the authorities might then arrest them.

Meanwhile, his physicians were becoming concerned. On 13 November, Dr Andres Virchis, a haematologist at Barnet Hospital, reviewed his case. It was, he admitted, a 'bit of a puzzle'. A diagnosis of gastro-enteritis now seemed less likely. Litvinenko was exhibiting a whole set of different, troubling symptoms; his platelet count had fallen through the floor and then there was the alopecia – abrupt, alarming hair loss. Nothing really fitted together.

'It just struck me that he looked like one of my patients who had had chemotherapy,' Virchis said. 'If you look at cancer treatment, there's various levels of intensity. There's outpatient treatment, but there are patients with acute leukaemia, a serious form of blood cancer, given very intensive chemotherapy. He looked just like a patient of mine that had had treatment.'

The senior team managing Litvinenko started to explore other possibilities. The idea that he had been poisoned was beginning to look less fanciful. The next day, 14 November, Virchis began discussions with a toxicologist at Guy's Hospital in London; they agreed to test for heavy metals and to carry out a biopsy. Litvinenko was extremely unwell. Virchis thought he looked like someone with acute radiation sickness. He wrote in the medical file: 'Ask radiology re. check radioactive sources of poisoning.'

The doctors were groping slowly towards an answer. On 15 November they brought a Geiger counter over Litvinenko for the first time. It looked like a chunky pocket calculator; if it found beta or gamma emissions the instrument would emit a loud whine. There was nothing. The notes record: 'Geiger Counter – No Emission.' The hospital didn't have equipment to measure much rarer alpha radiation; the only institution capable of doing that was the British nuclear weapons centre at Aldermaston.

As news of Litvinenko's condition spread, visitors arrived. That evening, Goldfarb dropped by. He was worried by what he discovered. Litvinenko was neutropenic. Goldfarb was a microbiologist by training and perfectly understood what this meant: Litvinenko's immune system was in ruinous shape, and collapsing.

Litvinenko told him about his suspicion that Lugovoi was the culprit. Goldfarb felt it was imperative the police get involved. The next day Goldfarb returned to Barnet Hospital with George Menzies, Litvinenko's long-time lawyer. They spent two hours at his bedside. Though weak, Litvinenko was in no doubt who was behind the plot, croaking to Menzies: 'You see, they have poisoned me' – 'they' being Russia's secret services.

Litvinenko continued to ring his friends. But he was fading. During one conversation with Suvorov his voice slowed up 'like a gramophone'; his voice faltered; the mobile tumbled from his grasp. Suvorov promised to come and see him in 'three or four days' when he was better.

Later that day, Guy's poisons unit came back with news. The biopsy pointed to a provisional diagnosis of poisoning by thallium, a deadly metal. But the levels of thallium were weirdly faint and not much above environmental levels – 30 nanomoles per litre. The data were confusing. Further verification was needed.

The diagnosis sounded an alarm. Medical staff contacted Scotland Yard and said they suspected a malicious poisoning. Virchis talked to Litvinenko. Litvinenko confirmed that the Russian intelligence service uses radioactive thallium. Doctors began treating him with Prussian blue, an antidote and counter-poison.

Plans were drawn up, meanwhile, to shift Litvinenko from Barnet to a specialist ward at University College Hospital in Bloomsbury, round the corner from the London university of the same name, and a short walk through a green square of veteran plane trees to the British Museum.

Litvinenko arrived at University College Hospital on 17 November. Just before midnight, two detectives appeared at his bedside.

To begin with, the British police had a confusing picture – a poisoned Russian who spoke poor English; a baffling plot involving visitors from Moscow; and a swirl of potential crime scenes. Two detectives, DI Brent Hyatt and Chris Hoar, from the Met's specialist crime unit, interviewed Litvinenko in the critical-care unit on the sixteenth floor of University College Hospital. They address him rather quaintly as Edwin. He is a 'significant witness'. There are

Barnet and Chase Farm Hospitals NHS
NHS Trust
PATIENT HISTORY SHEET
Consultant
Date

E948340 04/12/1962
Mr Edwin Carter
140 Osier Crescent
Muswell Hill
N10 1RF 640 153 8716

(21)

17/11/06 17.30 pm
Pt. developed headache fever & rigors
For neuro exam
Spoke to Guys poisons unit – prussian blue is the only treatment indicated for thallium poisoning at this stage. They cannot identify the isotope not able to check for possible radioactivity. Other heavy metal assays awaited e.g. arsenic but unlikely to cause these symptoms
Spoke to Haematology reg. at UCH re possible future need for BMT. They have agreed to take patient when a bed is available. Will take patient tonight.

Plan
1. Transfer to UCH
2. Continue prussian blue 4g tds for 7 days until repeat urine thallium level available
3. Continue present anti-[illegible]

[signature]

H/C neuro exam

17/11/06 (1) 17[55]

		R	L
lower limbs:	inspection	[illegible]	[illegible]
	power	5/5	5/5
	tone	normal [illegible]	normal
	[illegible]	++	++
	plantars	↓	↓
	[illegible]	✓	✓
	[illegible]	[illegible]	[illegible]
	[illegible]	normal	normal
upper limbs:	inspection	normal	normal
	[illegible]	++	++
	[illegible]	[illegible]	
	[illegible]	[illegible]	[illegible]

eighteen interviews, lasting eight hours and fifty-seven minutes in total. These conversations stretch out over three days, from the early hours of 18 November until shortly before 9 p.m. on 20 November.

The interview transcripts were kept secret for eight and a half years, hidden in Scotland Yard's case file, and stamped with the word 'Restricted', white capitals on a stark black rectangular background. Revealed in 2015, they are remarkable documents. They are, in effect, unique witness statements taken from a ghost. But Litvinenko is no ordinary ghost: he's a ghost who uses his final reserves of energy to solve a chilling murder mystery – his own.

Litvinenko was a highly experienced detective. He knew how investigations worked. He was fastidious too: neatly collating case materials in a file, always employing a hole punch. In the interviews he sets out before the police in dispassionate terms the evidence of who might have poisoned him. He acknowledges: 'I cannot blame these people directly because I have no proof.'

He's an ideal witness – good with descriptions, heights, details. He draws up a list of suspects. There are three of them: the Italian Mario Scaramella; his business partner Andrei Lugovoi; and Lugovoi's unpleasant Russian companion, whose name Litvinenko struggles to remember, and to whom he refers wrongly as 'Volodia' or 'Vadim'.

DI Hyatt begins recording at eight minutes after midnight on 18 November. He introduces himself and his colleague Detective Sergeant Hoar, from the Met's specialist crime directorate. Edwin gives his own name and address.

Hoar then says: 'Thank you very much for that, Edwin. Edwin, we're here investigating an allegation that somebody has poisoned you in an attempt to kill you.' Hoar says that doctors have told him Edwin is suffering from 'extremely high levels of thallium' and 'that is the cause of this illness'.

He continues: 'Can I ask you to tell us what you think has happened to you and why?'

Medical staff had pre-briefed Hoar that Litvinenko spoke good English. In fact, Hoar discovered, this wasn't the case. Litvinenko's answers were sometimes spotty and confusing; after this first nocturnal session they took a police interpreter, Nina Tupper.

Despite these hurdles, Litvinenko is able to give a full account of his career in the FSB, his deepening conflict with the agency, and his unhappy encounter in 1998 with Putin. The case file records his words: 'I have meeting with PUTIN, face to face. About forty minutes. I bring to PUTIN material about criminal inside FSB. PUTIN invite me to his team. I refuse. I know who is PUTIN. I have operation material against PUTIN in some … PUTIN have contract with one criminal group.'

Litvinenko talks of his 'good relationship' with the Russian journalist Anna Politkovskaya, another Putin enemy, and her fear she was in danger. In spring 2006, they met in a branch of Caffè Nero in London. Litvinenko asked her what was wrong. She told him, 'Alexander, I'm very afraid,' and said that every time she said goodbye to her daughter and son she had the feeling she was looking at them 'for the last time'. He urged her to leave Russia. She said she couldn't, citing her 'old parents' and kids. In October 2006, the journalist was shot dead in the stairwell of her Moscow apartment. Previously, in 2004, Politkovskaya was herself poisoned after drinking tea served on a plane to the North Caucasus. She had been on her way to mediate with Chechen terrorists who seized a school in Beslan in North Ossetia. The poisoning was the work of the FSB, she wrote.

Politkovskaya's murder in October left Litvinenko 'very very shocked', he says, adding: 'I lost a lot of my friends' and that human life in Russia is cheap. He tells detectives about a speech he made in the Frontline Club the previous month in which he accused Putin directly of having Politkovskaya killed.

From time to time, the interviews stop: the tape runs out; nurses come in to administer drugs; Litvinenko, suffering from diarrhoea, has to go to the bathroom. Mostly, though, he battles on. He tells Hyatt: 'Meeting you is very important for my case.' Litvinenko describes his encounter with Scaramella and gives a pocketbook description of the Italian: smart, grey suit, 'crooked hair', dark complexion, 1 m 72 cm – a typical man from Naples, with a light beard, and a 'little bit fat' round the middle.

The meeting, Litvinenko explains, was exasperating. Litvinenko says he was unimpressed by Scaramella's fondness for cloak and dagger – they had agreed to meet at Piccadilly Circus next to the statue of Eros. Litvinenko got there first and found himself wondering about the 'irony' of the situation. 'Why play the spies? To my mind, all these James Bonds verge on madness,' he tells Hyatt.

In the Itsu restaurant, Scaramella delivers a list. It includes both their names. Supposedly, those who feature are targets for assassination by the Russian state. Litvinenko says he isn't terrified by this development (which, in hindsight, appears to be a bizarre coincidence).

Rather, he's offended by the grubbiness of the A4 sheet Scaramella handed him. 'It was all dirty. I've worked a lot in my life with documents … When I am given papers like this I feel squeamish taking them into my hands,' he says. He shows the two detectives his own working notebook. It's immaculate, without any stains, even after two years. 'Look how I make notes,' he tells them.

But it is the two Russians who are at the centre of his suspicions. Litvinenko recounts his meeting with them at the Millennium Hotel. He says that he hadn't been to the hotel before and had to find it on a map. He insists this 'special' information remain secret – not to be made public or shared with his wife Marina. 'These people, it's interesting. Most interesting,' he muses. Litvinenko's logic is that if Scaramella is the culprit he can easily be arrested in Italy. But if it's the Russians they will be trickier to catch: 'If this Andrei and Vadim from KGB poison me, if I speak it, KGB cover it [up].'

With time running out, Litvinenko is working furiously to solve the conundrum. The transcript reads:

CARTER [LITVINENKO]: Only these three people
  can poison me.

DI HYATT: These three.

CARTER: Mario, Vadim [Kovtun] and Andrei.

After four or five hours of interviews, the case begins to cohere. There are moments when it appears that there are three officers hard at work: Hyatt, Hoar and Litvinenko, the punctilious ex-cop. By this point Litvinenko is speaking Russian. The investigation gains new momentum. Information is passed back to SO15, the counter-terrorist command at Scotland Yard, headed by Detective Superintendent Clive Timmons.

Litvinenko explains that his most important papers are kept at home, in the lower shelf of a large cupboard. The papers include critical information on Putin, and the people around him, from newspapers and other sources, as well as background on Russian criminal gangs. He gives the police his email password and bank account. He tells them where they can find receipts for two Orange SIM cards, bought for £20 from a store in Bond Street – in a black leather wallet on his bedside table. Litvinenko explains that he gave one of the SIMs to Lugovoi; they used these secret numbers to communicate. He hands over his diary.

It was, Litvinenko says, Lugovoi who insisted the pair of them meet at the Millennium Hotel on 1 November. They were originally scheduled to meet the following day, at the offices of security company Global Risk. Litvinenko shows Hyatt his note of the appointment. He uses a code for 'Lugovoi' – tragic in hindsight – calling him 'Friend 2'.

'We were to meet on the second. But he called me in the morning and said he had already arrived and he would like to meet me for a short time on the first,' Litvinenko says.

DI Hyatt produces a map of central London. With a little difficulty, Litvinenko retraces his probable route to Grosvenor Square – north along Old Bond Street, along Grafton Street, and then Berkeley Square.

He describes meeting Lugovoi in the Millennium lobby and going with him to the Pine Bar. Lugovoi was dressed, Litvinenko says, in clothes he had bought three months earlier on a shopping trip to Harrods, London's most famous department store – 'a kind of cardigan', dark blue and orange. Litvinenko said he didn't think much of Lugovoi's expensive, flashy style. 'We were in Harrods … I said to him then, "Why do you need this Harrods?"' There were further details – Lugovoi was wearing greyish jeans, 'fashionable' shoes, 'but not English make', and a big gold watch with a black face. 'It was very visible. Before he [Lugovoi] had told me that this watch cost $50,000.'

Ever helpful, Litvinenko phones his wife and asks her to locate a photo of Lugovoi at their home. Hyatt suspends the interview to secure the photograph. Lugovoi is now a prime suspect. Litvinenko describes him like this: 'Andrei is a pure European, and even he looks a little bit like me, sort of. The same type as like me … I am 1 m 77 cm, 1 m 78 cm, so he is probably 1 m 76 cm. He is two years younger than me, light hair.' He has a small, 'almost invisible' bald patch.

The transcript says:

DI HYATT: Edwin, do you consider Andrei to be a friend of yours, or a business associate? What, how do you describe your relationship with Andrei?
CARTER: He is not a friend. He is a business partner.

At the end of his second day of interviews, on 19 November, Litvinenko describes getting a lift back home with his Chechen friend Zakayev: 'Now the paradoxical thing is that I was still feeling very well but then somehow I had some kind of feeling that something might happen to me in the nearest future. Maybe subconsciously.' The detectives turn off the tape.

It's a full and frank account of events leading up to his poisoning – with one exception. During these two days Litvinenko doesn't mention his secret life and his job working for British intelligence. It's only the next day that he speaks of his meeting on 31 October with his MI6 handler 'Martin', in the basement café of the Waterstone's bookshop on Piccadilly. Litvinenko is chary, evidently reluctant to discuss his undercover MI6 role.

The conversation runs:

CARTER: On 31 October at about 4 p.m. I had a meeting arranged with a person about whom I wouldn't really like to talk here because I have some commitments. You can contact that person on that long telephone number which I gave you.
DI HYATT: Did you meet with that person, Edwin?

CARTER: Yes.

DI HYATT: Edwin, it could be absolutely vital that
   you tell us who that person is.

CARTER: You can call him and he will tell you.

The interview abruptly stops. It's 5.16 p.m. Hyatt dials
the long telephone number, reaches 'Martin', and tells
him that Litvinenko is gravely ill in hospital, the victim of
an apparent poisoning by two mysterious Russians.

It appears to be the first time that MI6 – an
organisation famed for its professionalism – learns of
Litvinenko's plight. Litvinenko, of course, wasn't a full-
time employee. But he was a salaried informant, with his
own encrypted cell phone, and MI6-provided passport.
The agency appears not to have classified Litvinenko as
being at risk, despite numerous threatening phone calls
from Moscow and the firebomb attack on his north
London home.

MI6's reaction is unclear. The British government has
still refused to release the relevant files. One can imagine
panic and embarrassment. And the agency shifting into
full-blown crisis mode. The transcripts show that after
speaking to DI Hyatt, 'Martin' scrambled to Litvinenko's hospital bedside. He talked to his poisoned agent,
and left around 7.15 p.m. The police interview then
resumes; Litvinenko continues his account of his Waterstone's meeting with 'Martin' in coy terms:

DI HYATT: Was that a meeting that was pre-arranged
   or was it a meeting that happened by chance?

CARTER: No, we called each other in advance and met up.

DI HYATT: OK. I don't want you to tell me the name of that person, Edwin, but can you tell me if that person is the person that I've been speaking to in your presence in this hospital around about fifteen minutes ago?

CARTER: Yes, that is absolutely correct.

The final exchanges deal with earlier threats against Litvinenko from the Kremlin and its emissaries. The detectives ask if there is anything Litvinenko would like to add.

DS HOAR: Can you think of anybody else who may wish to do this sort of harm to you?

CARTER: I have no doubt who wanted it, and I often receive threats from these people. This was done ... I have no doubt whatsoever that this was done by the Russian Secret Services. Having knowledge of the system I know that the order about such a killing of a citizen of another country on its territory, especially if it is something to do with Great Britain, could have been given by only one person.

DI HYATT: Would you like to tell us who that person is, sir? Edwin?

CARTER: That person is the president of the Russian Federation, Vladimir PUTIN. And if ... you of course know, whilst he's still President, you won't be able to prosecute him as the main person who gave that order, because he is the president of a huge country crammed with nuclear, chemical and bacteriological weapons. But I have no doubt whatsoever that as soon as the power changes in Russia or when the first officer of Russian Special Services defects to the west he will say the same. He will say that I have been poisoned by the Russian Special Services on Putin's order.

Litvinenko returns to the theme of Putin's culpability in his last two interviews, at 8.06 p.m. and 8.39 p.m. respectively. He is moving and lucid. And perceptive: Litvinenko is aware that his case raises a major dilemma for western governments. How should they deal with the head of a powerful, energy-rich state who, apparently, has his enemies murdered?

CARTER: I wouldn't like you to think that this is some kind of pompous political statement, but since all this happened I would like you to know very clearly what my position regarding this matter is. As you understand last month I was granted British citizenship and I very much love this country, and its people, although unfortunately I haven't learnt English language completely yet. I am proud to be able to say that I'm a British citizen. Yes, they did try to kill me and possibly I may die, but I will die as a free person, and my son and wife are free people. And Britain is a great country.

Litvinenko says western politicians are to blame for treating Putin as a respectable international leader:

> CARTER: I understand that this case is not a criminal one. I understand that everybody will be regarding this case as a political one. No, rather, I understand that this case is going to be perceived by everyone as political, but this case is not political, this case is criminal. I feel very upset that this criminal PUTIN sits at the G8 as its Chairman, at the same table as the British prime minister Tony BLAIR. Having sat this murderer next to themselves at the same table western leaders have actually untied his hands to kill anyone anywhere.
>
> INTERPRETER: To kill what?
>
> CARTER: To kill anyone anywhere. And of course I understand the west wants to get gas and oil from Russia, but one shouldn't be involved in political activity if one doesn't have political beliefs. And beliefs can't be traded for gas and oil. Because when businessman is trading he's trading with his money but when a politician is trading he is trading with the Sovereignty of his country and the future of his children.

The buzzer sounds, signalling the tape is finishing. Litvinenko tells Hyatt:

> CARTER: I have a request for you, Inspector. I trust you completely … In case there is from the top,

> administrative pressure for political reasons, I am
> asking him [Hyatt] to be firm in his position and
> to bring this case to the end, as far as it is possible.

Litvinenko's remarks would turn out to be prescient. The Scotland Yard detectives seem touched by his faith in them. DI Hyatt promises to 'do absolutely everything within my power to ensure that this case is properly investigated'. He adds: 'I know that this process has been extremely difficult because of your medical condition, and I just want to thank you for your time, your patience and your help with getting as much information to us as possible in the way that you have done.'

Litvinenko's condition was rapidly deteriorating. On 20 November, the same day as his last police inter-view, doctors moved him to intensive care. Here it was easier to monitor the patient and, if necessary, to inter-vene. His heart rate was becoming abnormal; his major organs failing.

The medics treating him were in unchartered territory. Litvinenko's case was problematic: he wasn't behaving like a patient who had ingested thallium. He had severe bone marrow failure and gut damage, which fitted. But he lacked one key symptom of thallium poisoning – peripheral neuropathy, pain or numbness in his fingers and feet. 'It was still a bit of a mystery,' one doctor said. Professor John Henry – an expert on poisoning – exam-ined Litvinenko twice. He found that his handshake was still extremely firm. Henry had previously told Sky TV that Litvinenko was a victim of radioactive thallium. Now he had doubts.

Meanwhile, those close to Litvinenko were reluctantly concluding he was unlikely to survive.

The Kremlin would subsequently accuse Berezovsky and Goldfarb of cynically exploiting Litvinenko as part of their long-running public-relations campaign against Putin. In fact, Litvinenko made it abundantly clear – as the Scotland Yard transcripts show – that he held Putin personally responsible for his poisoning. And he wanted to send this message to the world.

Litvinenko's lawyer, George Menzies, began drafting a statement on his behalf. Menzies later said that the ideas in it were wholly Litvinenko's. 'I was doing my best, in personal terms, to represent what I truly believed to be Sasha's state of mind and sentiment,' he said. Its themes – Litvinenko's pride in being British, his love of his wife, his belief as to the source of his illness – mirrored what his client thought, Menzies said.

Goldfarb and Menzies took the draft to the hospital. They showed it to Marina. Her reaction was negative. She believed her husband would pull through and that writing a last testament was tantamount to giving up on him. Pragmatically, they told her: 'Better to do it now than later.'

Menzies consulted with Tim Bell, chairman of the London PR firm Bell Pottinger. Bell's company had worked for Boris Berezovsky since 2002, helping the exiled oligarch through various legal scrapes, and had assisted the Litvinenkos as well. Bell said he thought the text was too gloomy and read like a 'deathbed statement'.

'I didn't think it was the right thing to do because I still hoped and believed Sasha would live,' Bell said.

Goldfarb read out the A4 sheet to Litvinenko in intensive care, translating it from English to Russian. At one point Goldfarb made a movement with his arms, mimicking the flight of an angel flapping its wings. Litvinenko endorsed the statement in its entirety, confirming: 'This is exactly what I want to say.' Litvinenko then signed and dated it – 21 November 2006, his signature trailing off into a raised black swirl.

The statement read:

I would like to thank many people. My doctors, nurses and hospital staff who are doing all they can for me; the British police who are pursuing my case with rigour and professionalism and are watching over me and my family. I would like to thank the British government for taking me under their care. I am honoured to be a British citizen.

I would like to thank the British public for their messages of support and for the interest they have shown in my plight.

I thank my wife, Marina, who has stood by me. My love for her and my son knows no bounds.

But as I lie here I can distinctly hear the beating of wings of the angel of death. I may be able to give him the slip but I have to say my legs do not run as fast as I might like. I think, therefore, this may be the time to say one or two things to the person responsible for my present condition.

You may succeed in silencing me but that silence comes at a price. You have shown yourself to be as barbaric and ruthless as your most hostile critics have claimed.

You have shown yourself to have no respect for life, liberty or any civilised value.

You have shown yourself to be unworthy of your office, to be unworthy of the trust of civilised men and women.

You may succeed in silencing one man but the howl of protest from around the world will reverberate, Mr Putin, in your ears for the rest of your life. May God forgive you for what you have done, not only to me but to beloved Russia and its people.

TV cameras and media had gathered outside the hospital's main gate, waiting for news. They'd been there since Monday morning, 20 November, in the wake of an interview given by Litvinenko to the journalist David Leppard and published the previous day by the *Sunday Times*.

Sixteen floors above them, Litvinenko asked Goldfarb if he was a big story. He was – but not much was known about Litvinenko, other than that he was a prominent critic of Putin's, and desperately ill. Goldfarb said: 'Sasha, if you really want the message to be seriously put across, we need a photo.' Marina was against the idea, and saw it as an invasion of privacy. But Litvinenko agreed, and said: 'Yes, if you think it's needed, let's do it.'

Goldfarb rang Bell Pottinger and spoke to Jennifer Morgan, Bell's liaison. Morgan in turn called a photographer she knew, Natasja Weitsz. Weitsz arrived at the hospital and was escorted upstairs past a police guard. She was with Litvinenko for mere minutes. He pushed his green hospital gown to one side so as to reveal the electro-cardiagram sensors attached to his heart. Weitsz shot a couple of frames of Litvinenko: bald, gaunt and defiant, staring with cornflower-blue eyes directly at the camera lens. The image was cropped around its haunting subject. It went round the world.

Litvinenko was aware his time was running out. His friend Zakayev had been visiting him in hospital every day; they had talked of Chechnya, religion and Zakayev's Muslim faith.

Litvinenko told Zakayev: 'One day when I die, will you promise to put my body in Chechen ground?' Zakayev agreed – given the circumstances, it would have been impossible to refuse. A precondition of burial was that Litvinenko convert to Islam. Zakayev asked Marina if he could bring an imam. She assented; the imam visited intensive care and performed the ceremony at speed.

Litvinenko's father Walter flew in from Moscow and arrived at his son's bedside. Litvinenko informed him: 'Dad, what do you think? I've converted. I'm now a Muslim.'

Walter was an Orthodox Christian. In his later years he'd become more of a believer. He took this development in his stride. And replied: 'It doesn't matter, at least you're not a communist.'

By the next day, Wednesday, 22 November, doctors treating Litvinenko had scrapped their diagnosis. Their notes read: 'We DO NOT feel this gentleman has or had inorganic thallium poisoning.'

At midday, a top-level meeting was convened at the Metropolitan Police's counter-terrorism command. It involved SO15 detectives, led by Detective Superintendent Timmons, medical staff, a scientist from the UK's Atomic Weapons Establishment, the Forensic Science Service and Dr Nick Gent from Porton Down, the UK's military science facility. The latest urine test had revealed the presence of a new radioactive isotope – polonium-210. But this was marked down as an anomaly, caused by the plastic container used to carry Litvinenko's urine.

According to Timmons, the specialists discussed five theories which might explain Litvinenko's baffling poisoning. Most were esoteric. They included Stevens–Johnson syndrome, an idiosyncratic reaction to drugs; an intake of cytotoxins, cancer-fighting medicines; and exposure to an external radiation source, such as cobalt-30. Another possibility was natural causes. Or an internal radiation source, such as polonium. This last theory was seen as unlikely. The experts decided to investigate further and to send a litre of urine to Aldermaston.

Back in the intensive care ward, Litvinenko was drifting in and out of consciousness. The Russian-German filmmaker Andrei Nekrasov visited him. Nekrasov had previously conducted several interviews with Litvinenko; he shot the video on condition that it would be released only with Marina's approval. It's the last photograph.

Litvinenko lies on his bed, a vanquished soul, around whom the world is closing and darkening. A drip is attached to his nose; his cheeks are hollow; his eyes are open – just. There is pale afternoon light.

'He was conscious, but was very, very weak,' Marina said. 'I spent almost all day sitting close to him, [to] make him just be calm and more relaxed.' At 8 p.m. Marina got up to leave, and told her husband: 'Sasha, unfortunately I have to go.'

She said: 'He smiled so sadly, and I started to feel I'm guilty because I'm leaving him, and I just said, "Don't worry, tomorrow morning I will come and everything will be fine."'

Litvinenko whispered back to her: 'I love you so much.' Marina wanted to exit on an optimistic note; she joked that she hadn't heard those words for a long time.

At midnight the hospital called to say that Litvinenko had gone into cardiac arrest, not once but twice. They managed to resuscitate him. She returned to University College Hospital, getting a lift with Zakayev, and found her husband unconscious and on a life-support machine. She spent the following day, 23 November, at his side; Litvinenko was in an induced coma. That evening she went back to Muswell Hill. An hour after arriving home the phone rang. It was the hospital telling her urgently to return.

Litvinenko suffered a third cardiac arrest at 8.51 p.m. The consultant on duty, Dr James Down, tried to revive him but at 9.21 p.m. pronounced life extinct. When Marina and Anatoly arrived at the hospital they were taken not to the ward but to a side-room. Ten or fifteen minutes later, the doctor told them that Litvinenko was dead. He added: 'Would you like to see Sasha?', to which Marina replied: 'Of course.'

For the first time in several days, she said, she was allowed to touch and kiss him; Anatoly ran from the room after half a minute.

Six hours before Litvinenko's death, at about 3 p.m., Timmons received a phone call from the Atomic Weapons Establishment. It had the results from the latest tests. They confirmed that Litvinenko was 'terribly contaminated', as Timmons put it, with radioactive polonium.

7

Ruslan and Lyudmila

Mayak nuclear complex, Ozersk, Russia,
1952–2006

'On the curved strand a green oak grows'
RUSLAN AND LYUDMILA, ALEXANDER PUSHKIN, 1820

Every good Russian student knows the beginning of Alexander Pushkin's much-loved mock-epic poem *Ruslan and Lyudmila*. It concerns a young prince, Ruslan, whose bride Lyudmila is seized from him on his wedding night by an evil dwarf, Chernomor. To get her back, Ruslan has to go on a knightly quest. Along the way he defeats a rival suitor. He meets a giant talking head and finds a golden sword.

The dwarf, meanwhile, tries in vain to woo Lyudmila, his prisoner. She manages to disappear using an enchanted hat. There is fighting. Ruslan grapples with Chernomor as they fly through the air. He later rescues Kiev from enemy attack. And there is a happy ending, with a little help from healing water and a magic ring.

The poem begins in a translation by Peter France:

On the curved strand a green oak grows
On the green oak a golden chain
And on it round and round there goes

The cat of knowledge, night and day –
Goes to the right and sings a ditty,
Goes to the left, begins a tale.

Published in 1820, the mock-heroic fairy tale made the young Pushkin famous. He started writing it at the age of seventeen, a student at the lyceum near St Petersburg. He finished it three years later, a junior official at the ministry of foreign affairs. The poem is playful, luminous, sparse and strange. Pushkin admired Lord Byron; *Ruslan and Lyudmila* has witty and colloquial touches reminiscent of the British poet.

It is also a very Russian work. It blends elements from Russian folklore and ordinary life; as well as a fantasy garden there is a scene in a bathhouse. It's subtle, too. Pushkin both enters into this fairytale universe and simultaneously stands outside and coolly assesses it. The low-tonality vowels of the opening have a haunting quality. What emerges is a new and vibrant literary language.

In the Soviet Union every educated citizen read Pushkin's epic verse at school. So, it was unsurprising that scientists working at a Soviet nuclear facility deep in the Urals decided to call two of their nuclear reactors there 'Ruslan' and 'Lyudmila'. The names were playful, half-nodding towards the strange and magical world of nuclear science. 'Ruslan' and 'Lyudmila' was also a lively, if ghoulish, shorthand – a way of referring to the clandestine work that went on inside the guarded perimeter fence. The Mayak complex was top secret, like other state institutions engaged in the assembly of nuclear weapons. What better way of defusing Mayak's threat than jolly familiarity? In Russian, *mayak* means 'light-house', humorous given its invisibility.

The two reactors were built at the tail end of the Soviet Union. Ruslan is a pool-type light water reactor that has operated since 1979, undergoing a major over-haul in 1998–9. Lyudmila is a heavy water reactor that has been in operation since 1988. Lyudmila is bigger, with a power of 1,000 megawatts.

The Mayak complex sprang from the Cold War, and the post-1945 nuclear arms race between the world's two superpowers, the US and the Soviet Union. After the American atomic bombings of Nagasaki and Hiro-shima, Stalin accelerated the Soviet nuclear programme. The nuclear physicist Igor Kurchatov directed research, while Lavrenty Beria, head of the NKVD secret police, was put in charge of efforts to steal nuclear secrets from the US, Britain and Canada.

These efforts worked. The Soviets were able to recruit a network of agents from among the scientists designing the US atomic bomb in Los Alamos, New Mexico – Robert Oppenheimer, Enrico Fermi, Leo Szilard. In Britain, Donald Maclean, part of the Cambridge spy ring, told Moscow that the British were developing a uranium bomb too. It was an exhaustive international espionage operation that allowed Moscow to catch up.

Money and privileges flowed towards physicists and engineers who worked in this new and covert field. They included Andrei Sakharov, a gifted nuclear scientist and future dissident, and the physicists Yakov Zeldovich and

Lev Landau. With many others, they successfully designed a Soviet H-bomb. A network of secret Atomgrads – closed cities – was built. These cities were dedicated to nuclear weapons research and development.

Mayak was located 43 miles (70 km) north-west of the city of Chelyabinsk and south of Yekaterinburg. The spot was chosen for its remoteness: it was in the geographic centre of Russia, far away from any front line, and protected by the Ural mountains to the west and Siberia to the east. In a mere eighteen months, Kurchatov built the USSR's first plutonium production reactor, Anachka. Some 70,000 gulag labourers were used. More reactors followed. The site was based around the closed towns of Ozersk and Snezhinsk.

Many of the people who worked in Russia's fledgeling nuclear industry had fled from war zones further west; they came from Belarus, Ukraine, Poland. Some were Jews who escaped the Nazis. Within a few years, Chelyabinsk was a booming industrial city, home to engineers, metallurgists and mathematicians. Another principal atomic facility was constructed at Sarov, 450 miles (725 km) south-east of Moscow near the Volga river. Sarov specialised in atomic weapons design and research. Sakharov worked there from 1950.

Officially, neither Mayak nor the Sarov complex existed: they didn't appear on maps. Residents of closed cities weren't permitted to leave for holidays until the 1950s. Sarov was codenamed Arzamas-16; Mayak Chelyabinsk-40, and later Chelyabinsk-65. They were closed to Soviet citizens, unless they had a good reason to be there.

And, of course, off-limits to foreigners. This made them objects of allure for western powers. (In 1960, American pilot Gary Powers was photographing the Mayak atomic plant when his CIA spy plane was shot down.)

Soviet physics was a beneficiary of Stalin's determination to match the US bomb. But there was a price. Little attention was paid to the environmental consequences of handling large quantities of fissile material. For example, radioactive waste water from Mayak was pumped out into small lakes nearby and the Techa river. The complex itself was the scene of mishaps and dangerous small leaks.

In September 1957, a cooling tank storing tens of thousands of tonnes of dissolved nuclear waste overheated and blew up. A cloud of radioactive material was set free. It contaminated over 300 square miles. Radiation was found in the Arctic Sea. It was one of the worst accidents of the nuclear age, on a par with the disasters at Chernobyl and Fukushima. In 1967, there was another catastrophe when Lake Karachay, used as a mid-level nuclear waste dump, dried out. Wind threw radioactive dust over a huge area.

The Soviet authorities responded to these accidents predictably, with denial and cover-up. (It took thirty years before Moscow acknowledged the Kyshtym disaster, as the 1957 Mayak explosion was known.) Troops were sent to evacuate some villages; soldiers fenced off the Techa river with barbed wire. But locals weren't told what had happened: the leak was a state secret. In summer, children still swam in the river; farmers watered their cattle; women drew water from the wells; locals cut hay.

Gradually, the toxic legacy from Mayak became impossible for the Kremlin to conceal. People were dying. The disasters of the fifties and sixties exposed at least half a million to radiation poisoning. Symptoms were ubiquitous: intestinal illnesses, nose bleeds, food allergies. There were respiratory and skin problems. Cancers were rife. In some of the worst-affected areas, it was unusual for villagers to live beyond fifty. Some were dead at twenty. Chronic radiation sickness affected future generations.

Paula Chertok, who grew up in Chelyabinsk, and later emigrated to the US, recalls: 'Nearly everyone I know from Chelyabinsk had cancer of one sort or another. Many had blood disorders. My mother's best friend, a doctor, died young from leukaemia. Every woman I know had breast cancer. And we didn't live in the villages, we lived in Chelyabinsk proper. The environment was utterly contaminated and we never knew a thing.' She added: 'We drank the water, played near the rivers and lakes.'

By the 1990s, the local population was still suffering from health problems, although the rules for visiting closed nuclear cities were somewhat relaxed. However, finding once-secret Snezhinsk is something of a challenge: the turn-off point to the town isn't marked with any signs. A high and rather rickety wooden fence surrounds Snezhinsk, with a checkpoint manned 24/7 at its only exit and entrance. A sign in a field in Russian and English warns non-authorised visitors not to go any further.

Meanwhile, the state that built Mayak disappeared. The demise of the Soviet Union made life difficult for all Russians, but for scientists it was a disaster. State institutions were unable to pay their employees; some moonlighted as taxi drivers; others flogged their possessions on the street. Atomic-weapons laboratories continued to function and academic visitors noted a high level of professionalism still. But with the apparent end of the Cold War their future looked bleak.

It was a moment when Boris Yeltsin's Russia believed in dialogue with the outside world; after all, Moscow was broke. In the US and Europe there were worries about what might happen to the former Soviet Union's nuclear technicians. Worst-case scenario: the experts would go off and work in Iran, Iraq or Libya. Russian scientists were given grants. A team from Princeton University advised closed cities like Sarov on how to transform their production lines from nuclear bomb manufacture to non-weapons activity.

Some of these US–Russian initiatives worked. The secret Avangard laboratory in Sarov, for example, moth-balled weapons production and began manufacturing civilian radioactive isotopes instead. It exported them to foreign markets, including America. This was, in effect, a job-creation scheme for the town's shrinking scientific workforce, down from 4,800 employees in the 1980s to 3,300 by 2000.

Avangard became the only place in the world where one particular isotope was made. It had been manufactured there since 1952. Not many people had noticed. The quantities involved were tiny, the export market practically non-existent. But then the isotope was very rare and highly unusual: an intensely radioactive silver-coloured metal.

Polonium.

On 18 July 1898 Marie and Pierre Curie discovered polonium while experimenting with the mineral pitchblende. Pitchblende contained uranium. They repeatedly heated it, and dissolved the residue in acid. This process allowed them to isolate a new and unknown substance. It had extraordinary properties. It was 400 times more radioactive than uranium. Curie called this new element polonium.

The name was in tribute to Curie's lost homeland, Poland, which hadn't existed as an independent state since the late eighteenth century. Three imperial powers – Russia, Prussia and Habsburg Hungary – had partitioned it into non-existence. Curie's family actively supported Polish nationalist movements; her father, a mathematics and physics teacher, was sacked from his job for pro-Polish sentiments. It would take two decades, strikes and street battles in Warsaw and Lodz in 1905, plus a world war, before Poland was reconstituted in 1918 as a sovereign territory.

Polonium was so rare it was impossible to make in any quantity. There were 100 microgrammes of polonium per ton of uranium ore. In the 1930s scientists found that under the right conditions they could manufacture polonium in a nuclear reactor. The technique involved irradiating another element, bismuth or Bi, by bombarding it with neutrons. (Specifically, Bi-209 absorbs a neutron and becomes Bi-210. It then beta-decays to Polonium-210, or Po-210.)

An isotope is a particular version of an element, depending on the number of neutrons. This resulting isotope was strange. Po-210 emits extraordinarily high levels of alpha particles, one of three types of radiation. A single gram produces 140 watts of energy, an enormous amount. Polonium is a source of much weaker gamma radiation. The element has a half-life of 138 days, which means that over this period half of the material will decay.

The right equipment can detect tiny quantities of polonium, so intense is its emission of alpha particles. It's possible to detect amounts as small as a few picograms, one millionth of a millionth of a gram.

In the century since the Curies' discovery, polonium never found much of a foothold in the real world. Nuclear states including the US, USSR, UK and France used polonium as a trigger for the first generation of nuclear bombs; it had a niche role in the Soviet space programme. In 1970, Moscow sent *Lunokhod 1* – an ingenious space rover that looked like a giant bathtub on wheels – to the moon. (It's still there.) During the lunar nights, Po-210 kept its components warm.

By the 1970s, polonium was more or less obsolete. Weapons scientists replaced it as a trigger with a more efficient tritium 'gun'. State-run nuclear laboratories in the US, UK and Canada stopped making polonium. (In the 1950s and 1960s Britain produced it at civilian nuclear sites. According to the defence ministry in London, any surviving stocks would have completely decayed to

Pb-206 – lead – by the early 1980s.) China abandoned polonium in the 1990s.

The only country that continued to produce it was the Russian Federation. The Avangard facility exported Po-210 on a commercial basis, for use in anti-static devices. The amounts involved were extremely small.

By the time Lugovoi and Kovtun came to kill Litvinenko in London in 2006, polonium was something of a forgotten chemical oddity. It was present on the periodic table, hanging in dusty chemistry classrooms, atomic number 84, found between bismuth and astatine, marked with a hazard sign.

Faced with what looked like a mini-nuclear bomb, a case with obvious political and diplomatic implications, and an international media frenzy, the British government sought expert advice on polonium. Where had it come from? Was it possible to buy polonium on the open market? How much would it cost? Did the UK have its own stockpiles? Could criminal gangs be involved? And just how dangerous was it?

One knowledgeable source was Norman Dombey, an emeritus professor of theoretical physics at the University of Sussex, set on a pleasant campus above the seaside town of Brighton. Dombey had published about a hundred scientific papers and was an authority on the nuclear weapons programmes of the UK, US and former Soviet Union. He also knew Russian. In 1962–3 he spent a year at Moscow state university on one of the first academic exchanges with the USSR, when he visited Soviet scientific institutions. He went back to Moscow in 1988 during Glasnost. He invited the nuclear scientist turned dissident Sakharov – by this point recalled by Mikhail Gorbachev from internal exile in Gorky – to the UK to collect an honorary degree. In 1992, Dombey visited the St Petersburg Nuclear Physics Institute. Subsequently he toured other physics institutions in Russia, as well as Armenia and Georgia, where professional scientific life had collapsed.

White-haired, approachable, lucid, modest, Dombey displayed a credibility that was enhanced by the fact that he was one of very few who predicted that Saddam Hussein didn't have weapons of mass destruction. In September 2002, in the run-up to the Iraq war, he wrote an article entitled 'Saddam's Nuclear Incapability'. His thesis – there was no nuclear threat from Baghdad – contradicted the apocalyptic assessments coming from the Bush–Cheney administration in Washington, as well as from its ally in London, Tony Blair. Dombey, as history shows, was right.

The professor's report on polonium – originally commissioned by Marina Litvinenko – was disturbing. The only comfort for investigators was that polonium was so intensively radioactive it was easy to track. The trail of those who brought it to London could be 'easily established', he believed.

The bad news was that what investigators were dealing with was an extremely hazardous substance – dangerous to handle in even milligram or microgram amounts, and requiring special equipment and strict control. Weight for weight, polonium was 2.5×10 to the 11 times as toxic as hydrocyanic acid.

Dombey's suspicion was that the polonium had come from Russia. He also realised Litvinenko's murder was not meant to be discovered. One version was that the use of polonium was showy: it sent a chilling message to Berezovsky and other émigré critics of the Russian regime. The other: that the isotope was the perfect undetectable weapon. Dombey inclined strongly to this second view. 'It was meant to be a mysterious poisoning. That was because polonium was an alpha emitter which Geiger counters didn't pick up,' he said.

To be certain of the polonium's origin, the professor had to make further inquiries. He wrote to senior nuclear officials in Moscow, the US, Canada and France. As he suspected, all countries other than Russia had ceased the manufacture of polonium. The only surviving polonium line was at Avangard in Sarov. Its director, Radii Ilykaev, confirmed the plant was exporting 0.8 grammes of polonium to the US a month, on a contractual basis.

Logically, there were only three ways of making polonium, Dombey reported. The first was to extract it from uranium ore, as the Curies did. The second was to irradiate a small sample of Bi-09 in a research reactor suitable for preparing isotopes. The third was to irradiate a large quantity of Bi-209 in a powerful high-flux reactor.

In his meeting with Lugovoi and Kovtun, Litvinenko drank 26.5 micrograms of polonium, it was established – or 4.4 gigabecquerels (GBq). This was an infinitesimally small amount, less than a grain of sand. A report by three radiation experts – John Harrison, Dr Nick Gent and Stuart Black – estimated that Litvinenko absorbed about

10 per cent of this dose – 0.44 gigabecquerels – into his bloodstream. It was more than enough to kill him

The actual amount put in the teapot, though, was larger – at least 50 micrograms, and probably 100 micrograms, including the undrunk tea left in Litvinenko's cup and the remaining tea in the teapot.

It would be impossible to extract this amount of polonium from natural uranium ore, Dombey calculated. Nor could it be prised out of commercial supplies sent to America. You would need to buy or steal 450 anti-static devices containing polonium without anyone noticing. Moreover, the tiny amount of polonium inside was impossible to extract unless, as Dombey put it drily, those performing the extraction 'wished to commit suicide'.

In the wake of Litvinenko's murder, Russian officials said that any nuclear research reactor was capable of making the isotope. There are about thirty research reactors worldwide. But again the amount that could be generated was far smaller than the amount of polonium put in Litvinenko's tea – mere picograms, at least 20,000 times smaller than the dose that killed him, via cell death in his body tissue and organs.

Dombey's conclusions – made public in 2015 – were succinct. He wrote:

a) The Po-210 used to poison Mr Litvinenko was made at the Avangard facility in Sarov, Russia. One of the isotope-producing reactors at the Mayak facility in Ozersk, Russia, was used for the initial irradiation of bismuth.

b) In my opinion the Russian state or its agents were
   responsible for the poisoning.

Dombey believed it was 'highly unlikely' that the reactor
used to irradiate the bismuth was in Sarov. None of
the reactors there had a sufficiently high neutron flux.
Instead it began its journey to London from the Mayak
facility near Chelyabinsk.

Litvinenko was undoubtedly Mayak's most spectacular victim. But there were thousands of anonymous
others in Chelyabinsk province and beyond who were
consigned to agonising leukemias and premature deaths.
Their suffering played out at home and in hospitals,
largely unnoticed, beyond a small circle of family and
friends, before an indifferent world.

The operation to kill Litvinenko was complex, covert and
extra-territorial. It involved an esoteric nuclear poison, two
hand-picked – if incompetent – assassins and a logistics
chain that stretched from the Ural mountains via several
intermediary points to the streets of London's Mayfair.

It was also full of hazards. As part of his investigation, Dombey examined previous cases of polonium
poisoning. In 1925, Nobus Yamada, a Japanese scientist who had been working at the Curies' laboratory in
Paris, fainted suddenly on his return to Japan. He had
been handling polonium. Yamada died eighteen months
later. In the summer of 1927, a Polish researcher, Sonia
Cotelle, who had also been preparing polonium, suffered
severe side effects. The Curies' daughter Irene wrote that

Cotelle was in 'very bad health', had stomach problems and had experienced 'a very rapid loss of hair'. She carried on working for several years until a vial of polonium shattered in her face. She died two weeks later.

These were accidents, but Litvinenko's death was deliberate. Given polonium's rapid decay, the dose used to kill him must have been made in a relatively brief period before his killers travelled to London.

Dombey said: 'Whoever poisoned Mr Litvinenko and brought polonium to Britain would only have done it if it had been tested in advance, because polonium is so radioactive that if they got their numbers wrong it wouldn't work.' He went on: 'On the higher side it could have produced a major public health problem.'

With little data to go on, Dombey asked a colleague to check if there were any suspicious deaths in Russia with the same symptoms as Litvinenko's? The colleague said there were. He mentioned two similar cases. The Russian press had featured both of them.

The first involved a Chechen guerrilla commander called Lecha Ismailov. Ismailov was captured, put in Lefortovo Prison, and tried. He got nine years. According to Akhmed Zakayev, Russia's spy agencies put pressure on Ismailov to switch sides. He refused their offer to work for the FSB.

On the morning of his transfer from Lefortovo to a regular jail, the two people who had failed to recruit Ismailov summoned him for a friendly chat. They suggested he drink a farewell cup of tea. They also offered him a snack. Ismailov drank the tea. He began to feel ill after five minutes, as warders took him to his cell. He was moved to a hospital in Volgograd, where his Litvinenko-like symptoms – hair loss and massive blisters – bewildered doctors there. Twelve days later he was dead. His relatives told journalists they suspected Russia's security agencies may have poisoned him.

The other possible precedent involved a figure from Vladimir Putin's early years in St Petersburg, Roman Tsepov. In the 1990s, Tsepov worked as a bodyguard for Putin and for the city's mayor Anatoly Sobchak. Allegedly, he was the liaison between politicians and the Tambov crime gang. Tsepov co-founded a private security company, Baltic-Escort. His partner was Viktor Zolotov, the future head of Putin's personal bodyguard. According to some accounts, Zolotov was the president's brutal enforcer and an individual of enormous physical strength.

Tsepov had friends in high places. And, unfortunately perhaps, he knew their secrets too well. In September 2004, he stopped by at the local FSB office for a cup of tea. He fell violently ill. He was admitted to Hospital No. 31 in St Petersburg, an institution that formerly treated the communist elite. Tsepov's symptoms were unusual: vomiting and diarrhoea but also a catastrophic fall in white blood cells. He died shortly afterwards.

The investigative paper *Novaya Gazeta* quoted sources in the St Petersburg prosecutor's office who said a post-mortem examination revealed 'high quantities' of radioactive contamination in Tsepov's body. This wasn't told to law-enforcement bodies. No cause of death was established.

Dombey's report traced the source of the polonium to Mayak, in the form of irradiated bismuth. From Mayak it went to Sarov. But one link in the chain was missing. The polonium made on Sarov's production line was in metallic form. Sealed in a special container, it was difficult to extract. The polonium used to kill Litvinenko, by contrast, was soluble.

According to Dombey, a 'state organisation' would need to convert the metallic polonium to soluble polonium. Only then could it be deployed.

That the KGB had its own specialist poisons laboratory was a well-established fact. Numerous former officers – some retired, some defectors – had confirmed its existence.

Pavel Sudoplatov, the former chief of Stalin's foreign-intelligence service, who coordinated the atomic espionage operation against the US and Britain, mentions the lab in his 1994 memoir, *Special Tasks*. The poisons factory was set up in 1921. It went through several changes. Its core function – experimenting with poisons and other lethal substances on behalf of the state – remained the same.

Western intelligence experts believe its efforts were originally directed towards using poison on the battlefield. Tests were unsuccessful. The KGB concluded that poisons were better used to eliminate individuals.

The KGB had a track record of killing in Britain. Oleg Kalugin, a former high-ranking KGB officer and defector, now living in the US, said that the KGB's poisons unit was involved in one of the most notorious murders of

the Cold War. In September 1978, the Bulgarian dissident and writer Georgi Markov was waiting for a bus at
Waterloo Bridge in London. He was on his way to his
job at the BBC. Markov felt a sharp pain on his leg from
what he thought was an insect bite; next to him he saw a
man stooping to pick up a dropped umbrella.

Markov's assassin had fired a pellet of ricin into
Markov's leg from close range. Four days later he was
dead. According to Kalugin, the then head of the KGB,
Yuri Andropov, agreed to a request from the Bulgarian
security services to facilitate the assassination. Kalugin
told Radio Free Europe: 'Through the KGB laboratory
we transferred the poison that was used in the umbrella.
There was literally a milligram of poison, a small drop of
ricin placed in a capsule at the tip of the umbrella.'

In the 1980s, the KGB's lab was still operational.
Litvinenko's co-author Yuri Shvets, at the time an
upwardly mobile KGB colonel, recalls meeting a laboratory staffer in Moscow. Against Shvets's judgement, his
KGB bosses had decided to use a truth-telling drug on
his American source, codenamed 'Socrates'. The secret
KGB laboratory was at No. 1 Academician Varga Street,
in south-west Moscow.

Shvets describes the use of speciality drugs as 'among
the most delicate of intelligence operations'. Documents
relating to such operations were stamped with a 'Special
Importance' classification. The Technical Operations
Directorate of the KGB had to approve any use. The lab,
Shvets wrote, produced a wide variety of drugs, including
poisons, narcotics and psychotropic substances.

The drug used on 'Socrates' was SP-117 – concentrated alcohol dropped into his champagne glass. After ten minutes, the subject was drunk. At that point he was ready for interrogation. Shvets nicknamed the 'small, portly' lab worker who briefed him on the chemical side of the operation Aesculapius, after the Greek god of medicine. He noted that if this drug was number 117, the KGB's arsenal probably included at least another 116 potions.

Political killings – of domestic opponents or troublesome exiles – were a hallmark of the Soviet Union and Russia from 1917 onwards. Under Yeltsin, these murders dwindled. But from 2000, prominent critics of the Kremlin once again began to meet mysterious deaths. The evidence of official complicity in these crimes was circumstantial. Defectors claim the KGB's special poisons department was back in business, under a new and deliberately anonymous name, the FSB research institute.

The lab was in the same building as before. Its formal title is Nauchno-Issledovatelsky Institute No. 2 – Scientific-Research Institute No. 2. Or NII-2, for short. Photos of the institute show a squat, gloomy, beige

edifice, dating from the Andropov era, built in impregnable isolation, with lights visible through its windows and a few scrawny trees.

According to locals, it's a quiet spot. There is a guarded perimeter fence. When the building first went up in the 1980s, they assumed it was a hospital for injured Soviet veterans from the war in Afghanistan.

As well as Ismailov and Tsepov, there were others who appear to have been poisoned. The FSB admitted that it was behind a deadly poisoned letter sent in 2002 to Amir Khattab, a militant living in Chechnya. Journalist and Duma deputy Yuri Shchekochikhin died in July 2003. His cause of death was mysterious: his skin peeled off and his internal organs had swollen up. According to Dombey, radioactive thallium probably poisoned him. In 2004, Viktor Yushchenko, the pro-western presidential candidate in Ukraine, narrowly survived an assassination attempt. He was poisoned with dioxin; his face erupted in blisters.

Dombey's report went to the heart of the row over who had killed Litvinenko and the question of state responsibility. In the days immediately after Litvinenko's gruesome death, Kremlin regulatory officials told the media that Russia's nuclear facilities were under tight control.

Sergei Kirienko, the head of Rosatom, the state agency in charge of Russia's nuclear facilities, said that 'control over production is very strict'. He added: 'I don't believe that someone stole from it.' Boris Zhuikov, head of the radioisotope laboratory at the Nuclear Studies Institute, echoed this: 'Everything connected with polonium production and application is controlled by governments … It is regulated and checked by many people.'

Dombey's view was that such statements were true. Polonium was a state affair: made using reactor and production facilities belonging to the Russian state, supervised by the state. The facilities used to irradiate bismuth – a process involving highly radioactive materials – belonged to the state as well. These facts didn't diminish the theory that the state was involved. Instead, they confirmed it, and led Dombey to conclude that the Russian state or its agents were responsible.

Litvinenko's friends agreed. Goldfarb described the plot as an 'interdepartmental effort'. Rosatom, formerly the atomic ministry, was an 'extremely powerful' organisation with its own hierarchy, Goldfarb said, pointing out that the agency's chief Kirienko is a former prime minister. It was improbable the FSB would call him up and ask for a special delivery of polonium.

Something of this nature would require Kremlin authorisation. Since Rosatom officials stressed that no polonium had been withdrawn from their system there would need to be some sort of cover-up. 'It would really be a very serious bureaucratic exercise,' Goldfarb said.

As Yuri Felshtinsky put it: shooting someone in the head was one thing. Anybody could do that. Killing someone with a rare nuclear isotope was another. It would require collaboration between ministries and spy agencies as well as 'coordination from the very top'.

All Scotland Yard had to do was to get the evidence.

8

An Inspector Calls

Moscow, December 2006

'What one man can invent another can discover'
SHERLOCK HOLMES, IN *THE ADVENTURE OF THE
DANCING MEN* BY ARTHUR CONAN DOYLE

In early December, nine Scotland Yard detectives flew to Moscow. The weather when they landed was noticeably colder than in London – a sharpness that pricked the lungs. The sky was a forbidding grey. British embassy staff met them at Domodedovo Airport. The press was there too: TV cameras, lots of them, and noisy reporters. Litvinenko's murder was front-page news around the world. The men from the Met declined to comment.

They were driven north towards the centre of Moscow, along a forest of silver birch trees bent under snow. The route passes Gorky Leninsky, an official sanatorium used by Lenin, and rows of wooden dachas. Once you are inside the capital's orbital motorway the landscape grows urban: there are depressing ranks of dull tower blocks and the blue domes of a neo-Byzantine church. Then, in the centre, a giant titanium statue of Yuri Gagarin and the Moskva river, already white and encrusted with plates of ice.

The British embassy is a modern building on Smolenskaya embankment; new diplomatic flats overlook the river. Here the visitors got security passes and a temporary office. Outside is a bronze statue of the great sleuth Sherlock Holmes and Dr Watson; Sir Arthur Conan Doyle has many fans in Russia. Poems by British and Russian authors are displayed on stone tablets in the embassy wall.

Even before Litvinenko's killing relations between the UK and Russia were sticky. They were about to get a lot stickier.

Scotland Yard's mission was diplomatically sensitive. The detectives' main task was to interview Lugovoi and Kovtun and to collect as much evidence from Moscow as possible. At this point, the two Russians were officially witnesses, not suspects. But the detectives knew Kovtun and Lugovoi were in the frame for murder. This was an unprecedented international inquiry. Seemingly the trail led back to the Russian state itself.

The Kremlin had promised to 'actively assist' the UK government in its inquiries. The Russian prosecutor general's office offered 'full support'. It even hailed the 'constructive and dynamically developing cooperation' between law-enforcement agencies in both countries.

At the same time, senior Russian politicians from Putin downwards had noisily denounced Litvinenko as a nobody and 'third-rate small fry' – in short, as someone not worth murdering. Sergey Ivanov, a spokesman for Russia's foreign-intelligence agency, claimed his service hadn't assassinated anybody since 1959 and the operation to kill the Ukrainian nationalist leader Stepan Bandera. Why start now? The police should turn their attention, Ivanov suggested, to Litvinenko's entourage in London.

Others suggested that Litvinenko had it coming. During a debate in the Duma a day after his death, deputy Sergei Abeltsev said: 'The traitor received the punishment he deserved. I am confident that this terrible death will be a serious warning to traitors of all colours, wherever they are located. In Russia, they do not pardon treachery.'

Abeltsev was a member of the ultra-nationalist Liberal Democratic party. Its leader Vladimir Zhirinovsky, a clever clown licensed by the Kremlin to send out politically useful messages, called Litvinenko a 'scoundrel'. MI6 killed him, Zhirinovsky said. Gennady Gudkov, a Duma deputy and ex-FSB colonel, accused Berezovsky. Nikolai Kovalyov, the former FSB chief, observed that high-profile defectors to the west like Gordievsky (in Britain) and Oleg Kalugin (in the US) still enjoyed 'good health'. No one had murdered them.

Then there was the polonium. Senior figures argued that the use of polonium demonstrated that Moscow had nothing to do with his death. As Sergei Lavrov, Russia's foreign minister, put it, why make a spectacle? Lavrov told the *Trud* newspaper: 'Why would the intelligence services spend millions [on polonium] in order to send to kingdom come a former rank-and-file agent, whose absurd accusations against them have long ceased to be taken seriously?'

These statements made a kind of sense – if the aim of Litvinenko's murder was to make a spectacle. They were less persuasive if Litvinenko's assassins – and those in Moscow who sent them – had assumed the poison used to murder him would never be found. These were early days. But to the inspectors – now encamped in the Radisson Hotel, overlooking Europe Square and the frozen Moskva, from where cruise boats depart in summer – this seemed the most likely version.

The British police force is an egalitarian organisation, with a fine disregard for rank when it suits. The team in Moscow included senior officers from the Yard's SO15 counter-terrorism unit: Chief Superintendent Timothy White and Inspector Brian Tarpey. White dealt with the embassy and the Russian authorities; Tarpey was in charge of day-to-day operations. There were three Russian-speaking constables. The investigators took with them standard police equipment: recording devices, tapes, notebooks.

The next morning, 5 December, they headed to the Russian prosecutor's office. The building in Tekh- nichesky Lane is in the same part of town as Lefortovo Prison, the FSB pre-detention and investigation centre where Litvinenko spent eight months in jail. The area on the east side was once Moscow's foreigners' quarter. The young Peter the Great held all-night drinking parties there with his Swiss mercenary friend and mentor Franz Lefort.

Waiting in the prosecutor's office was a high-level Russian delegation. It included Russia's deputy chief prosecutor Alexander Bastrykin, later promoted to head the investigative committee. He was one of the men linked to the Russian mafia in Spain by Grinda, the Spanish special prosecutor for corruption and organised crime. It also included senior investigators, the head of the legal assistance division, and other specialists. Twelve people in all.

This, surely, was a good sign?

The detectives, however, soon found that the Russian authorities intended to manage all parts of the investigation. Bastrykin announced a series of rules. Scotland Yard wouldn't be allowed to question witnesses directly. Russian officials would do that. The British side could submit questions – in writing and in advance. Scotland Yard's tape equipment wasn't needed; only the Russian side would be permitted to carry out audio recordings. 'I found that a little bit strange,' Tarpey said.

This initial meeting set the tone for what followed. Over the next two weeks the Scotland Yard team found itself in a bizarre and sometimes ridiculous bureaucratic pantomime. 'We were very obviously being railroaded into a situation where we had little or no control,' Tarpey said. He reluctantly agreed to the prosecutor's conditions. The Kremlin's apparent goal was to give the impression of cooperation – while sabotaging the investigation where necessary.

Moscow was insisting that Lugovoi and Kovtun, Litvinenko's assassins, were actually victims. In reality, both men were fine; they, after all, hadn't ingested radioactive polonium. The Russian authorities claimed that their condition was 'rapidly deteriorating'. This might be the only opportunity to talk to them.

Kovtun was being 'treated' in Hospital No. 6, a Moscow state clinic. The clinic was named after a USSR deputy health minister, Avetik Burnazyan, who helped to develop the Soviet atomic bomb. It specialised in radiation victims. Some of those affected by the Chernobyl disaster were sent there. The building – a Lego-like seven-storey block – is in the capital's Shchukino district, on a street of Khrushchev-era apartments and lime trees. Nearby is a wooded park with a lake and natural spring, from where pensioners fill plastic water bottles; this would shortly become my Moscow jogging route.

The detectives set off for the hospital, following a lead Russian vehicle. It drove at high speed – and then seemingly got lost. Tarpey was informed that only one of his officers – Russian-speaking constable Oliver Gadny – would be allowed to see Kovtun. After two hours in heavy traffic they arrived at the federal clinic. It was 8.45 p.m. The official in charge, Vadim Yalovitsky, said that under Russian law a witness couldn't be questioned after 10 p.m.

Gadny was ushered inside. He met the hospital's chief doctor, Konstantin Kotenko, who appeared nervous, and discussed with the Russian investigator Alexander Otvodov the list of questions. The mood between the sides was 'cold and suspicious', Gadny said. The constable donned a protective suit. He was escorted into cabinet number eight.

There was Kovtun – dressed in cream-coloured pyjamas and wearing a paper face-mask and a blue plastic head covering.

Kovtun seemed tired but not visibly ill. Kovtun's hair might have been shaved off but it was difficult to tell, Gadny thought. He had dark rings under both eyes, two bags under the right, one under the left. He was almost blind in the right one – an injury going back to a brawl with Russians, according to his ex-wife. His breathing was normal. In his notebook, Gadny wrote: 'KOVTUN was a white male, with (yellow) tanned skin; aged mid thirties; with brown eyes, full brown eyebrows and full eyelashes.' And: 'He had a 5 mm round pock-like scar on the right side of the bridge of his nose.'

It seemed Kovtun was unperturbed by the accusations against him. He offered a 'look of resignation bordering on boredom, particularly when being addressed by the Russian prosecutor,' Gadny said.

Otvodov asked the questions in a rapid, stern manner, speaking clearly and loudly.

Kovtun described seeing Litvinenko in the Millennium and said that he and Lugovoi were with him 'for half an hour'. On first meeting they had hugged, as is the Russian custom. After leaving the bar, they chatted for eight minutes near the hotel entrance, Kovtun said. Litvinenko's poisoning was a mystery, he added.

OTVODOV: What do you know about the reasons for Litvinenko's illness?

KOVTUN: About this I do not know anything.

OTVODOV: Do you know about polonium-210? Do you know anything about this substance?

KOVTUN: Now I know, yes. Polonium is a radio-active isotope, with which one can be infected through respiration or food. Its half-life is a period of 130 days. I know no one who knows more details about this subject.

OTVODOV: Did you have anything to do with this
  substance?
KOVTUN: I never had anything to do with polonium.

After ten minutes, the chief doctor announced the interview had to end imminently. Gadny protested and was
allowed to ask a couple of questions. Then:

OTVODOV: How are you now?
KOVTUN: Very nervous. I feel serious weakness.
OTVODOV: What is the matter with your hair?
KOVTUN: I shaved it bald. Don't pay any attention
  to that.

And that was that. The party left and went down a
corridor to a small conference room. There they were
tested for alpha radiation. An older doctor waved a
scope – a kitchen-roll-sized tube with a flat circular plate
– over Gadny's skin. The detector made an irregular
high-pitched beep. There was no contamination. The
constable left the hospital. It was dark. He rejoined his
colleagues, who had been waiting in the car park. Back at
the embassy, he photocopied his notes and put them in a
tamper-proof evidence bag.

The interview had lasted a mere thirteen minutes.
From the 118 questions submitted to Russian prosecutors Kovtun answered eighteen.

Meanwhile, Scotland Yard's attempts to meet
Lugovoi were going nowhere. The next morning, 6
December, the team arrived outside the prosecutor's

office. Staff allowed only one person inside – Detective Superintendent Alan Slater – taking him on an odd circuitous tour of the building. Inside, officials berated Slater about SO15's alleged failings. The complaints concerned minor administrative details; Slater felt them overblown. 'I think I'd been summoned there just to be told off,' he said.

The sergeant asked when he might talk to Lugovoi. The reply: you can talk to him for one hour, when doctors permit.

That evening in London, the press office of New Scotland Yard announced that Litvinenko's death was being now treated as a murder inquiry. The news went down badly in Moscow. Detectives had been due to interview Lugovoi on 7 December. The interview was cancelled, rescheduled and cancelled again. Russia announced its own criminal inquiry into Kovtun's 'poisoning' – a counter-move. There were further delays, and a meeting in which Russian prosecutors claimed that Litvinenko had aided Berezovsky's 'bogus' claim for UK asylum.

In Britain – actually on sabbatical in Oxford, learning Russian ahead of my *Guardian* posting to Moscow – I received an email from British Airways.

It said:

Dear Mr Harding
    As a valued customer I am writing to give you the latest information regarding the forensic examination of three of our Boeing 767 aircraft.

You may be aware that these three aircraft were identified by the UK government as part of the police investigation into the death of Alexander Litvinenko.

The email went on to say that initial tests revealed 'very low traces of a radioactive substance' on board two of the planes. It said the UK's Health Protection Agency had concluded there was no risk to passengers from one of them, and that 'monitoring is continuing on the second aircraft'. BA listed the affected planes on its website. It gave the number of an NHS Direct helpline.

I checked BA's website: my wife Phoebe and I had flown on a polonium plane. I called NHS Direct. The helpline wasn't terribly enlightening – it gave general information and suggested that if concerned I should go and see my doctor. I hung up. After all, I was feeling fine.

Behind the scenes, the British authorities were trying to identify all of the aircraft used by Lugovoi and Kovtun in their journeys to and from the UK. In addition to their BA flights, they had travelled on 16 October from Moscow to London with Russian carrier Transaero. They sat in seats 16F and 16E on the outward leg, and in 26F and 26E on the return trip two days later. The police identified the Boeing 737 planes involved, EI-DDK and EI-DNM.

The UK Foreign Office asked the Russian authorities for help. It suggested that, given the potential risk to public health, they test both aircraft for radioactive contamination. The reply was prompt. Russia's chief public health minister Gennady Onishchenko told the British embassy in Moscow that extensive checks had been carried out. He was happy to announce that no radiation had been found on either plane.

Despite these reassurances, teams from the Atomic Weapons Establishment were made ready. Scotland Yard wanted to examine the aircraft for evidence. In early December, experts tested the second Transaero plane, EI-DNM, after it landed at Heathrow. To their surprise they found low-level traces of polonium – eight becquerels per centimetre squared. Onishchenko's remarks – widely reported in the Russian press – were a lie.

The results were passed to COBRA, the UK government's emergency response committee. A request was sent to the Russian foreign ministry asking for permission to test the first Moscow–London plane. This was likely to show higher levels of contamination, since the polonium had originated in Russia. The plane never arrived. It appears the Kremlin instructed Transaero to cancel the flight. EI-DDK never came back to UK airspace.

As for BA 873 – the plane used by Lugovoi and his family to fly to London on 31 October – polonium was found here too. The highest readings came from Lugovoi's seat, 23D. Contamination was discovered on the BA aircraft in which they flew back to Moscow on 3 December, especially in seat 16D. The very expensive poison had left a very detectable signature.

Back in Moscow, British detectives were finally granted an audience with the man himself, again in Hospital No. 6. DI Slater travelled with Otvodov in a van with blacked-out windows, its blue lights flashing. They arrived, entered via a rear entrance, and went up the stairs to a room with a table.

Lugovoi was dressed in a hospital gown, as befits a patient receiving medical treatment. Underneath, Slater noticed with surprise, Lugovoi was wearing an expensive designer T-shirt, black with a white motif. The gown, it appeared, was for dramatic purposes.

Doctors had claimed Lugovoi was gravely ill. To Slater, he looked positively fit and healthy – and appeared to have been driven to the clinic from outside. Slater had instructions to check Lugovoi's eyebrows and arms; if he'd been suffering from radiation sickness his hair would have fallen out. He had a full head of hair.

Lugovoi's interview lasted longer than Kovtun's and he gave better answers. He talked about his family – he was estranged from one of his daughters, Anastasia, who lived in the city of Kursk. He spoke of his business activities – his factory in Ryazan province which made *kvas*, beer and wine. And he gave an account of his three trips to London in October and November, including his dealings with Litvinenko.

According to Lugovoi, he and Kovtun had arrived back at the Millennium Hotel at 4 p.m. We know this is untrue: CCTV footage shows them arriving half an hour earlier, with Lugovoi and Kovtun both making separate visits to the gents' toilets, later found to be heavily contaminated with polonium. 'We didn't go upstairs but went straight to the bar to wait,' he said. 'About ten minutes later, Litvinenko arrived in the lobby and I invited him to sit.'

Litvinenko spoke mostly to Kovtun about Hamburg, Lugovoi said. The meeting broke up, he added, when his daughter Tatiana appeared at the entrance to the Pine Bar and his son Igor came in: 'I introduced him to Litvinenko. Maybe they shook hands.' Lugovoi said he'd known Kovtun for thirty years, and that Kovtun lived in Moscow.

After one and a half hours, a doctor told Slater the interview was over. The detective hadn't finished. Nevertheless, Lugovoi got up and left, telling Slater breezily in English:

'Goodbye, see you later.'

The encounter had yielded some useful information. It confirmed Lugovoi's movements in the UK, and gave a sharper picture of his contacts and associates. But many questions were unanswered. Slater drew up a list. Among them: 'Clarify Millennium meeting. Who sat where at the table? Can you draw a sketch plan? How was the meeting arranged? What telephones were used?'

The next day, Slater returned to the prosecutor's office to agree a transcript of the Lugovoi interview. He'd taken notes and typed them up. Otvodov produced the official Russian version of the meeting. Some of what Lugovoi said was missing. It had been edited from the protocol.

It appeared that the Kremlin wanted to remove all references to the Russian mafia in Spain and its links with Russian politicians. Lugovoi's account of his conversations with Litvinenko about Spain had disappeared. Litvinenko had described how he had helped arrest Zakhar Kałashov, known as Shakro, a leading Russian mafia boss. He had also told Lugovoi about 'Jorge', his contact in Spanish intelligence.

The omission was significant. Lugovoi had mentioned Spain before Litvinenko's work for the Spanish security services had become public knowledge. It meant that the Kremlin knew Litvinenko was investigating an organised crime syndicate linked to Putin and to corruption at the top of Russian power. It also knew that Litvinenko was a key witness in a future possible trial.

The now-vanished passage quoted Lugovoi as saying: 'Litvinenko knew I wanted to go to Spain and we discussed it. He said he had a friend in Spain. Litvinenko told me that Russian criminal elements were buying property in Spain. On the 26th and 27th [October], Jorge called Litvinenko and Jorge speaks Russian. Litvinenko told me that Shakro, a criminal, was arrested in Russia, the same kind of operation is going to be done in Spain. It's connected with money-laundering.' Litvinenko had said the sums involved were large – $250 million.

Slater raised the missing section with Russian officials. They brushed away his concerns. Slater reluctantly

Alexander Litvinenko, at home in Moscow, Russia, with his small son Anatoly. A year later, in 1998, Vladimir Putin would fire him from the FSB after Litvinenko exposed corruption inside the agency. Putin, the FSB's then boss, soon to be prime minister and president, viewed Litvinenko as a traitor.

Litvinenko in exile in the UK with his wife Marina and Anatoly. He escaped from Russia in 2000, slipping into Georgia and fleeing to Turkey on a false passport. On his arrival at Heathrow airport he asked for political asylum, and said: 'I am KGB officer.'

Litvinenko never mastered English but quickly took to his new home. Here, he poses with Anatoly and two bobbies in Hyde Park. He became a journalist – and part-time consultant with MI6, the British spy agency, which paid him £2,000 a month.

Litvinenko in Cambridge visiting Vladimir Bukovsky, a Soviet dissident. Bukovsky became Litvinenko's guru and educated him about the evils of the Stalin era. With him are Anatoly and his mother-in-law.

Polonium levels

Low ▭ ▭ ▮ ▮ High

Andrei Lugovoi and Dmitry Kovtun's first attempt to poison Litvinenko, in a Grosvenor Street boardroom in October 2006 (*above*), failed. The killers put polonium in his cup – the area marked in purple by Scotland Yard – but he didn't drink.

The two killers on 1 November 2006 at the Millennium Hotel in Mayfair, London. CCTV captures them on their way to the gents' toilets, where they prepared the poison in a cubicle.

Litvinenko (*above*) in the hotel lobby, dressed in a denim jacket with fawn collar, minutes before his fateful meeting with Lugovoi and Kovtun in the Pine Bar.

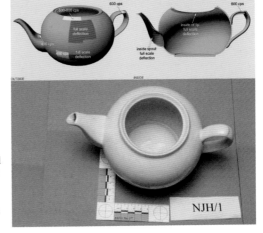

Kovtun or Lugovoi stirred radioactive polonium-210 into a pot of green tea. Litvinenko drank just 'three or four sips'. Hours later he fell violently ill.

```
==========================================
              Pine Bar
303 David
TBL 1   /1   CHK 6513        GST 3
01NOV'06 16:33
- - - - - - - - - - - - - - - - - - - - -
   3 Tea                    11.25
   3 Gordon's               17.25
   3 Tonic                   4.50
   1 R. Julieta no1         15.00
   1 Champagne Cocktl        9.00
   1 Gordon's                5.75
     12.5 %
     OPTS GRATS              7.85
     441/LUGOVOY
     Room Charge            70.60
     TOTAL                  62.75
     TIPS                    7.85
     PAYMENT                70.60
- - - - - - CHECK CLOSED 17:53 - - - - - -
==========================================
```

Lugovoi murdered with a certain breezy style. As well as the deadly tea, he ordered gin, champagne and a cigar. The bill, paid on his credit card, came to £70.60.

RECORD OF INTERVIEW

Number: Y11

Enter type:
(SDN / ROTI / Contemporaneous Notes / Index of Interview with VIW / Visually recorded interview)

Person interviewed: CARTER, EDWIN REDWALD

Place of interview: University College Hospital, Critical Care Unit

Date of interview: 19/11/2006

Time commenced: 1704   Time concluded: 1750

Duration of interview: 46 minutes   Tape reference nos. (→) CH/10

Interviewer(s):   DI HYATT , DS HOAR

Other persons present: Ms TUPPER (Interpreter)

Police Exhibit No: CH/10A   Number of Pages: 10

Signature of interviewer producing exhibit

Tape counter times(↵)	Person speaking	Text
0.09	DI HYATT	I'm Detective Inspector Brent HYATT from the Specialist Crime Directorate of the Metropolitan Police Service. This is a continuation of the interview of Mr Edwin CARTER at the University College Hospital, London. He's being interviewed as a significant witness. The date is the 19th of December 2006.
	DS HOAR	November.
	DI HYATT	Sorry my apologies, November, the 19th of November

Litvinenko's symptoms baffled doctors. Transcripts of his interviews (*left*) with Scotland Yard's officers are remarkable. Litvinenko helps solve a chilling murder mystery: his own.

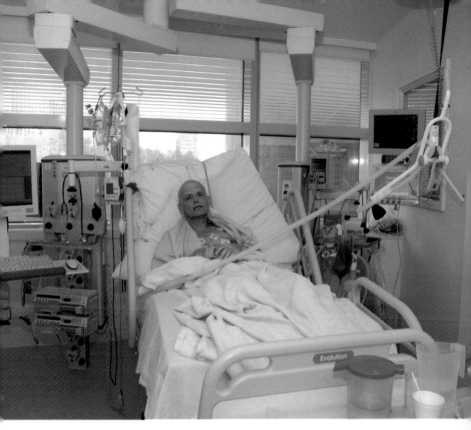

Litvinenko in the critical care unit of University College Hospital, London, three days before he died. The photo shows him bald, gaunt and defiant. Released with his permission, it went round the world.

In a deathbed statement Litvinenko accused Russia's president of ordering his murder. Putin denied the claim and responded with macabre levity, remarking, 'Mr Litvinenko is, unfortunately, not Lazarus.'

(*Top left*) Boris Berezovsky, Litvinenko's mercurial patron, led a campaign to overthrow Putin. He fought a billion-pound legal battle with his one-time friend Roman Abramovich (*right*) … and lost. He was found dead in 2013 in Berkshire.

Alexander Perepilichnny (*left*), a Russian whistleblower, collapsed and died in November 2012 outside his home in Surrey. A rare Himalayan fern, *Gelsemium elegans*, used by Chinese and Russian assassins, was found in his stomach: the likely cause of death.

The Russian opposition leader Boris Nemtsov at a rally. Nemtsov was a fearless critic of Vladimir Putin. He exposed official corruption and the president's covert war in Ukraine in a series of dissenting pamphlets.

… And lying dead. In February 2015 a Chechen assassin shot Nemtsov a few hundred metres away from the Kremlin, as he walked home with his Ukrainian girlfriend. Fifty thousand mourners came to his funeral, filling Moscow's embankment.

In spring 2014, Putin seized Crimea and choreographed a pro-Russian rebellion in eastern Ukraine. He sent tanks, weapons and undercover soldiers to help rebels – and a Buk anti-aircraft missile system, seen (*circled in red*) trundling through the Ukrainian countryside.

On 17 July 2014, the Buk's crew shot down Malaysian Airlines MH17, en route to Kuala Lumpur, with 298 people on board. They mistook it for a Ukrainian military aircraft. All perished. It was a terrible mistake, and one that flowed from Putin's contempt for Ukraine's sovereignty.

Marina Litvinenko (*above*) arriving at the High Court in London for the much-delayed public inquiry into her husband's murder. Britain's Conservative-led government initially opposed the inquiry, fearing it would annoy Putin. There were sixty-two witnesses. Much of the evidence, which ran to 10,000 pages, had been kept secret for eight years.

In September 2015, Putin bombed Syria and (*below, in December*) opposition-controlled parts of Damascus in support of his ally President Bashar al-Assad. It was the first time since the Cold War that the Kremlin had launched a major military action outside the borders of the ex-Soviet Union.

signed and added a dissenting note saying the protocol was incomplete.

During the second week in Moscow, the detectives got access to other witnesses. They included Lugovoi's wife, Svetlana; Sokolenko, the third man at the Millennium Hotel; Lugovoi's personal assistant Angelina Idrisova; his lawyer and doctor.

Svetlana Lugovaya's interview took place at the prosecutor's office. Her answers were curt.

DC HALL: Did your husband discuss with you some theories as to [the death of] Litvinenko?

LUGOVAYA: No.

DC HALL: Nothing at all? No theories, nothing? I find it very strange you have not spoken to your husband about this case.

LUGOVAYA: I do not find anything strange because of all of the versions of it and the mix-up.

DC HALL: And which versions are these?

LUGOVAYA: We have to know what to discuss precisely? We do not know exactly what has happened.

DC HALL: What?

LUGOVAYA: None. Simply papers, television. We read the papers but we do not discuss anything.

Under the surface, the Lugovois' marriage looked to be in trouble. What, if anything, did Svetlana suspect? She and her children had all been exposed to polonium and were treated at a private hospital; little Igor had shaken Litvinenko's hand. Her husband had put their entire family in peril. What kind of monster would do that? Lugovoya would later divorce her husband. In April 2013, aged forty-six, Lugovoi married again, to a 23-year-old named Ksenia; two years later they had a son.

Sokolenko, meanwhile, said he'd flown to London to attend the CSKA Moscow–Arsenal match. His trip had been touristic, he said. It included beers with other fans who'd flown in from Austria, a bus trip, and a visit to Madame Tussauds. He went shopping with Lugovoi and Kovtun. They visited a toyshop, where Lugovoi bought cartridges for a computer game as a present for Igor. Sokolenko purchased teddy bears. He said he knew nothing about polonium.

By 19 December the detectives had wrapped up. All that remained was for them to collect the interview tapes from their Russian counterparts. Tarpey went to the prosecutor general's office. He was surprised to find, for once, no media outside. An official escorted him to a third-floor room. Inside he saw an array of reporters from Russian state TV.

Tarpey said he was 'totally unprepared' for cameras and would have objected, given a chance. Russian officials insisted he make a small speech, thanking the Russian prosecutor for his help and assistance. Tarpey muttered a few polite words. He was taken to a table, where officials presented him with lever-arch file binders containing the interview tapes. The cameras whirred and clicked; Tarpey signed a receipt.

It was a nice little piece of television and proof, surely, that Moscow was as keen as London to uncover the truth? For much of the mission, the Kremlin had led Scotland Yard investigators by the nose. It had been a difficult, high-profile trip in which officers had found themselves uncomfortably under the media's glare. Their task was to collect evidence and often this hadn't been possible.

Still, Tarpey thought, at least he had the audio-recordings.

When the detectives got back to Scotland Yard they found one final unpleasant surprise. Seven of the tapes were fine. But when they played the eighth, the recording of the interview with Lugovoi, no sound came out. The tape was blank.

From his fifth-floor office, Thomas Menzel had an impressive view of Hamburg. The city's police headquarters were located in the green suburb of Alsterdorf. The detectives who worked there nicknamed the HQ 'Polizei-Stern' or Police Star because of its unusual ten-sided design. Through his large corner window, Menzel could see a light athletics track stadium, cranes, a line of trees and a police training building immediately below him.

Menzel was aware of Litvinenko's case from the German press. It was, he thought, an extraordinary business – reminiscent of the Cold War, and involving a substance he had never come across before in many previous murder inquiries. Menzel was the head of the criminal investigation department in Hamburg's *Kriminalamt* and the director of its organised crime unit. His officers were used to the darker and more extreme aspects of human behaviour: murders, drug violence, rapes.

This was something else.

The German news magazine *Der Spiegel* had devoted six pages and its cover to Litvinenko's strange death. The date was 4 December 2006. Menzel picked up a copy and began reading. Halfway through he stopped. He reached for the phone. *Spiegel* reported that Kovtun had spent four days in Hamburg before meeting Litvinenko in London. Scotland Yard hadn't been in touch but it was evident London's problem was now Hamburg's headache too. It was, seemingly, the biggest case since the discovery that some of the 9/11 terrorists led by Mohamed Atta had been living quietly in the city.

Menzel quickly established a few basic facts. Kovtun was registered in Hamburg, had an ex-wife in the city, and appeared to have lived in Germany for twelve years. The German authorities had no experience of polonium; nobody did. 'We didn't know what this substance was,' he told me.

Menzel contacted two other federal agencies – the office of criminal investigation, known as the BKA, and the office of radiation protection. Soon, he had 600 officers on active duty. Journalists spotted lights burning in the Polizei-Stern over the weekend. Something was up.

Menzel's team came up with a name for the unusual operation. They called it 'Der Dritte Mann' or 'The Third Man', after the black-and-white 1949 thriller set in divided post-war Vienna. '*Der Dritte Mann* is a film classic. We thought the title appropriate. We had three men who had gone to London and the atmosphere around it had some-thing of the Cold War about it,' Menzel said. He added: 'It was very unusual. It had a political dimension like no other case I've been involved in.'

Within a short period, Hamburg police were able to reconstruct Kovtun's movements in the city – from his ex-wife's flat in Hamburg-Altona to the town hall where he filled in and signed his new foreigner registration docu-ments. They found traces of polonium under his photo; indeed everywhere they looked. Officers lugged away evidence in boxes from Wall's apartment in Erzberger-strasse and from D3's home. Menzel opened a criminal case. Kovtun was accused of unlawfully smuggling nuclear material into the Federal Republic of Germany.

Washington was paying attention. Duane Butcher, the US consul general in Hamburg, met Menzel on 14 December. In a confidential dispatch to the US State Department, later leaked, Butcher gave an account of Menzel's findings. He noted: 'Investigators hope to find out more about Kovtun as an individual – what he did for a living, what his personal background was – and whether he had worked at the Russian consulate in Hamburg in the past.' Kovtun had met an Italian national in Hamburg – D3. Perhaps there was an Italian connection, Menzel told Butcher.

German and British investigators were agreed: the forensic evidence against Kovtun and Lugovoi was plen-tiful and damning. Butcher quoted Gerhard Schindler, deputy director general for counter-terrorism at the German interior ministry:

'Kovtun left polonium traces on everything he touched – vehicles, objects, clothes, and furniture. German investigators concluded Kovtun did not have polonium traces on his skin or clothes; Schindler said that polonium was coming out of his body.'

As the investigation made progress, D3 found himself in a terrifying nightmare. After Kovtun flew to London he devoted no further thought to his friend's wild story of traitors and poisons. Two days later, he called Kovtun to see how he was getting on. Kovtun didn't pick up. A little later, and apparently back in Moscow, Kovtun called back, and said everything was fine.

Two weeks after that, D3 picked up a copy of either the *Hamburger Morgenpost* or *Bild Zeitung* – he can't remember which. Splashed across it was the story of Litvinenko's poisoning and death. Kovtun's name was mentioned; he appeared to be the prime suspect. D3 read the story and, as he put it, felt the ground give way beneath his feet.

What he'd dismissed as another of Dmitry's quixotic idiocies had materialised into a cold-blooded international killing. D3 was afraid and confused. He thought about going to the police. But what if this situation somehow rebounded upon him? He decided to do nothing. Perhaps detectives might solve the case on their own.

Then, Kovtun called from Moscow as D3 was out on his bike. The line was poor; they agreed Kovtun would ring again in the evening, which he did. Kovtun asked if

D3 had read the newspapers. D3 asked him: 'Was that you?' Kovtun said the story was rubbish, adding that the English police were going to question him. 'If that wasn't you, you don't need to worry,' D3 replied.

Try as he might, D3 could not banish the poison conversation with Kovtun from his mind. In December, German police interviewed him for the first time. They searched his flat and took away his contaminated mattress. He gave them an account of his meeting with Kovtun. But he said nothing about Kovtun's confession as they had walked together towards Steindamm.

As D3's torment grew, Kovtun's seemingly lessened. On 11 December, Kovtun phoned from Moscow. 'He was quite jolly. He was in a good mood,' D3 said. Kovtun said he was fine, apologised for causing inconvenience, insisted he was innocent, 'marked' by someone else and the victim of a media smear. D3: 'I asked him what kind of arsehole he is to do this with Marina and the children? I was very angry but tried to remain calm.' Upbeat, Kovtun was again talking of the Moscow flat he soon expected to receive.

They didn't speak again.

D3 wasn't afraid of Kovtun as such. But he understood that he was now a witness, an important one. And therefore – the logic had a dark certainty to it – a vulnerable one as well. It was a frightening position. Even if Dmitry were not capable of murder, perhaps others around him were? Twelve days passed. Unable to bear it any more, D3 told a lawyer what had happened. The lawyer contacted the police. 'This awful feeling became so great that I had to get it off my chest. I had to say it, I could not go on,' D3 said.

He told detectives the affair had left him uncertain and edgy. And added: 'I curse him [Kovtun] every day, because of the conversation, because of the whole story, and because of other persons whom he has presumably also contaminated. And perhaps because of the mattress.' His fear that something might happen to him or his family came and went, he said, adding: 'I am frightened quite suddenly for no reason.'

Asked what might befall him, D3 gave a simple answer. 'I may also be killed. I heard something,' he said, adding that he felt guilty 'because it then actually happened'. It never occurred to him to go to police immediately after the conversation, he explained, because he didn't consider what Kovtun told him was actually possible.

German detectives were reluctant to believe D3's account. They were sceptical for several reasons. First, they thought it unlikely that assassins sent by Moscow on a complex mission would be scrambling around at the last moment looking for a cook. Second, what kind of killer would suggest in the same breath that he and his ex-wife might strip off for a porno mag? It was … well, illogical. And improbable. And therefore dubious.

It wasn't until 2010 that Scotland Yard – using cellular data and interviews with D3's colleagues – established he was telling the truth.

In conversations with his friends and ex-in-laws in Germany, Kovtun stuck to the script: he was blameless. He called Eleanora Wall, his former mother-in-law, and said: 'Please do not think that I did this.' She believed him. 'Dmitry is not a brutal person who kills people. No member of the KGB would have put poison in Dmitry's hands,' she told Hamburg detectives. 'I do not believe when he visited us he knew he was giving off radioactivity.'

Only once did Kovtun let his guard slip – and then in ambiguous terms. Back in Moscow he was receiving regular infusions, he told Wall, as well as other medicines whose names he couldn't reveal. Kovtun said he'd been exposed to some of the poison that did for Litvinenko. And told her: 'These arseholes have probably poisoned us all.' He didn't explain who the arseholes were.

While Kovtun was calling Germany, the Russian authorities were busy covering up their role in the murder. Similar to the Metropolitan Police, Menzel tried to test the Aeroflot plane Kovtun had taken from Moscow to Hamburg. A team was got ready to ground it as soon as it arrived. Somehow, Russia's spy agencies learned of the plan and at the last minute Aeroflot swapped planes. Kovtun's plane never came back.

In Hamburg and London, the threads were coming together. The Met has been the focus of much public criticism but its investigation into Litvinenko's murder was painstaking and exemplary. Around 100 detectives were involved, together with 100 uniformed officers.

Teams were sent out across the capital. Their job was to collect CCTV, identify potential witnesses and to find members of the public who may have been contaminated.

The public-health picture was a horrifying one. Forensic tests showed the murderers left radioactive traces at every location they visited: offices, restaurants, hotel rooms, toilets and aeroplanes. Scientists revisited each location with specialist detection equipment. They scanned every inch – leaving stickers with radiation readings in different locations.

This information was fed back to Scotland Yard's computer-aided modelling bureau. It reproduced the findings in graphic form. Scientists also tested hair samples from Litvinenko. The results were revealing: they gave a window of dates for the two occasions on which he was poisoned. These coincided exactly with the dates of his meetings with Lugovoi and Kovtun.

The polonium appears on the hair as an area of darkness – first as a constellation of light dots and then as an intense, banded black region. The hair of a dead man.

I arrived in Moscow in January 2007, as the *Guardian*'s new Moscow bureau chief. My wife Phoebe and our two small children, Tilly and Ruskin, came too. We moved into a cramped temporary apartment in a tower block in the suburb of Voikovskaya. The kids' new British international school was within walking distance; in the frozen courtyard youths were drinking from tins of beer. The cold felt sharp; it hit you in the face; you breathed it.

It was an inauspicious moment to be a British corre-spondent in Russia.

When Putin first became president in 2000, relations between Britain and Russia were positive. Putin's first foreign trip was to London. Russia's new leader – at this point an enigmatic figure, and the subject of the question 'Who is Mr Putin?' – called into Downing Street for talks. The prime minister Tony Blair hailed his guest as a fellow moderniser and defended him in the face of criticism over human-rights abuses and the new war in Chechnya. Putin even met the Queen at Windsor Castle.

The estrangement began in 2003, when a British judge granted Berezovsky political asylum. A court turned down Russia's extradition request for Zakayev, whom it accused of terrorism. Putin took these decisions as a personal snub.

In the Russian system, judges typically do what the Kremlin expects of them. Putin interpreted the court's rulings as a betrayal by Blair, who had failed to ensure the correct result. Russia lodged twenty-one applications for the extradition of Russian citizens from the UK. All were unsuccessful. Judges refused them on the understandable grounds that the individuals were unlikely to get a fair trial back in Russia and were, in many cases, being perse-cuted for their anti-government views.

Relations with the west in general were cooling, too. The Kremlin didn't perceive the pro-western revolutions in Georgia, in 2003, and in Ukraine, in 2004, as popular movements for democratic reform. They were, it claimed to believe, the product of a US-engineered conspiracy.

And a further sign of America's insidious encroachment in Russia's post-Soviet neighbourhood. US president George W. Bush – an early enthusiast for Putin – found that Russia's president was a prickly and unpredictable adversary, opposed to Bush's Iraq misadventure and much else.

From these alleged slights flowed a series of hostile actions by the Russian government. The British side did some daft things, too. In January 2006, Russian state TV broadcast footage showing an alleged British intelligence officer retrieving information from an artificial 'rock' concealed in a Moscow park. The 30-cm rock looked like a small, innocuous light brown boulder – the kind of boulder familiar to fans of *The Flintstones*. The FSB claimed UK diplomats used the rock to communicate with their Russian 'agents'. (Jonathan Powell, Blair's special adviser, later admitted the spy rock was genuine.)

Berezovsky remained a toxic figure for Putin's administration. Just how toxic I found out for myself in April 2007. Two colleagues interviewed him in London. Berezovsky told them he was plotting nothing less than a revolution. He was, he said, bankrolling people close to the president who were conspiring to mount a palace coup. 'We need to use force to change this regime,' he said. Democratic methods were pointless – they wouldn't work.

Berezovsky acknowledged that such statements were risky: 'I don't have any doubts that the Putin regime has become criminal, killing those they calculate as their personal enemy.' Why? 'Because they [the regime] identify themselves as Russia. Putin's understanding is who is against him is against Russia.'

The oligarch's latest claims were incendiary. He'd said similar things before but in less vehement tones. My bosses at the *Guardian* asked if I might get a reaction from the Kremlin. I reached Dmitry Peskov, Putin's spin-doctor, and faxed over the key quotes to his office inside the president's HQ. I had visited Peskov there before, soon after taking up my new Moscow job; he'd told me it was a sadness that the country's opposition was weak.

The story appeared on the *Guardian*'s front page the following day, with a photo of Berezovsky and the head-line: 'I am plotting a new Russian revolution'. Peskov's comments were included: 'In accordance with our legis-lation [his remarks] are being treated as a crime.' My by-line – Luke Harding in Moscow – appeared on the story, placed third, behind that of my two colleagues who'd done the work. At this point I'd never personally met Berezovsky or had any dealings with him.

A more self-assured regime would have dismissed Berezovsky's claims as self-aggrandising baloney. They were ridiculous. Berezovsky didn't have a secret army working inside Russian power. The FSB's purpose, however, was to uncover plots against the state. Here – in lurid black and white – seemingly there was one. Someone inside the spy agency decided to hunt the conspirators. A good place to start, he thought, would be with the *Guardian*'s Moscow reporter.

I woke up the next morning to find myself inside a sort of sub-John le Carré spy novel. Over the next few weeks a succession of FSB agents followed me round the streets of Moscow. They were easy to spot: unpromising young men wearing cheap leather jackets and brown shoes. Once I met a friend in the deserted basement of a café. Two FSB operatives turned up ten minutes later and, ignoring the many empty tables, sat right next to us. They didn't order anything; the spy agency doesn't pay expenses for its officers on duty, I discovered. We laughed, and left.

It became obvious that someone was listening to my phone calls. The *Guardian*'s bureau was a ground-floor apartment in a block close to Moscow's Belorusskaya train station. Two low-ceilinged apartments knocked into one. From the tiny kitchen you could see a small area of green where locals walked their dogs. I had a large desk with a landline. Whenever I called London and mentioned the word 'Litvinenko' or 'Berezovsky' the connection was cut. There was an ominous crackling. The same thing happened if I made jokes about Putin.

Other western correspondents experienced eaves-dropping too; the Brits and Americans were routinely monitored, it seemed. The KGB had perfected these techniques during the Cold War. Female agents listened to targets for hours on end in secret chambers dotted around Moscow. (This was tedious low-level work; it took hours to transcribe conversations.) A caller from the presidential administration, meanwhile, asked for my cellphone number. It looked as if someone had hacked my Gmail account too. Emails tagged with Berezovsky disappeared and then reappeared in my inbox.

None of this was perhaps surprising. Litvinenko's murder had put a deep chill on UK–Russian relations; I was a British correspondent. The KGB taught its recruits that all western journalists were spies. The belief flowed from mirror thinking: in Soviet times, correspondents abroad, like the talented Yuri Shvets, used journalistic cover to conceal their real jobs as KGB operatives.

What was more unusual in my case were the break-ins by the FSB – a series of intrusions into the apartment where I lived with my family. These were sinister and unwelcome. They became a recurring feature of our Moscow life.

The first took place soon after the Berezovsky story was published. My wife was away. I had been at dinner with friends. I returned with Tilly and Ruskin to our apartment. We'd moved shortly before to a new tenth-floor flat in the suburb of Voikovskaya. From the living room there was a view of a park – birches and a municipal lake in one direction, where we swam in summer; a courtyard in the other.

That someone had broken in was obvious. My son's single Ikea bed was next to a low window. We kept the window double locked. Now the window was unlocked. It had been left propped open – with a 15-metre drop to the yard below. We peered down. 'Has there been a burglar?' my son wondered. 'I don't know,' I replied. It seemed unlikely you would survive a fall from such a height. The message appeared to be: take care, or your son might meet with an accident.

At 4 a.m. that night, I was woken by a loud beeping from next door. I turned on the light, and groped towards the sound. An alarm clock with a digital display was ringing in the living room. I hadn't set the alarm. We'd inherited the clock from our landlord, Vadim, but never used it. It appeared my intruders had decided to play a sinister prank on us. Evidently, this wasn't a conventional burglary. I checked the kitchen. I'd left several thousand dollars in a drawer to pay next month's rent. The cash was still there.

Putin's secret policemen were carrying out a different mission: to intimidate and scare us. Berezovsky, Litvinenko's polonium murder, the FSB's secret poison factory – all these were apparently taboo themes. I had crossed a line. There would be further break-ins, and further warnings.

Shortly before this covert harassment started, I attended Putin's annual press conference. The venue was a giant two-tiered auditorium inside the Kremlin. This was a remarkable set-piece event – attended by 2,000 mostly Russian journalists and screened live on state television. They shouted softball questions. What did the president think about gardening? How should Russians bring up their kids?

Putin was also asked about Litvinenko. His dismissive response: that Litvinenko was a small-time agent who'd been fired from the FSB for beating up suspects and who 'didn't possess any secrets at all'.

In May 2007, the UK's Crown Prosecution Service charged Lugovoi with Litvinenko's murder. This, from Putin's perspective, was another provocation. He refused Britain's request to hand over Lugovoi. Putin said that Russia's constitution forbids the extradition of its citizens. The request was a sign of Britain's 'arrogance' and a 'no brains' colonial mentality, he added.

In the wake of the CPS's charge, Lugovoi held a press conference. It took place in the Moscow office of the Russian news agency Interfax. This was the same room where in 1997 Litvinenko had accused the FSB of ordering him to snuff out Berezovsky. A photo of the famous event hung on a wall in the corridor. It was a hot day; I turned up in shorts. The room was full. Lugovoi walked in with Kovtun. Lugovoi was wearing a grey pinstriped suit and pink tie. Kovtun's hair had grown back. Lugovoi began with a polite 'Good afternoon, ladies and gentlemen.'

He said he'd called a press conference to defend himself from swirling accusations made by the 'western mass media'. They had initiated 'a real war against me and against Russia', he said.

What followed was a lengthy denunciation – of Berezovsky, MI6 and the UK government, which had 'hidden traces of the crime' and 'made me a scapegoat'. Lugovoi said that MI6 had tried to recruit him. He wasn't a murderer, or as he put it: 'Some Russian James Bond, infiltrating a nuclear centre and poisoning his mate in cold blood, contaminating himself, his wife and children along the way!'

Vesti-24, the state-owned TV news channel, broadcast this live. According to Lugovoi, British intelligence had murdered Litvinenko, one of its agents.

This was a serious allegation. I asked Lugovoi if he had any proof.

Lugovoi replied: '*Yest!*' – There is proof!

So what was it?

Lugovoi didn't offer details.

My question had annoyed him.

He said: 'The British public must take a serious interest in what some Russian-born people are doing in the UK. They are engaged in recruiting Russian citizens, they sell British passports. The British nationality is for sale, esteemed BBC ... sorry I don't know what other English mass media companies are present here. Your nationality is sold like Chinese rags in a market, and you are doing nothing about it whilst thigh-slapping! I do apologise for the rough expression.'

Afterwards, the Kremlin announced that Lugovoi's vague accusations – clearly based on talking points supplied to him by others – were worthy of 'further investigation'.

Later that day, Britain's ambassador to Moscow, Tony Brenton, sent off a confidential eGram – a diplomatic telegram – to the foreign office in London. Brenton summarised Lugovoi's claims, noting that Kovtun 'was present but said little'.

He concluded: 'Lugovoi's story sounds like nonsense to us, but is shrewdly judged for its plausibility to Russian ears – particularly in view of the "rock" incident last year. The fact that he was given nearly two hours on a government news channel to make his allegations strongly suggests official involvement in the stage management of his "revelations".'

Britain's security agencies compiled their own report on the murder, based on police evidence and secret sources. Its contents have not been divulged. The conclusion, it appears, is that this was a Russian state-sponsored assassination – not just an unfriendly act, but one involving dangerous nuclear material, which potentially endangered hundreds of lives.

In July 2007, the new UK foreign secretary, David Miliband, expelled four Russian diplomats from London. This was in protest at Moscow's refusal to hand over Lugovoi. Miliband told parliament he believed the FSB was involved. He severed cooperation with the Russian spy agency and introduced a new visa policy for Kremlin politicians travelling to London. Up until this point MI6 had communicated with the SVR, its Russia's foreign-intelligence counterpart. These channels were cut as well, even though the SVR was apparently not involved in Litvinenko's poisoning, an FSB operation.

The Kremlin's response was comparatively restrained. It expelled four diplomats in turn from the UK embassy in Moscow.

The mood among British diplomats based in Moscow was understandably embattled. They found themselves at the front end of the worst stand-off in relations since the Brezhnev era. Brenton held regular breakfast briefings for journalists. The ambassador's residence was just off the Old Arbat – a nineteenth-century building in Bolshoi Nikolopeskovsky Lane that had once belonged to a merchant or senior official.

Brenton admitted that the Litvinenko case made better relations with Moscow impossible and said that there was no prospect of an early meeting between Putin and Gordon Brown, the UK's new prime minister. 'I don't know what happens next. Lugovoi remains a wanted man,' Brenton said. Lugovoi's support came from the top and from 'quite influential chunks of the Russian state', he said, adding: 'This guy is a suspected murderer. In normal places you don't find a government giving support and encouragement to such a person.'

It was the use of a radioactive nucleotide that convinced the UK government this was a Kremlin plot, Brenton said. 'Our private judgement is that you have to be a state or state organisation to get hold of polonium in the quantities it was used.'

The day after Litvinenko's death, Lugovoi and Kovtun had visited the British embassy. They met Brenton's deputy Sian MacLeod and his security officer David Chitty. The two Russians insisted they had nothing to do with the murder – and signed declarations to that effect.

Subsequently, the room was tested for contamination. Scientists picked up traces of polonium. The highest readings came from Kovtun's chair – four to five becquerels per centimetre squared. They found it at the table in front of which Kovtun had been sitting, and in the storage hole where he'd left his mobile phone. 'He sat in a chair. We had to burn the chair,' Brenton said.

Actually this wasn't quite true. Embassy staff locked the conference room used by Lugovoi and Kovtun, with the chairs still in it. Only a small number of diplomats knew about the radiation. Paul Knott, the embassy's second secretary, told his colleagues the room wasn't available because he'd 'lost the key'. The atmosphere

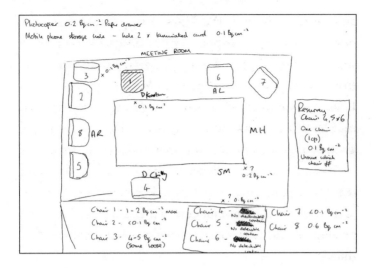

at the time was 'sort of Le Carré', he said, adding: 'We had that Cold-War-is-here-again feeling. We knew things were worsening. But to do what they did in the heart of London seemed to us incredible.'

Brenton was an unusually frank diplomat. His reward was a campaign of Kremlin-sponsored harassment: the pro-Putin youth group Nashi picketed his public events, jumped in front of his car, and waved unflattering placards outside the embassy. The placards bore a photo of the ambassador with the word 'Loser' stamped in red ink across his forehead.

Days after my first break-in I had had my own meeting with MacLeod and an embassy security officer. I'd reported the intrusion to the *Guardian* and mentioned it to the embassy's press attaché, who suggested I drop by. The venue for our chat was the embassy's secure room from which mobile phones were banned. It looked rather like a music studio; a map of the Russian Federation hung on a wall. The room appeared to be the only part of the building which Putin's security agents were unable to bug.

The conversation was helpful. And demystifying. It turned out the embassy knew all about FSB burglaries. They were Moscow's worst-kept diplomatic secret, I learned. British and US diplomats and Russian nationals working for western missions found themselves on the receiving end of demonstrative break-ins. So, I later discovered, did Russian opposition activists. Recently, the break-ins had grown more frequent. 'We don't talk about it publicly. But no, you're not going mad,' the officer told me. 'There's no doubt this was the FSB. We have a thick file of similar cases. Generally we don't make a fuss.'

The FSB's tactics were weird, to say the least. They included defecating in loos, and not flushing afterwards; turning off fridges while the occupant was away on holiday; and introducing items of low value, like a cuddly toy, which hadn't been there before. Sometimes a TV remote control would vanish, only to reappear weeks or months later. The same break-in team would install listening devices. Apparently, our flat was now bugged. 'There's not much you can do about them. Trying to identify or remove them will merely trigger the FSB's return,' the officer said.

On the surface, the FSB's methods looked like bad-taste practical jokes. Actually, the KGB knew that such tactics – repeated over time – could have a destructive effect. The KGB developed and codified these techniques in the 1960s and 1970s. They had a name: operational psychology.

The Stasi, East Germany's secret police, and the KGB's sister organisation, employed the same tactics against dissidents, church leaders and others. One former Stasi officer told me proudly: 'We always did it better than the Russians.' Such methods were wonderfully deniable. It was easy to deride anyone who complained of sprite-like intrusions by unknown third parties as paranoid and mad.

I discovered that Stasi officers had written entire theses about what they called *Zersetzung*. The word in German means corrosion or decay. The goal of this harassment – in which the state's hand remained hidden – was to 'corrode' a target so he or she ceased all hostile anti-state activity. With me, that appeared to be writing articles on themes the FSB deemed unacceptable. In the GDR, *Zersetzung* became a pseudo-scientific discipline. Putin had certainly come across *Zersetzung* when he served as a junior KGB spy in Dresden.

The embassy officer told me there was no evidence the agency hurt children, despite the ominous window left open next to my son's bed. This was somewhat consoling.

That summer I received a letter from the FSB. It said that the agency had opened a criminal inquiry into Berezovsky's *Guardian* interview. It added that Berezovsky had taken part in activities against state power, an offence under Russia's penal code, article 278. An FSB agent called our Moscow office. He informed me I was being summoned as a 'witness' in connection with the case. I was to report to Lefortovo Prison. Oh, and I'd need a lawyer.

Three weeks later, I turned up outside Lefortovo jail. The letter had indicated the address – Energeticheskaya St 3a – useful since Lefortovo didn't appear on maps. The building was as forbidding as I'd imagined, set among anonymous grey apartment blocks. There was a single tree in the courtyard. I entered through a heavy metal door with my lawyer, Gari Mirzoyan. Inside there was a large waiting room. It was devoid of tables and chairs. The agent on duty sat behind a silvered one-way window. He could see us; we couldn't see him.

A hairy hand shot out and took my passport. Since there was nowhere to sit, we stood. After five minutes we were told to proceed to room 306, where Major Kuzmin was waiting for us. We walked down a corridor. The carpet was a worn red-green. I noticed an old-fashioned lift, with a heavy metal grille. It sank to the prison's lower depths where Litvinenko had been kept. Above us were old-style security cameras. The atmosphere was one of shabby menace and institutional gloom. Seemingly little had changed since KGB times.

Major Kuzmin was younger than I expected: late twenties perhaps, with blond hair, neatly cut, and wearing a dark olive-green uniform. Lying on his desk was a colour photocopy of the *Guardian*'s front-page Berezovsky scoop. I had explained that my role in the affair was a small one. Nonetheless, Kuzmin wanted to know under what circumstances the interview had taken place. Who was present? Was there a recording? Kuzmin typed my replies – there wasn't much to say – two-fin-gered onto a computer.

It occurred to me that Kuzmin probably wasn't the officer's real name. Was he the guy who had been organ-ising my apartment break-ins? There was nothing in the room that gave clues to his personality – no photos, one small spider plant. On the table in front of me was a bottle of fizzy water and a glass. Drinking didn't seem like a good idea. The glass was engraved with four sets of initials in Cyrillic letters: Cheka, OGPU, KGB and FSB. These were the names of the Kremlin successive counter-revo-lutionary agencies, beginning with Dzerzhinsky's *Cheka*.

After fifty-five minutes, the interview was over. Kuzmin gave me a witness statement to sign. We shook hands. He offered me a gift: a copy of the 'Investiga-tions department, Lefortovo Prison' 2007 FSB calendar. It featured the FSB's sword and shield logo, in dark red, against a purple background. Mirzoyan and I walked out into the corridor. It was empty. There was no noise or office chatter – merely a smooth and unnerving silence.

Despite the apparent end of the Cold War, the FSB clearly saw itself operating in the same tradition of Bolshevik conspiracy as its predecessors. The KGB's and FSB's goals were the same: to protect the state against all enemies. The agency's neuralgic reaction to a single newspaper article suggested the Kremlin continued to view Berezovsky as its enemy in chief, a sort of modern Trotsky. Apparently I'd been marked down as Trotsky's mini-helper and accomplice.

*

The FSB's Lefortovo summons had the opposite reaction to what the agency may have intended. The Litvinenko case was inherently fascinating – and I was being told, through unsubtle KGB-style break-ins, not to investigate. The Kremlin's extreme sensitivity to the topic suggested there was a lot to uncover. With digging and a little tenacity, perhaps it might be possible to find some answers.

In the summer of 2007, I met Dmitry Peskov, Putin's urbane English-speaking press spokesman. It was a moment when the Kremlin still cared about Russia's image abroad, one the Litvinenko affair had dented. A group of western correspondents had been summoned to one of Moscow's fancier Italian restaurants. Peskov explained the affair from the Russian government's perspective.

In his version of events, the Kremlin was a blameless victim: a reasonable and forbearing partner, surrounded by hostile and irrational actors. Miliband's decision to expel four Russian diplomats was 'totally unexpected', Peskov said, and a throwback to the bad old days of Cold War confrontation. 'We consider it unfortunate,' he added smoothly, his tone – this was classic Peskov – one of faux innocent regret.

Peskov stated that Moscow 'strongly rejected' any suggestion of Russian state involvement. Where was the proof? Litvinenko's death was a 'terrible crime' and not a political murder, he said. He reeled off Moscow's many grievances against London – unsuccessful extradition requests, 'Mr Berezovsky, Mr Zakayev…' One quip had annoyed him. Peskov recalled how he flew first-class with

British Airways from New York to London. The stewardess had served him a cup of tea with the words: 'No polonium this time, Mr Peskov.'

According to Peskov, London was succumbing to the kind of virulent 'Russophobia' more usually associated with Eastern European countries like Poland. 'You want me to encourage my citizens to go to London?' he asked, adding: 'It takes two to tango.' He was adamant the Kremlin was reacting to the aggressive behaviour of others. 'We weren't the initiators of this crisis,' he said. 'This mirror response [the expulsion of UK diplomats] was actually something we regret, and something we were forced into.'

Peskov's performance reminded me of the writer and critic Clive James's observation in his book *Cultural Amnesia*: truly unprincipled states never blush.

Meanwhile, the FSB sent me a further letter. Its investigation was going well; officers had concluded that I didn't meet Berezovsky. I was therefore 'not of interest' to the agency, it wrote. In August we flew back to the UK for our annual summer holiday and a week on a Cornish beach. Later that month I returned to Moscow without my family, who were staying on.

The post in Moscow was unreliable; sometimes packages arrived, sometimes not. I had hand-carried a video taped by a friend, the poet Heathcote Williams. He had recorded two documentaries he thought might be of interest. One was a BBC *Panorama* investigation into Litvinenko's death, *How to Poison a Spy*, presented by the journalist John Sweeney. The other was *My Friend Sasha*

– *a Very Russian Murder* by Andrei Nekrasov, the film-maker who had shot the deathbed footage of Litvinenko.

I dumped the tape under the TV, and forgot about it. Williams had Sellotaped programme notes to the side of the cassette, including the photo of Litvinenko in intensive care. One Sunday evening I slotted the video in to watch. The recording began normally – a slice of BBC *Newsnight* hosted by Jeremy Paxman. After this, something very strange. The Litvinenko documentaries had been erased. Instead of pictures, there were scratchy black-and-white lines; the sound, just audible, was a high-speed squeak.

It was hard to be sure, but it appeared the FSB had broken in again, taken umbrage at the tape's contents, and deleted them. I emailed Williams. He'd checked the tape before he sent it; it played fine. The *Panorama* documentary, I found out later, featured interviews with all the major players. Peskov – who else? – denied Kremlin involvement.

There was also a clip from an interview with Litvinenko. In it, he remarked: 'There were two ideologies in the Soviet Union, communist and criminal. In 1991, the communist ideology ceased to exist and only the criminal remained. The KGB was renamed, it became the FSB, but nothing really changed. Everything stayed the way it was before. The only difference was that a KGB officer killed for his ideology while an FSB officer kills for money.'

Lugovoi had friends in high places; that was obvious. They were keeping a close eye on his case. I caught up with the man himself four months later. He was on the campaign trail, embarking on an unlikely career as a deputy in Russia's parliament. Lugovoi was number two on the federal list of the Liberal Democratic Party of Russia (LDPR), an outfit set up by the KGB and led by the flamboyant Zhirinovsky. In his new role as a would-be politician, Lugovoi zigzagged across the country, traveling to the Far East, the Urals and European Russia.

It seemed that Lugovoi was going to make the best of his notoriety. His campaign, such as it was, had an anti-British flavour.

I went with Lugovoi to Manturovo, a village 60 miles (100 km) outside the western city of Kursk. It was always good to get out of Moscow; here were crumbling dachas, snow-covered fields and poplar trees. Lugovoi toured a farm, peered into its cowshed and visited an orphanage. That evening he talked to locals in a pink-walled hall decorated with an icon and a bust of Lenin. His audience listened politely.

Lugovoi, it struck me, wasn't a natural politician. With his modish suit, purple tie with swirls and Italian shoes, he cut an incongruous figure. Since elections in Russia were fake political exercises – vote rigging on behalf of the ruling United Russia party was rampant – this didn't matter. At a press conference in his hotel, the Nightingale, Lugovoi blamed Britain for Russia's woes. The British had invaded Crimea, forged the Zinoviev letter in 1924 and carried on behaving like 'Anglo-Saxon imperialists'.

I scribbled his remarks in my notepad. 'If you look at Russian–British relations, the Cold War never started and never ended,' he declared.

Locals seemed bemused by his performance. Did it matter that Lugovoi was accused of murder? 'It's difficult to say,' Viktor Shumakov, a veteran of the Soviet war in Afghanistan, told me. 'In Russia many strange things happen all the time.'

A year after Litvinenko's death, Lugovoi was elected as a deputy to Russia's Duma. His meteoric rise, most observers in Moscow felt, could have happened only with the Kremlin's endorsement. Lugovoi, meanwhile, gave numerous audiences to the domestic and foreign press. They took place in Moscow, on the remote and beautiful Kamchatka peninsula, and while he sat on the back of a horse.

My own on-off investigation into Litvinenko's murder had not met with a breakthrough. But there were clues. I went to see Olga Kryshtanovskaya, an expert on elite politics, and a researcher in sociology at Russia's academy of sciences. Kryshtanovskaya was an interesting figure, who would go on to became a United Russia MP. She had described how under Putin former KGB officers rose to senior positions – by 2007, 42 per cent of those in top Kremlin jobs had a military or intelligence background. She had good contacts inside Russian intelligence.

I asked her about Litvinenko. She said that FSB officers had privately admitted that his murder must have been one of their operations. They had no regrets about the target – Litvinenko was a traitor and merited the punishment – but expressed surprise at the shoddy way in which his execution was carried out. These things were done much more tidily by the KGB, in particular when Yuri Andropov – the only KGB officer to lead the Soviet Union – was communist party general secretary.

'My FSB friends told me that this [Litvinenko's bungled poisoning] would never have happened under Andropov,' Kryshtanovskaya told me. 'They told me the KGB was much more efficient at murdering back then.'

Lugovoi and Kovtun may have been third-rate killers, but they continued to enjoy support from where it mattered. In April 2008, I interviewed Lugovoi for the first time. The location was his first-floor office in Moscow's Radisson Hotel in Kievskaya, the same place where the detectives from Scotland Yard had stayed.

Despite his contempt for the British 'establishment', Lugovoi turned out to be an Anglophile. He was a fan of English literature; the works of Arthur Conan Doyle sat in a glass-fronted cabinet case. 'I've read all Conan Doyle. I'm very fond of *The Lost World*,' he explained. His son went to the same British school in Moscow as my son, though at a different campus. His daughter spent a year on an English course in Cambridge.

Lugovoi's assistant, Sophia, brought us tea. On the wall was a photo of Putin shaking hands with Berezovsky; another jokey montage showed the president chopping the head off the exiled oligarch Mikhail Khodorkovsky. There were framed snaps from Lugovoi's days in the Federal Protection Service, when he accompanied Kremlin politicians including Boris Yeltsin and prime minister Yegor Gaidar. I spotted two photos of his trips with Gaidar to Washington.

I asked Lugovoi why he had joined the KGB's ninth directorate, responsible for government security. 'They invited me. Any normal Soviet officer would take it as an honour to be in the KGB. It means that you are the best.' Lugovoi denied that he was ever a spy and said his job in the early 1990s, as head of a Kremlin platoon, was rather boring. Instead of intelligence work he trained new recruits to perform ceremonial drills in Red Square.

What happened in London? Lugovoi's answer: nothing much. He claimed Litvinenko insisted on a meeting, picked the Millennium Hotel as venue, and called him 'at least five times'. This was, as phone logs later demonstrated, untrue: it was Lugovoi who called Litvinenko. As for the tea: 'I've always said I can't remember whether we ordered tea at all. I remember that I drank some whisky or gin. Then Litvinenko arrived. He said next to nothing. He was very excited.'

Not all of what Lugovoi said was deceitful. He recounted how Litvinenko rang him at 8.30 a.m. on 2 November and explained he was feeling ill and couldn't make their meeting later that morning. Lugovoi phoned Litvinenko in hospital on 7 November ('We had an excellent conversation') and on 13 November – the last call before his death. Lugovoi said Litvinenko had told him he worked for British intelligence: 'He was definitely an agent of the English security services.' Lugovoi took a dim view of MI6, which recruited its agents 'in the pub'.

It was strange. Lugovoi had a certain charm. In person he was disarming. His tale of virtuous innocence and wrongful insinuation even seemed plausible, until you remembered the chilling facts. He smiled, joked, made rueful expressions with his face, and tossed the occasional word of English into his Russian ('absolutely'). He was wearing the same kind of clothes – a pink shirt, fashionable cuffs, grey business suit – that had prompted hotel staff in London to snigger.

By this point, Lugovoi had given dozens of interviews to journalists. In each, he stuck to the same blameless formula: he wasn't a murderer but the victim of conspiracy. At key points, his recall of events was fuzzy. Why couldn't he remember what drinks he ordered at the Millennium Hotel? It wasn't an encounter you would forget. He was lying, there was no doubt. Underneath his smooth persona was something cold, cruel and terrifying.

Before my interview with Lugovoi, I bumped into Kovtun outside the office. When I emerged he was waiting for me. He had the air of someone with not much to do. Though he didn't say so, he seemed jealous of Lugovoi's fame and obvious material success. In the wake of the CPS's murder charge, Lugovoi became, for many Russians, a national hero. Kovtun – not charged until 2011 – was a footnote.

We chatted for ten minutes. Kovtun said his situation frustrated him. His attempts to clarify whether he was under suspicion had been unsuccessful. He wanted to go back to Germany but not if that meant arrest and jail. 'There are no guarantees. I don't want to risk it,' he told me. Kovtun said that he was still on good terms with his ex-wife Marina, who had visited him in Russia over New Year. She'd remarried, had kids, started a new life.

Kovtun said he ended up in the Pine Bar because of a series of coincidences – in Germany his passport renewal went quicker than he expected; he and Andrei sat in the bar because Lugovoi's family hadn't returned from Madame Tussauds. But what about the polonium? The trail went to his hotel bedroom, didn't it? 'By the time the polonium was found, twenty days had passed. There was plenty of time for the British intelligence services to organise lots of things,' he replied.

Kovtun wrote down his mobile number for me. He was stuck in Russia, but felt things could be worse. 'We go on holiday in Siberia and Altai,' he said. 'It's a big country.'

Not long after our conversation, Kovtun broke off all contact with Lugovoi. After 2009 they maintained no relations whatsoever. The two murderers, for whatever reasons, had fallen out.

One of Russia's most popular social networking platforms is LiveJournal.com. Alex Goldfarb ran a page on the site devoted to the Litvinenko case. One day, Goldfarb received an intriguing email. Its sender, 'thepotemkin', said he had information that might be of interest. It concerned polonium.

Goldfarb suggested that he and the source – his name was Alexei Potemkin – communicate via Skype. Potemkin explained his background. He was, he said, an FSB agent working undercover in Austria. He claimed to have met

Litvinenko in the mid-1990s. And been part of the transportation chain that smuggled the polonium from Russia to London.

Goldfarb was wary. Was this an FSB set-up? He met Potemkin in Austria four times. It turned out Potemkin was disillusioned with his job – spying on Austria's Chechen diaspora – and wanted out. Potemkin said that in 2006 an FSB courier delivered a sealed container with radioactive markings. His job was to deposit it with left luggage at Innsbruck Station. The package was the size of a photo. In it was a sealed vial. The vial had a coded lock.

According to Potemkin, the FSB began to carry out espionage missions abroad from 2000. The SVR, Moscow's foreign-intelligence agency, resented this. Potemkin said his ultimate boss was Mikhail Nechaev. Nechaev, a three-star general, was the head of the FSB's counter-intelligence operations department and a very powerful figure.

This was fascinating – but, as Goldfarb recognised, meant little without documents. Potemkin said that in 2003 he'd attended a meeting with Nechaev in Moscow in which polonium was discussed. It had a codename: 'chemistry'. A representative from the FSB's research institute in Moscow described it as 'a perfect poison'. It couldn't be detected by standard police or hospital equipment, the officer said, and was 'harmless unless ingested'.

Potemkin gave Goldfarb internal FSB waybills. They appeared to confirm what Professor Dombey claimed – that the polonium came from the Russian nuclear production facility at Sarov. From there, it was sent to another nuclear complex at Balakovo, 250 miles (400 km) away. A driver from the FSB's garage in Yaroslavl collected the polonium, and delivered it to the FSB's research institute in Moscow. The shipment took place six to eight weeks before Litvinenko was poisoned.

Goldfarb believes Potemkin's story is genuine. 'My personal sense is that there is no sense in him inventing all this,' he said. 'It would be too dangerous.' Potemkin agreed to seek asylum in the UK, holing up for a week at a pension in Vienna, but then changed his mind. He went to ground in a secure place somewhere in Europe. The last contact was in late 2010.

Others are not so sure. Andrei Soldatov, a Moscow-based journalist and expert on Russia's spy agencies, says that some details on the documents are wrong. For example, one is stamped 'FSB counter-intelligence service'. At the time, back in 2003, it was still an FSB department, not becoming a service until 2005.

And what of General Nechaev, the man who may have masterminded the Litvinenko operation? In December 2007, he died. He was fifty-six. Potemkin told Goldfarb he didn't believe Nechaev's death in Moscow was due to natural causes. Rather, it was punishment for the fiasco in London. Polonium was never meant to be discovered. Nechaev's team was disbanded, Potemkin said.

The FSB posted Nechaev's obituary on its website. The citation was brief. 'Mikhail achieved significant results in the confrontation with foreign intelligence agencies,' it wrote.

*

Back in Moscow, the intrusions at our apartment continued; the FSB would typically break in after I wrote something which displeased them. The UK Foreign Office raised my case privately with their Russian counterparts. The harassment would stop, only to resume a few months later. By 2010, I wondered how my Moscow assignment might end. Perhaps I would leave normally, when it was time to move on. Perhaps not.

My newspaper was on a roll: publishing a series of articles in collaboration with WikiLeaks, based on leaked US military logs from the wars in Afghanistan and Iraq. That autumn I flew back to London to take part in a third investigation. There was another leak. It was sensational – more than a quarter of a million secret and classified dispatches sent from the US's embassies and consulates around the world, back to the US state department in Washington.

My task was to examine the cables on Russia and the former Soviet Union. There were 3,000 of them. I and other correspondents worked in an airless room – the air conditioning was broken – on the fourth floor of the *Guardian*'s Kings Cross office. A search engine allowed you to enter a term that would spill out a set of results. You could also specify which US mission was of interest – Moscow, Paris, Berlin etc. I took a breath. I entered a search term – 'Litvinenko'.

At a glance, the results were disappointing. The secret cables didn't reveal who ordered Litvinenko's murder; apparently Washington didn't know. Or, if it did, this wasn't a subject for diplomatic traffic. I looked again. Bingo! The most interesting material came not from the US embassy in Moscow but from elsewhere. I found the secret Madrid cable citing Litvinenko's work for Spanish intelligence and his thesis that Russia was a 'virtual mafia state'.

Another intriguing telegram came from the US mission in Paris. It suggested the White House believed Putin knew about, and probably approved, Litvinenko's murder. Sent on 12 December 2006, it noted a meeting between the US assistant secretary of state, Daniel Fried and Maurice Gourdault-Montagne, a French presidential adviser to Jacques Chirac. The French blamed Litvinenko's poisoning on 'rogue officers'. They doubted the Kremlin was involved.

Fried disagreed: 'Fried, noting Putin's attention to detail, questioned whether rogue security elements could operate in the UK, no less, without Putin's knowledge. Describing the current atmosphere as strange, he described the Russians as increasingly self-confident to the point of arrogance.'

There were other striking cables. I discovered that I wasn't the only one suffering from covert FSB tricks. In 2009, the US ambassador John Beyrle, complained that 'harassing activity against embassy personnel has spiked in the last several months to a level not seen in many years'. It included libellous attacks against US staff in the Russian media, and claims – made to family members – that their loved ones had met accidental deaths. Beyrle also said: 'Home intrusions have become far more commonplace and bold.'

The Russia WikiLeaks material was terrific. It was known that the country suffered from corruption and misrule. The cables went further. They suggested the US shared Litvinenko's gloomy conclusion that Russia had morphed into a full-blown kleptocracy run along mafia lines. In December, the *Guardian* ran a front-page story with the headline: 'Inside Putin's "mafia state"'. An article citing the Fried cable together with a photo of Litvinenko ran on page two. I was the author; they appeared with my by-line.

Before I flew to London the press and information department of Russia's foreign ministry summoned me to a meeting. I'd been informed my press accreditation and visa would not be renewed. The British embassy succeeded in postponing this decision – I had to leave by December 2010 – for six months. This would give us enough time to pack up our home, find new schools for the children, and move back to the UK.

In the meantime, the WikiLeaks articles had enraged someone in the FSB, or the presidential administration, or both. In February 2011, I flew back from London to Moscow, and found myself dumped out of Russia. Officials from the Federal Migration Service cancelled my Russian visa, locked me briefly in a cell, and then escorted me back to the plane I'd just arrived on. My four years as Moscow bureau chief ended in expulsion.

9

Death of an Oligarch

Commercial court, Rolls building,
Fetter Lane, London, October 2011

'A genius gambler'

YULI DUBOV ON HIS FRIEND BORIS BEREZOVSKY, 2011

Eight months later, that October, I found myself inside London's Rolls building. I was no longer reporting from Moscow. But, as with Litvinenko's dramatic murder, it seemed that Russian feuds had a habit of spilling over into London. The building was Britain's new commercial court. There was something in the air: the unmistakeable whiff of very large amounts of cash.

Up on the third floor I found two rival entourages. There were supporters in shiny suits, relatives, friends, PR consultants, journalists and a glamorous Russian woman dressed in black, her blonde hair piled into a chignon. There were lawyers, dozens of them. And there were bodyguards, outsize figures with earpieces.

At the centre of all this were two Russians. Once they were friends and business partners. Now they were bitter enemies. They walked separately into courtroom 26 and sat on opposite sides. One of them was a short, balding man in his mid-sixties, the possessor of an immense and restless energy, which compelled him to speak, move, fidget and gesture. His mind was said to be like a powerful computer. His mood – at this point sunny – was written all over his face.

The other was two decades younger, in his mid-forties. This second man seemed quiet, shy, calm and politely aloof. He appeared oblivious to the teeming drama around him. And sympathetic, too: with a boyish face, light beard turning grey, and a clear, open-eyed expression. His suit was smart yet understated. He sat placidly in one corner, listening to the proceedings via headphones, a reluctant participant with a bemused smile.

The first Russian was Boris Berezovsky. Berezovsky may have caused my departure from Russia, but this was the first time I had seen him. The second man was Roman Abramovich, owner of Chelsea football club in west London. Both were billionaires and among the richest people on the planet.

The dispute between the two of them was the biggest private litigation battle in UK history. At stake was an awful lot of cash. Berezovsky claimed that Abramovich had cheated him out of over $5 billion (£3.2bn). He said that he and Abramovich were partners back in the 1990s in the oil firm, Sibneft, and that he had been forced later to sell his share at a considerable loss. Abramovich denied the claim.

The case was more than a feud over billions. It was the latest instalment in the bitter decade-long public war between Berezovsky and Putin, Abramovich's friend and political boss. Putin wasn't in court but scowled above the hearings, which would go on for twelve weeks, like a malevolent ghost. The dispute was also about what exactly happened in the 1990s when President Yeltsin, in effect, gave away state assets to a handful of insiders, the oligarchs.

Both litigants had submitted witness statements to the judge, Mrs Justice Gloster. They made fascinating reading. Berezvosky's gave an account of his relations with Putin, a tale of friendship and – as both men saw it – betrayal. The two were once close. They first met in late 1991 when Putin was head of St Petersburg's external-relations committee and Berezovsky was trying to expand his LogoVAZ car franchise. 'During this time we became friends,' Berezovsky wrote. They went on holiday together in Russia and abroad, he said. In the early 1990s, Putin stayed with Berezovsky at his chalet in Gstaad in Switzerland for several days.

In his statement, Berezovsky took credit for Putin's rapid rise in politics. He said that he introduced Putin to Yeltsin's team, and supported his appointment as FSB chief. When Litvinenko revealed the plot to kill Berezovsky, the oligarch was 'disappointed' by Putin's cool reaction. Nevertheless, they remained friends. In February 1999, Putin turned up to the birthday party of Berezovsky's partner Elena Gorbunova. Later the same year, Berezovsky backed Putin as prime minister. He even flew to Biarritz that summer to persuade him to take the job – shades here of a reluctant Julius Caesar refusing to take the crown.

Like many others, Berezovsky appears to have found in the inscrutable Putin what he wanted to see. There were warning signs but he chose to ignore them. During one meeting, he spotted that Putin had a statue of Felix Dzerzhinsky, the head of the Cheka, Lenin's murderous secret police, in his office. Berezovsky was astonished but said: 'He [Putin] had never before seemed to be a *chekist* – someone who believed that the security organisations were entitled to do as they pleased.'

Once Putin was in the Kremlin, these tensions escalated into full-blown conflict. 'I am not the kind of person who can remain silent when someone, even the president, is acting politically in a way with which I disagree,' he told the court, truthfully.

The end came when Berezovsky's ORT TV station criticised Putin for his apparent indifference over the sinking of the Russian submarine *Kursk*. The navy vessel suffered an explosion in the Barents Sea; everybody on board drowned. Putin, meanwhile, was on holiday near the resort of Sochi, riding around on a jet ski. Berezovsky said he rang Putin and told him he had to get back to Moscow, otherwise the criticism would get worse. Putin was furious.

During their last meeting in August 2000, Putin told Berezovsky to sell ORT or go to jail. The president accused Berezovsky of 'hiring prostitutes to pose as the widows and sisters of sailors killed aboard the *Kursk* to attack him verbally'. The allegation was crazy, probably invented by the FSB, and Berezovsky said so. Putin's parting words were stiff: 'Goodbye, Boris Abramovich,' he said, using the formal patronymic. Berezovsky's sorrowful reply, addressing Putin's informally, was: 'Goodbye, Volodya.'

In October 2000, and under criminal investigation, the oligarch left for France and then Britain, never to go back.

Berezovsky's fall coincided with Roman Abramovich's rise. By the late 1990s, Abramovich was a Kremlin insider in his own right. (In 1999, he allegedly approached Berezovsky and suggested they buy Putin a $50 million yacht as a present. Berezovsky declined; Abramovich bought the yacht anyway.) By 2000 – according to Berezovsky – Abramovich 'played a central role in the selection of members of President Putin's cabinet', and had the power to open and shut criminal cases.

Abramovich took advantage of his position, Berezovsky said. In exile he was compelled to sell his interest in Sibneft at a 'gross undervalue'. His stake was worth at least $7 billion, Berezovsky claimed. Abramovich paid him a measly $1.5 billion. Berezovsky didn't think much of Abramovich's intellectual gifts either. But, he said, his former friend had one magical talent: everyone liked him. Berezovsky wrote: 'He is good at psychology in this way. He is good at appearing to be humble. He is happy to spend days socialising with important or powerful people if that is what is needed so that he can get closer to them.'

By the time of Litvinenko's poisoning, Abramovich was a Kremlin insider and loyal functionary, serving as governor of Chukotka, a barren and backward federal district on Russia's remote north east Pacific coast. He ploughed many of his millions into the territory – apparently at Putin's request. Unlike Berezovsky, Abramovich obeyed the rule laid down by Putin at a meeting with

Russia's plutocrats in summer 2000. It said, in essence: keep your mouth shut and obey the state.

Abramovich's witness statement was a chunky white booklet. He disputed practically everything Berezovsky said. His main claim was that he'd hired Berezovsky as a top-level Kremlin fixer because of Berezovsky's connections with Yeltsin. A Russian word defined this arrangement – *krysha*, or roof. In return for his political services, Abramovich paid Berezovsky 'more than $2.5 billion' and funded the latter's lavish lifestyle. This meant yachts, planes, a villa in France and jewellery for his girlfriend. Abramovich said he didn't owe Berezovsky anything. He rejected his financial demands as 'fantastic'.

As Abramovich told it, Berezovsky was someone who came to believe he was invincible – intellectually brilliant, but inconsistent, easily distracted, and obsessed with grandiose and ultimately pointless schemes. He was uninterested, Abramovich said, in the quotidian detail of running a company. Moreover, Berezovsky behaved like a child. Often he said the first thing that came into his head, Abramovich claimed in his statement, adding: 'He would quite often convince himself that something was true, only later to convince himself of the opposite.'

The Chelsea FC owner was certainly right about one thing – that this was, as he put it, 'a uniquely Russian story'. It hinged on what kind of agreement had been struck between the two participants many years previously. Berezovsky said the Sibneft deal had been made orally – a typical arrangement in Russia at the time, he argued, where business was done on the basis of personal trust and a handshake. Abramovich maintained that Berezovsky was never his partner.

This, then, was the story of two oligarchs – one loyal to the Putin regime, another actively plotting its overthrow.

The case began on a blue-skied October day. It was an alluring spectacle. Here were two figures who had played a key role in shaping the history of modern Russia – robber barons or respectable entrepreneurs, depending on your point of view – facing off against each other in the rule-bound setting of an English courtroom.

The question was: which of them would Mrs Justice Gloster believe?

Over the years, the Kremlin had tried various strategies to destroy Berezovsky. It had sought unsuccessfully to extradite him from Britain. There had been criminal prosecutions in Russia, trials *in absentia*, guilty verdicts. And of course the exemplary murder of Litvinenko, Berezovsky's friend and lieutenant.

At some stage, his enemies noticed that he had a fondness for going to law. Berezovsky had served his writ against Abramovich after spotting him out shopping in the London branch of Hermès. Berezovsky was confident that Abramovich would settle, never believing he would turn up in a British court.

Now the case was about to start. According to Berezovsky's friend Yuli Dubov – they had known each other since 1972 – the oligarch hadn't actually read his own witness statement. Nor had he bothered to wade through 1,500 pages of court documents. What was going on?

'He was a genius gambler,' Dubov told me later. 'It wasn't fascinating for him to win. He had to win against the odds. If there is something that has to be done by midnight he would start doing it at 11.55 p.m.' Berezovsky had always done impossible things – getting a PhD in the 1970s Soviet Union at a time of prejudice against Jews, winning elections for Yeltsin, bringing Putin into the Kremlin. Why should this time be different?

Berezovsky's preparations, then, had been woefully inadequate. 'He thought that he could go into court and after five minutes everybody would be charmed by his personality,' Dubov said. Further, he had misjudged Abramovich in the same way he misread Putin. Berezovsky had known Abramovich as a callow young man. In the intervening years Abramovich had grown up, got serious.

'Boris had a very high estimate of himself and a low estimate of his opponents,' Dubov said. He added: 'It's the surest way of losing when you go into a fight.'

Abramovich had spent months preparing for the case. He hired a top legal team. Representing him was Jonathan Sumption, a stellar QC and now a UK Supreme Court justice. Often described as one of the cleverest men in Britain, Sumption is a scholar of medieval history. He is also the owner of a handsome French chateau, complete with dreamy towers, turrets and ramparts, in the Dordogne.

Sumption's fee was rumoured to be more than £5 million. Berezovsky's lead barrister was the South African-born Laurence Rabinowitz QC. Both took up positions in front of their respective clients. The judge,

Mrs Justice Gloster, came in. She sat beneath the royal coat of arms: a lion and unicorn, a heraldic shield, and the motto in old French: 'Evil be to him that evil thinks'.

Rabinowitz told the judge that the two Russians had worked together to acquire a shared asset, Sibneft, which made both of them wildly rich. After Berezovsky fled to London, Abramovich could remain loyal to his old friend or 'profit from his difficulties'. He took the second option, the QC said. He conceded that the case was 'incredibly complex'.

It wasn't helped by the fact that several of its participants were dead. Berezovsky's Georgian business partner Patarkatsishvili died of a heart attack in 2008; the British lawyer Stephen Curtis, who took notes at a crucial business meeting, perished in a helicopter crash in 2004 in Dorset. Rabinowitz added: 'The case is rather lacking in contemporaneous documents. But some shine out like a beacon.'

At the end of day one, Berezovsky was in good cheer. The case seemed to be going his way. Marina Litvinenko had turned up to support him. We had met over lunch that summer, introduced by a former lecturer in Russian, Martin Dewhirst. I liked her immediately.

The next day, Berezovsky took to the witness box. He looked relaxed, in charcoal jacket and open shirt, and declared himself ready to answer everything and anything. Berezovsky opted to speak in English. After over a decade in the UK, Berezovsky's English was fluent. It didn't always make sense, though: his sentences were often ungrammatical, with muddled tenses, articles that tended to go awol, and errant prepositions. He had a strong Russian accent.

He began by sketching his relations with Yeltsin – good, he said, after he got friendly with the president's daughter Tatiana.

Sumption, Abramovich's star lawyer, got to his feet. The barrister pointed out that in 2001 Berezovsky had sued *Forbes* magazine after it said that he had influenced Yeltsin through his daughter. Now Berezovsky had just admitted this was true. Sumption read from Berezovsky's earlier witness statement. 'Why did you deny it and then sign a statement of truth in support of your denial?' he asked. Visibly flustered, Berezovsky gave a smile. He replied: 'It's a good question.'

The court laughed. Mrs Justice Gloster was unimpressed. She chipped in: 'Well, could you answer it, please?' Berezovsky said his lawyers had prepared the document, and he hadn't paid too much attention to it.

The rest of the day was less painful. Berezovsky agreed with Sumption's description of 1990s Russia as the 'wild east'. (The barrister further likened the lawless post-communist era to 'fourteenth-century England', his expert period.) The oligarch admitted that corruption was widespread, but said that he personally 'wasn't corrupt'. He said that, under Yeltsin, Russia was significantly less corrupt than today under Putin's authoritarian leadership, which scored ten out of ten for corruption compared with Yeltsin's 'three or four' out of ten.

The hearings settled into a routine. Berezovsky attended every day. Outside the courtroom he chatted to journalists, many of them Russian; he shook hands, greeted well-wishers. I introduced myself. Berezovsky muttered something; a bodyguard gave me his business card; the great man moved on. At lunch he ate sushi with his legal team in a third-floor consultation room.

Abramovich, by contrast, didn't mingle. It was as if an invisible bubble protected him. The two men politely ignored each other. In the corridors and the lift they kept apart, their teams occupying different parts of the wavy glass court complex.

For onlookers, the case was the best free show in town, not least because it offered a glimpse into the weird world of the super-rich. *Forbes* estimated Abramovich's then fortune at $13.4 billion. Giving evidence, he admitted to owning a string of properties. They included a multi-million-pound chateau in France, once belonging to the Duke and Duchess of Windsor; a 420-acre estate in West Sussex, Fyning Hill; and a 'large and expensive central London' home in Lowndes Square, Knightsbridge.

Asked if he had an extravagant lifestyle, Abramovich said: 'Well, yes, possibly. I agree, yes, one could put it that way.'

According to Abramovich, he and Berezovsky had been friends, but not close friends. Instead their relationship was one of 'protectee' and 'protector'. Once Berezovsky fell out with Putin, Abramovich considered their *krysha* arrangement defunct. He said he continued to hand over large sums to a greedy Berezovsky because he felt some loyalty to him.

The reality, though, was Berezovsky's epoch was over. 'Russia had moved on. I had moved on,' he said. Meanwhile, Abramovich said he'd never aspired to be a public person. He said he was taken aback that buying Chelsea FC in 2003 had made him a figure of global interest. In 2005, Abramovich said he sold his share in Sibneft to Gazprom, an arm of the Russian government. He got $13 billion for it.

Rabinowitz did his best to pull Abramovich's story apart. But the oligarch was well prepared. He gave his evidence in Russian. Mostly, Abramovich replied to the QC's questions with a single word: '*Da*'. His style was minimalist. (At one point, having failed to receive an answer, Rabinowitz prodded him with the words: 'Could you say "*Da*", please.') The court adjourned in January 2012 while Mrs Justice Gloster went away to write her judgment.

Eight months later, on the last day of August, the judge came back. Berezovsky strolled into the Rolls building, as ebullient and upbeat as ever. I asked him if he was about to win his battle against his ex-friend? He told me: 'I'm confident. I believe in the system,' then we went through the metal detector together to the lift. We travelled up to the fourth floor.

At 10.30 a.m., Gloster walked into court. Everyone rose. There was a hush. The first three rows were packed with lawyers – the true winners in this multi-billion-pound struggle. Berezovsky sat in his old spot on the left near the door, two bodyguards behind him. Abramovich wasn't there. 'He's probably on his yacht in Corfu or Marbella,' someone whispered.

Berezovsky had always believed in British justice – which, after all, had granted his 2003 application for political asylum. It had handed him handsome libel victories, too. But on this occasion, the same system delivered him an almighty and humiliating kick. First, the judge dismissed his case and his claim that he was ever a partner with Abramovich in Sibneft. Then she gave her reasons.

They were withering, in the kind of remorseless language rarely heard in the High Court. Berezovsky, we learned, had destroyed himself early on in the witness box. 'On my analysis of the entirety of the evidence, I found Mr Berezovsky an unimpressive and inherently unreliable witness, who regarded truth as a transitory, flexible concept, which could be moulded to suit his current purposes,' the judge said.

Berezovsky clutched his face. She continued: 'At times the evidence which he gave was deliberately dishonest; sometimes he was clearly making his evidence up as he went along in response to the perceived difficulty in answering the questions in a manner consistent with his case.

'At other times, I gained the impression that he was not necessarily being deliberately dishonest, but had deluded himself into believing his own version of events. On occasions he tried to avoid answering questions by making long and irrelevant speeches, or by professing to have forgotten facts which he had been happy to record in his pleadings or witness statements.'

Berezovsky had been right about one thing. Abramovich had charmed the judge. She concluded that Abramovich was a 'truthful and on the whole reliable witness' – one who gave 'careful and thoughtful answers, which were focused on the specific issues about which he was questioned'.

The judge even absolved Putin of wrongdoing. She said that there was no evidence that Putin had bullied Berezovsky into selling his TV station, a remark that prompted laughter and incredulity from Russians sitting in the back row. Putin had held a grudge against the British judicial system ever since it granted Berezovsky asylum. Now it had delivered Putin a glorious victory.

A stunned Berezovsky appeared on the pavement in front of the cameras. The judge had tried to rewrite Russian history, he said, adding that his faith in the system had been badly shaken. Had he expected to win? 'Absolutely.' Berezovsky said he hadn't yet decided whether to appeal – a tricky step, given the judge's devastating comments. 'I'm absolutely amazed what happened today. I'm surprised completely,' he said.

He quoted Winston Churchill, who said that democracy was bad but that nobody had devised a better alternative. He said: 'English court is bad but there is nothing better.' The oligarch said he didn't regret bringing the case. He even attempted a note of stoicism, observing: 'Life is life.' He left in a black Mercedes.

Berezovsky had suffered a grievous blow. But friends pointed to his enormous appetite for life, politics and intrigue. They mentioned his love of women, and his wealth. His fortune was now much diminished. But he was still rich. They thought he would recover.

*

Gloster's verdict was peculiar. Juridically it was perhaps unanswerable. Berezovsky had contradicted himself in the witness box; any court would take a dim view of lying. For those who knew Russia in the 1990s, though, it seemed strange. There were no bad guys and good guys at that time; the privatisations that benefited a small group of oligarchs were surely all dubious and done at the expense of ordinary Russians; the absence of documentation from this period was unsurprising.

Berezovsky's friends felt an injustice had taken place. They considered appealing. Nikolai Glushkov, who gave evidence for Berezovsky, thought the judgment was deeply one-sided. He complained to the court authorities, without success. Frustrated, he showed me the letter he'd got by way of brush-off. Dubov took a slightly different view. He felt Berezovky had told the truth, broadly, but that much of the detail was wrong or invented retrospectively.

It was ironic. An English court had achieved something the Kremlin had been trying to do for a decade – shut down Berezovsky's anti-Putin London operation. As a result of his diminished wealth, Goldfarb closed down the International Foundation for Civil Liberties. Over twelve years it had disbursed $75 million on various causes – grants to the Sakharov museum in Moscow; full-page newspaper adverts depicting Putin as Groucho Marx during the 2006 G8 summit; Litvinenko's London rent.

The immediate casualty was Marina Litvinenko, whose legal costs Berezovsky had underwritten. She was faced with a problem. Where to find £300,000 so she could be represented at a forthcoming inquest into her husband's death? I agreed to help; we shot a video at the *Guardian*'s office. Marina told me she wanted to hang on to her legal counsel so she might uncover the truth behind the murder. 'I'm very grateful for all these things Berezovsky did for us. For six years he supported us,' she said.

By end of the year there was no word from Berezovsky himself as to whether he would appeal. In the past, Berezovsky had been happy to give interviews. As a result of his loss to Abramovich he'd ceased to be a public and political figure. He was uncharacteristically dormant. Sometimes he answered his mobile; more often he didn't. (I reached him once and he agreed to meet, but we never fixed a date.) He sold his home in Wentworth, Surrey – he faced £100 million in legal bills – and moved into his ex-wife Galina Besharova's place near Ascot in Berkshire.

Previously, Berezovsky had slept just four hours a night. He had thrown himself into multiple projects, exhausting all those around him. He travelled regularly to Israel and South Africa. In the wake of defeat, his world shrank. He would come down from his bedroom for breakfast, return to his room, and not emerge again until mid-afternoon. Friends suspected the verdict had sent him into a psychological decline; his normal energy and joie de vivre gone.

By early 2013, Berezovsky's family – two ex-wives, one ex-partner and six children – felt he was in better shape. He had, they thought, thrown off his depression. In February, Glushkov emailed me to say that he had quarrelled with Boris, but added that he was 'most positive' his friend would be 'back in public life' later that year.

In late March, his bodyguard, Avi Navama, went off to do some shopping, leaving Berezovsky alone in the Surrey house. It was a Saturday afternoon. Navama is an Israeli former special forces soldier. He'd spent six years living with Berezovsky and was at his side during the High Court hearings. Navama returned at 3 p.m. There was no sign of his boss. He saw Berezovsky's mobile phone lying on the table. There were missed calls. This was unusual. He went upstairs to the bathroom. No sound. The door was locked from the inside.

Navama kicked open the door. Inside, he found Berezovsky lying on the floor, his favourite black scarf twisted around his neck. The neck showed bruising. Next to Berezovsky was a broken shower rail. Navama touched Berezovsky's hand. It was cold. He retreated from the bathroom, shut the door behind him and rang the police.

By the time Berezovsky's ex-wife Galina arrived at the house, officers from Thames Valley Police were already there; they kept her, her two children and Navama downstairs in the kitchen. Berezovsky's friend Dubov arrived at 5 p.m. The police wouldn't allow him inside, so he sat on the road in a police car for the next twelve hours, awaiting news.

Berezovsky's death, in a secluded estate in southeast England, prompted a full-scale investigation. After Litvinenko's murder, the police were taking no chances. A paramedic, John Pocock, examined Berezovsky's body on the bathroom floor. Pocock was carrying a radiation detection device. It gave off a 'warning tone'. Detectives later said the device had a battery fault.

Government atomic energy scientists tested samples taken from Berezovsky for radioactivity. They were sent to the Atomic Weapons Establishment in Aldermaston. They found no traces.

Nor were there any signs of a break-in.

Instead, the police moved quickly to the theory that Berezovsky had killed himself. Chief Inspector Kevin Brown, the detective in charge, released a statement saying he was ruling out 'third party involvement at this stage'. His conclusions were apparently drawn from the medical evidence – there was no obvious sign of foul play – and from interviews with Berezovsky's associates.

The picture was of a depressed and broken man who in his final months had talked frequently of taking his own life. Navama told police that on one occasion Berezovsky had picked up a steak knife, and demanded: 'Where should I cut?' On another he asked his body-guard: 'What is the best way to die?' Berezovsky had also inquired how he might choke himself.

Marina Litvinenko was distraught. She emailed:

Dear Luke

   I am still not ready to talk about Boris. It is very painful. I can't believe this has happened. I am very sorry, just need some time.
   Marina

Those in Berezovsky's grieving circle were unconvinced by this official version of events. After several attempts to kill him, including by the FSB in the 1990s, they suspect he too was murdered, like Litvinenko. 'I don't believe in suicide. He could not do it psychologically. He wasn't this kind of person,' Dubov told me.

Dubov likened Berezovsky's death to the locked-room mysteries he used to read as a child growing up in the Soviet Union. He was a fan of the crime novels of the American writer John Dickson Carr, also known as Carter Dickson. Carr specialised in impossible situations, in which murderers would kill their victims from inside a sealed room and vanish without trace. There would be no sign of an exit from windows or a chimney; no footprints in the snowy yard below or roof above.

'Maybe I'm just influenced by reading too many stories all those years ago,' Dubov said. 'I think that given a certain kind of fantasy I could come up with a vision of how it was done.'

Glushkov, who had known the oligarch since 1989, said: 'I will never believe in the natural death of Berezovsky. The idea that he would have taken his own life is bullshit. You have the deaths of Boris and [his business partner] Badri [Patarkatsishvili] over a short period of time. Too many bodies are happening. I would say this is a little bit too much.'

Litvinenko's friend Viktor Suvorov agreed: 'That guy loved life so much. He loved women so much. For me it isn't possible to imagine he could kill himself.' Suvorov said he'd hated Berezovsky before he knew him, viewing him as a crook who had destroyed Russia and its chances of turning into a normal democratic country. 'When I met him I immediately melted. He was such a charming man. A negative genius.'

Some interpreted the circumstances of his death as a coded message from the Kremlin. Berezovsky had disagreed with Putin's war in Chechnya. In 1999, Putin said of the Chechen rebels: 'If we catch them on the toilet, we will wipe them out in the outhouse.' Did Berezovsky's death in a bathroom, not far from the loo, hark back to Putin's remark? Others believed Berezovsky may have been helped to commit suicide. They pointed to inconsistencies at the scene: what was Berezovsky's body doing on the floor?

Meanwhile, Yuri Felshtinsky said he'd spoken to Berezovsky on the phone a few months before his death. 'He didn't appear to be suicidal. He had been looking for private schools in the US for his daughter. Boris understood that the Kremlin aimed to destroy him,' Felshtinsky said.

The late French writer Gérard de Villiers – who specialised in turning real events into lightly fictionalised thrillers – devoted his last novel to Berezovsky. Called *Revenge of the Kremlin*, it postulates that Berezovsky was indeed murdered. A five-man squad neutralises the estate's security system, goes into the house, and immobilises Berezovsky before he can reach for his gun. They inject him with an undetectable poison that renders him unconscious, tie his prone body to the shower rail and escape.

These suspicions, of course, proved nothing. But they spoke volumes about the expectations of Kremlin behaviour. After Litvinenko's murder, the idea that the Russian government might assassinate a well-known political critic living in exile, in a country with which Russia was not at war, was all too believable.

In 2007, Scotland Yard had intercepted yet another plot to kill him. The alleged assassin was a Paris-based Chechen, Ruslan Atlangeriev. Police advised Berezovsky to leave the country for a few days; he flew to Israel. Atlangeriev was caught trying to break into Berezovsky's Mayfair office. He was deported back to Russia, where he disappeared.

There was also the strange matter of the T-shirt.

In July 2010, Berezovsky met with a business associate from his Moscow days, Rafael Filinov, in London. Filinov also knew Andrei Lugovoi. Filinov delivered a present from Lugovoi for Berezovksy – a black custom-made T-shirt printed on the front and back.

The T-shirt didn't win any prizes for subtlety. On the front were the words 'Polonium-210, CSKA, London, Hamburg, to be continued', around a red star logo of the CSKA football team. On the back: 'CSKA Moscow, nuclear death is knocking your door'.

Was this a sick joke? Or a warning that Berezovsky was next? The oligarch's assistant, Michael Cotlick, said Berezovsky held the T-shirt up and exclaimed: 'Look what Lugovoi has sent me.' They came to the conclusion that it wasn't a threat, though what it portended was unclear. Cotlick gave the T-shirt to Scotland Yard. It joined the mountain of evidence against Lugovoi.

The Kremlin had put enormous pressure on Berezovsky over a period of many years – though his courtroom defeat was surely self-inflicted. In Moscow, Dmitry Peskov, Putin's press spokesman, claimed that Berezovsky had written a letter to Russia's president shortly before his death requesting forgiveness. Berezovsky begged to come home to Russia, Peskov said. The letter was never published.

Meanwhile, a Russian reporter from *Forbes* claimed to have interviewed Berezovsky in London's Four Seasons Hotel the evening before his death. Berezovsky allegedly told the reporter, Ilya Zhegulev, he yearned for Moscow and had 'over-estimated' the west. Berezovsky drank a cup of tea with honey.

These Moscow-inspired media reports looked and sounded self-serving. Deconstructed, they amounted to a Kremlin morality tale: if you oppose legitimate Russian power, you end up in exile, broke, friendless and ultimately dead. Nikolai Kovalyov, the former head of the FSB, probably best summed up the Kremlin's real feelings towards the late oligarch. Kovalyov told Russian TV that Berezovsky had got what he and other traitors deserved – an unpleasant end.

Berezovsky's funeral took place in May 2013. Six weeks had passed since his death. Around thirty mourners – family, friends and lawyers – attended. There was tight security. The ceremony was in Brookwood Cemetery near Woking in Surrey. The service took place in a small brick chapel, overlooked by suitably Russian pines and silver birches, and under a dull, pearl-grey sky.

One guest arrived in a Bentley. There were several Mercedes. I travelled by rail, reporting on the event for the *Guardian*. Others dressed in black and bearing white lilies came on the same modest suburban train to Brookwood Station. Zakayev turned up with his son Shamil; we chatted briefly. Berezovsky's daughter Yelizaveta brought flowers. It was a strikingly understated send-off for a man who had lived and blazed in the public eye, in Russia and the UK.

'He was a friend. I miss him. I'm very grateful to Boris. Through him I felt the touch of history,' Goldfarb said. For better or worse, he added, Berezovsky had played a major role in the 1990s: advising Yeltsin, bringing peace to Chechnya and promoting Putin – his biggest error. One of the mourners was Rabinowitz, his QC. What did he make of Berezovsky? Rabinowitz, walking along a path lined with rhododendrons, and in meditative mood, told me: 'He was very Russian, like something from the pages of a Dostoyevsky novel.'

In March 2014, an inquest opened into Berezovsky's death. The two-day hearing in Windsor heard evidence that confirmed suicide. Dr Simon Poole, a forensic scientist, said that microscopic tests of the tissues on Berezovsky's neck revealed no sign of any restraint or defence injuries. Toxicology tests didn't turn up any poisons. Another scientist, Dr Raymond Fysh, said he saw no evidence that Berezovsky had been strangled.

A German forensic pathologist, Professor Bernd Brink-mann, disagreed. Brinkmann didn't examine Berezovsky's corpse but he did review autopsy photographs. He concluded that the businessman didn't kill himself. His report, commissioned by Berezovsky's family, said that a number of assailants may have murdered Berezovsky, suspending him by his scarf from the shower rail. 'The strangulation mark is completely different from the stran-gulation mark in hanging,' Brinkmann said. An assailant could have throttled him in a bedroom, he posited.

Brinkmann was an interesting witness. It was Brink-mann who had proved that the Italian banker Roberto Calvi – found hanging from Blackfriars Bridge in 1982 – had been murdered. Calvi's family had never believed the official version of suicide; Brinkmann's report two decades later led police to reopen the case as a murder inquiry. The killers appeared to be the Sicilian mafia. In 2005, five Italians were tried for Calvi's murder but acquitted.

This time, however, the coroner Peter Bedford was sceptical of Brinkmann's conclusions. Bedford said it was unlikely anyone could have attacked Berezovsky 'without any reaction' from him. Rather, Bedford said that there was convincing evidence that Berezovsky – depressed, and under financial pressure – was capable of suicide. However, Bedford acknowledged that Brinkmann was an eminent witness. He entered an open verdict.

This meant the cause of death was impossible to determine. It could be either murder or suicide. Thames Valley Police were privately irritated with the verdict and Brinkmann's evidence.

The family still believe Berezovsky was murdered. Yelizaveta Berezovskaya, daughter by his first marriage, pointed a finger at the Russian government. She told the inquest a number of people would be interested in having him killed. The motive, she suggested, was obvious: for more than a decade Berezovsky had warned that Putin wasn't merely a danger to Russia but was capable of menacing other countries too.

Recent events had proved him right. 'I don't think they liked what my father was saying. He was saying that Putin was a danger to the whole world. And you can see that now,' she said.

It was hard to disagree with that. Days earlier, Putin had annexed a large chunk of someone else's territory.

Putin seemed unstoppable. But just a few months before Berezovsky's demise, another mysterious death of a Russian émigré on British soil was to raise still further questions that were to resonate at the very top of international politics.

10

Gelsemium Elegans

St George's Hill, Weybridge, Surrey,
10 November 2012

'The only possible way to imitate a natural death
without arousing suspicion was to use poison.
An accident would not suit – they always
left a lingering odour of suspicion'

THE DEATH OF ACHILLES, BORIS AKUNIN, 1998

The names sound quintessentially English – Silverwood, Horsley, Bassett Lodge, Hawthorn Mill. Each refers to a mansion on the private St George's Hill estate in Weybridge. The houses here are large – think three-storey mock-Tudor mansions with dormer windows, sweeping driveways and triple garages. Their owners are rich people. Naturally enough, they value their privacy. Signs suggest that outsiders and those who are not members of the local golf club can piss off. Guardhouses limit access at the entrances. Branded estate vehicles buzz along the woody drives.

St George's is Britain's bucolic answer to Beverly Hills. Celebrities like this green corner of Surrey, immediately south-west of London. John Lennon, Ringo Starr, Elton John and Tom Jones have all lived here. Others keep a low profile for different reasons. There are hedge fund managers, City bankers, a Nigerian computer tycoon. Their personal accounts and investments – all legal and declared, of course – amount to millions. Contractors are used to installing bulletproof glass and panic rooms for some of the more particular residents.

Granville Road is a typical St George's address. At its entrance is a white barred gate. A notice in front of a large rhododendron says: 'Restricted access'. Fifteen-foot-high hedges of laurel and copper beech shield the houses and their enormous gardens from view. CCTV cameras are everywhere. As one police officer told the *Observer* newspaper: 'Even the security has security.' If you want to disappear this is a good spot, a wooded refugium of silver birch and pine.

On 10 November 2012, one St George's resident was returning from an early-evening jog. It was 5.15 p.m. The runner, dressed in a tracksuit, turned into Granville Road. Ahead of him was his home in exile, the Coach House, which he shared with his wife Tatiana and their two children. The property was at the end of a turning circle. The house was imposing – six bedrooms, £12,500 a month rent, a Porsche parked outside. In the garden was a kids' trampoline.

Fifty metres from his front door, the jogger collapsed. He didn't get up. He lay face down on the ground.

Police arriving at the scene jotted down a few details. The man's name was Alexander Perepilichnyy. He was a Russian citizen and forty-four years old. He had previously been in excellent health. Like Litvinenko, Perepilichnyy had fled to the UK from Moscow after a dispute with some powerful people there. Since 2010, he had been living anonymously and quietly with his family in St George's, avoiding trouble. Latterly, he'd been receiving some worrying messages from Russia.

Perepilichnyy lay motionless under a white sheet. A single lamp-post illuminated the darkness. Liam Walsh, a local chef, said that when he arrived at the scene the Russian wasn't breathing. 'We had to get him on his back and start doing CPR. He was probably dead for a while,' Walsh told Reuters. There was zero paramedics could do. No obvious cause of death. No obvious sign of foul play either. Unexplained, then.

It would take more than two years before the likely murder weapon was discovered, and then not by men in uniform. The weapon was a rare and deadly toxin. It had been on a journey as improbable as that taken by the polonium from a closed nuclear city in the Urals to the streets of Mayfair. Whoever was responsible had shown a high degree of cunning. Was this the FSB? The toxin came from a plant. A plant that grows on the hillsides of China.

If he'd been born a couple of decades earlier, Perepilichnyy might have been a professor. Maybe even a member of the Soviet Union's prestigious academy of sciences. He was a talented physicist and maths whizz. Born in Western Ukraine, he moved to Moscow in the 1980s to study at the Physical and Technological University in the faculty of molecular and biological physics. In his student days Perepilichnyy was a vertical, skinny figure, with gangling legs, jet-black hair and pale skin. He preferred black clothes. His expression was somewhat absent, as if he was thinking about something. He was an introvert, serious and deadpan, even when making a joke. Friends called him Stanek.

According to one friend, Yuri Panchul, Perepilichnyy dreamed of moving to the US. In 1989, he wanted to apply to an American university to do a post-grad in biochemistry or biophysics. Leaving the USSR was no longer a problem but he lacked cash. So Perepilichnyy began trading in computers. Gorbachev had allowed private ventures for the first time. Perepilichnyy began selling computers to government organisations, as well as fax machines, which the Soviet Union had effectively prohibited.

In seven months, between mid-autumn 1989 and spring 1990, Perepilichnyy earned a couple of thousand dollars, and then bigger sums. 'His perspective on life changed. Originally he was a quiet student who had good grades. He discovered this intense drive for earning money,' Panchul said. Perepilichnyy bought himself a black Mercedes. He parked it several blocks from his faculty so as not to embarrass his badly off lecturers. He was now an intermediary in the new private economy.

Perepilichnyy's teachers thought him a capable student and invited him to do a PhD. He declined and in 1991 began trading on the country's first commodity exchanges. 'He became a private investor,' Panchul said. 'He started to move in circles frequented by all sorts of sharks.' Many of his new contacts were busy acquiring fortunes through dodgy methods. Perepilichnyy, however, worked openly. 'He didn't have a criminal mentality,' Panchul added. 'He had some feeling of decency, some rules. He just happened to be in a place where these new rules were not mature.'

By the mid-nineties, Perepilichnyy was a successful investment fund manger. The promising student who played cards and read sci-fi novels now looked after the money of some extremely well-connected Muscovites, who believed him to be a financial genius. They included Olga Stepanova, a top Moscow tax official, and her husband Vladlen. Panchul last spoke to Perepilichnyy in the early noughties. He was doing well and had acquired a flat in London. He was still dealing with 'strange people' and 'taking risks' but hadn't lost his 'moral standards', Panchul said.

In 2007, Stepanova, and others in a circle featuring interior ministry officials, suddenly acquired very large sums of money. Perepilichnyy sprinkled some of it through accounts he managed on their behalf in Cyprus and Switzerland.

From where had this windfall come?

In 2005, Bill Browder, a US-born financier, was unexpectedly deported from Russia. Browder was the CEO of Hermitage Capital, an asset management company and a major investor in Russia. Browder had been a fan of Putin's in the early years, seeing him as an ally in the fight against oligarchic malfeasance. Like many others, Browder found the new president inscrutable. He had failed to appreciate that Putin wasn't interested in cleaning up corruption. Rather his aim was to redistribute the state's resources among his KGB friends.

The Kremlin-approved attack on Browder left Hermitage vulnerable. In 2007, a group of officials, led by a convicted fraudster, Dmitry Klyuyev, seized three Hermitage firms. They claimed the firms had lost $1 billion and were therefore entitled to a tax refund from the state. On Christmas Eve, a $230 million transfer was secretly approved in a matter of hours – by Perepilichnyy's client Olga Stepanova, the head of Moscow tax office No. 28. The stolen funds were then laundered though different countries using shell companies.

The criminals made only one mistake: they underestimated Browder. Browder is driven, obsessional and unrelenting. I got to know him after my forced departure from Russia. His personal story – told in a page-turning memoir, *Red Notice* – is interesting, too. The grandson of Earl Browder, the head of the US Communist Party in the 1930s, Browder had rebelled against his brainy left-wing family and become a capitalist, venturing into Eastern Europe after the collapse of the Soviet bloc.

Stuck in London, he hired a team to investigate back in Russia. It included an idealistic young anti-corruption lawyer called Sergei Magnitsky. In 2008, Magnitsky found out where the stolen money had gone. He filed a complaint to Russian prosecutors. The same officials who had carried out the fraud, including an investigator at the interior ministry, Major Pavel Karpov, had Magnitsky arrested. He was tossed into a freezing cell and refused medical treatment.

Magnitsky suffered from pancreatitis and gallstones, and spent months in pain. The officials wouldn't allow his family to visit. This state-sanctioned torture was meant to make him withdraw his testimony. He didn't. Threats were sent to Hermitage in London; one of Browder's colleagues received a text, quoting from *The Godfather Part II*, which said: 'History has taught us that anybody can be killed.'

In Moscow, Magnitsky's condition grew critical. In November 2009, guards put him in an isolation cell. There, they beat him to death. He was thirty-seven, married, the father of two small boys, and a representative of Russia's decent middle class. He had believed that the law would protect him, that Russia had said farewell to its Soviet ghosts. It was a tragic misjudgement. At least three other people who testified against the fraud in Russia died in unclear circumstances.

Browder began a global campaign to bring Magnitsky's killers to justice. Since they occupied mid-ranking positions in the interior ministry and FSB there was no prospect of this happening inside Russia's own legal system.

Perepilichnyy, meanwhile, was facing big problems of his own. His job, it appears, had been to offer semi-legal financial services to a range of clients, including corrupt ones.

During the 2008–9 financial crash he lost much of his clients' funds. They accused him of robbing them and demanded he repay their market losses. One of them was said to be Dmitry Kovtun, Litvinenko's killler. Kovtun and Perepilichnyy may have had business together.

More probably, though, Perepilchnyy's enemies invoked Kovtun's name in order to frighten him.

Perepilchnyy fled Russia and moved with his family to Surrey. In July 2010, he sent an anonymous email to Hermitage under a false Spanish name, Alejandro Sanches. The email began:

Dear Sirs,

Let me, first of all, express deep respect for your basic civic stand concerning events connected with the Hermitage case.

I am ready to donate some information and documents concerning compensation received by the management of a tax inspectorate for the illegal return from the Russian Federation budget of more than 5 billion roubles.

Perepilchnyy signed off as 'Sergei'. He said he couldn't give his real name 'as my relatives live in Russia'.

His information was astonishing – details of an alleged money-laundering ring involving the Russian mafia and state. It included the identities of those who had pulled off the fraud, print-outs from the Stepanovs' secret bank account with Credit Suisse, and an explanation as to where the money had gone – on Range Rovers, Moscow real estate and tacky properties in Dubai.

One mansion bought by the Stepanovs was on Palm Jumeirah, the world's largest man-made island, reclaimed from Dubai's coast. The island forms the shape of a palm tree as viewed from the air: some residents lived on its 'trunk', others on 'fronds'. The Stepanovs' villa, number 48, was on Frond F – out of the way by Palm standards, and at the end of a sun-bleached and desolate cul de sac. There are few shops and amenities here. Barriers, cones and a Filipino security guard keep out the uninvited.

At first, Hermitage was suspicious of this unknown Russian. Jamison Firestone, a US lawyer and ally of Browder's who had hired Magnitsky and knew him well, sent emails back. There was no immediate answer. In August, however, 'Alejandro' gave further details. And offered to meet in London.

The rendezvous took place in the upscale surroundings of the Westbury in Mayfair. The five-star hotel is close to Grosvenor Street and the scene of Litvinenko's twin poisonings. Firestone was waiting in the Polo Bar. Security guards had taken up positions undercover; they had already waved a Geiger counter up and down. Perepilichnyy sauntered in – now a chunky, somewhat dowdy figure, wearing a tracksuit and no tie. He was distinctly underdressed for his posh surroundings and not quite the 'minigarch', or minor oligarch, they'd expected.

According to Jamison, Perepilichnyy began by saying in Russian: 'It's really terrible what happened to your colleague. I admire your work.'

Gradually it became clear that Perepilichnyy was genuine, and someone from the inside. Someone with a grudge. Stepanov had used his wife's tax connections to destroy Perepilichnyy's business empire – and now

Perepilichnyy was retaliating. 'This was a move in a war to get the heat off, to get them [the Stepanovs] to back down,' Jamison said. 'It was a business dispute between partners. Perepilichnyy wanted to rip the legs from under them.'

There were further meetings in the same bar in London, over green tea and biscuits. According to Ivan Cherkasov, a Russian lawyer working for Browder, who fled Russia, Perepilichnyy was uninterested in his surroundings. 'He was someone who existed in a world of maths and logic,' he said.

Perepilichnyy turned over more documents. They included statements showing payments of several million euros to Stepanov's private Credit Suisse bank account. The money came from a Cyprus-based company, Arivust Holdings, also belonging to Stepanov. One source, who met Perepilichnyy several times, said: 'He was a nice chap. He was bright. He seemed rational.'

Hermitage gave this material to the Swiss attorney general. Some sources say Perepilichnyy ignored advice from his brother-in-law in Moscow to drop his complaint. Swiss prosecutors then froze Stepanov's account, containing €8 million. Other 'investors' using the same dubious schemes also saw their funds seized.

Soon afterwards, the threats from Moscow began. In 2011–12 Perepilichnyy told his Hermitage contacts that his situation was looking dangerous. 'He tried to be cautious. He was a bit fatalistic,' the source – who doesn't want to be named – said. Perepilichnyy's name turned up on a hit list recovered from a group of Chechen assassins arrested in France. The gang had a pretty accurate dossier on Perepilichnyy's whereabouts in the UK, though some details were out of date.

More warnings followed. Perepilichnyy met in Geneva with someone who presented himself as an informal representative of Russia's interior ministry. The representative passed on a message: that Perepilichnyy was to make a public statement saying that the wire transfers to Stepanov's offshore accounts were completely legitimate. Failure to do so would result in the authorities in Moscow opening a money-laundering case against him.

In May 2012, Perepilichnyy held talks with Stepanov's lawyer, Andrei Pavlov. Pavlov was on his way back to Russia; the venue was a café on the upper floor of London Heathrow Airport terminal five. It's unclear what they discussed – though Pavlov claims that Perepilichnyy said he wanted a reconciliation with the Stepanovs and other unhappy former customers in Russia.

As for Stepanov himself, he denies wrongdoing. In a public letter in 2011, he said that he and Olga were divorced. He claims that the value of his designer mansion near Rublyovka – Moscow's most exclusive district – has been overstated. Of Perepilichnyy, he said: 'This man owes me a lot of money. As a matter of fact not only to me but to scores of other creditors. He cheated me by pocketing my money and assets.'

On 5 November 2012, Perepilichnyy held his last meeting with the team from Hermitage. 'He was casually dressed. The photos of him are accurate, but the final time I saw him he was looking a bit skinnier,' the source said. Like Litvinenko in Spain, Perepilichnyy had agreed to testify in a forthcoming trial in Switzerland into the $230 million fraud, where he would be the star prosecution witness.

Next, Perepilichnyy took the Eurostar to Paris. He spent three or four days there. Some sources suggest Ukrainian women were involved. Perepilichnyy appears to have worried about his security. He booked into three different hotels: the five-star George V, the Bristol, and a three-star guesthouse. He spent €1,200 in a Prada shop.

He returned by train to London. Back at home, his wife cooked him some sorrel soup. He told her he was feeling somewhat groggy. He decided to run this feeling off. And then he collapsed.

Detectives in Surrey were slow to grasp Perepilichnyy's story – his links with shadowy figures in Moscow, his name on a Russian death-list, the emissaries and warnings. Instead, they treated his death as routine. There was, after all, no proof that this was murder. Nor were there any obvious suspects. Their assumption, it appears, was that Perepilichnyy's death was due to cardiac arrest.

For those who knew FSB methods, however, the case looked deeply suspicious.

Before Litvinenko's death, it might have seemed improbable verging on incredible that Russian assassins might murder someone on the streets of London. After Litvinenko, these doubts disappeared. Such murders had happened and were happening. The question for police was: was this one of them?

To Browder, the Perepilichnyy case looked like Litvinenko II. A week after his death, Hermitage's lawyers wrote to the police detailing their concerns and asking for extensive toxicology tests to be carried out. The police didn't reply. Another week passed. In frustration, Browder leaked the story to the *Independent*, owned by Alexander Lebedev, the Russian businessman and former KGB intelligence officer who had worked in the 1980s at the Soviet embassy in London.

There were many possible lines of inquiry. Hermitage's lawyers urged the police to cooperate with the French authorities, and to obtain video surveillance in Paris and from Weybridge. Other avenues to examine included the movements of members of the Klyuyev group (the criminal gang headed by fraudster Dmitry Klyuyev), some of whom had travelled to the UK. There was Perepilichnyy's possible dispute with Kovtun. And the fact that Eastern European contract killers were still entering the UK with ease.

Seven months earlier, a Moldovan assassin had ambushed another Russian in Canary Wharf in east London. The assassin, Vitalie Proca, had fired six shots into German Gorbuntsov, a 44-year-old Russian banker, as he returned home to his flat in Byng Street. Proca was caught on CCTV, gun raised. Gorbuntsov had fled to Moldova and then the UK after falling out – like Perepilichnyy – with wealthy clients in Moscow. They allegedly included senior figures in Russian Railways and the Solntsevo mafia gang. Gorbuntsov was badly wounded but survived.

The Surrey police investigation into Perepilichnyy's death continued for some months. Toxicology tests conducted after twenty-two days drew a blank. Two post-mortems failed to uncover a cause of death. In 2013, detectives announced that there was no evidence of 'third-party involvement'. The case – tragic, but apparently not homicide – was passed on to Surrey's coroner. Browder was furious. 'I'm certain he was murdered. The police kicked it into the long grass. This is a travesty of justice,' he told me.

It wasn't until spring 2015 that Browder's suspicions were confirmed, and in quite spectacular fashion. Shortly before his death, Perepilichnyy insured his life for £3.5 million. He took out a flurry of policies. One, with Legal & General, worth £2 million, became active just eight days before he died. The insurer was reluctant to pay out. It asked a plant expert at the Royal Botanic Gardens in Kew, south-west London, Professor Monique Simmonds, to conduct her own tests.

Simmonds was a figure who might have sprung from the pages of Agatha Christie – a distinguished botanist in late middle age, thin, dressed in a severe black trouser suit and with short cropped hair. She had previously been involved in some extraordinary cases. In 2001, the limbless and headless body of a boy had been found floating in the river Thames. Forensic tests at Kew revealed traces of the toxic calabar bean in the lower intestine. The plant trail led to West Africa, where witch doctors use the bean to paralyse their victims. The police concluded the boy – aged five or six – had been ritually murdered.

Simmonds' latest findings were similarly sensational. They were revealed at a pre-inquest hearing in Woking. She had tested samples taken from the dead man against a range of deadly plants. Perepilichnyy had been poisoned. He was the victim of a twining climber found in scrubby mountain forests.

The poison came from one of five possible varieties of the lethal gelsemium plant. The plant contains gelsemine, a compound similar to strychnine. The plant is a weapon of choice among Chinese and Russian assassins. Simmonds discovered traces of an ion linked to gelsemium in Perepilichnyy's stomach. The most toxic variety is *Gelsemium elegans*. It grows only in Asia. The poison's last known victim was Long Liyuan, a Chinese billionaire who died in 2011 after eating cat meat stew believed to have been laced with *Gelsemium elegans*.

This was a dramatic development. The focus now was on Perepilichnyy's last meal. What was it and who was his dining companion? There were clear parallels with

Litvinenko – here, once again, was an apparent reprisal killing of someone with potent enemies in Moscow.

But there were differences, too. Perepilichnyy's widow Tatiana insisted her husband wasn't murdered. There was no direct evidence, she said. She accused Hermitage of peddling 'lazy stereotypes'. Not every Russian exile who dropped dead was the victim of foul play, she added.

The case went on, disputed and unresolved, into 2016. Surrey Police continued to insist Perepilichnyy's death was wholly ordinary. At the same time, however, it refused to release forty-two documents, on the grounds of national security. Three years on, this was a surprising move. It raised another possibility. Before his murder, had Perepilichnyy talked to Britain's spy agencies?

In March 2009, the US secretary of state and future presidential candidate Hillary Clinton presented her Russian counterpart Sergei Lavrov with a small green box tied with a ribbon. The venue was Geneva; the mood was warm; there were smiles and handshakes from the American and Russian delegations.

Lavrov opened the box. Inside it was a red button on a yellow background, and the word *peregruzka*. As Lavrov noted with some glee, the word '*peregruzka*' actually means 'over-charged'. The Obama administration had meant to write *perezagruzka* – the Russian noun for 'reset'.

The blooper was emblematic of how US know-how on Russia had degraded in the post-Cold War era, as Washington became distracted with international wars (Afghanistan, Iraq); grappled with the hydra-headed threat after 9/11 of radical Islamist terrorism; and assumed that Russia, its defeated Cold War adversary, was moving slowly towards liberal democracy. It wasn't. The US State Department still had Russian area specialists, of course. But it appeared that none of them could spell.

During the presidencies of George W. Bush, relations with Moscow sank. Putin supported the US-led war in Afghanistan but opposed Iraq. The Russian president's list of grievances against Washington grew. Briefly summarised, they included Nato expansion, the US's putative missile defence programme in Europe, and the pro-western and pro-reform revolutions in Georgia and Ukraine, which Putin claimed were an American-inspired plot.

Relations reached a nadir in August 2008, when Mikheil Saakashvili, Georgia's president and a US ally, tried to seize back the rebel province of South Ossetia using military force. Russia responded with a full-scale invasion. It was a brutal lesson in regional geo-politics. And a practical articulation of the Kremlin's new big power doctrine: that it had 'privileged interests' in its post-Soviet back and front yards.

The Obama administration's decision to 'reset' relations with Russia was pragmatic. The goal was not to turn Russia into a progressive law-based state – an unlikely prospect that could only be achieved by Russians themselves – but to secure Moscow's co-operation on key international challenges. These were Obama's first-term priorities. They included Iran's nuclear programme; Afghanistan; the common threat from Al Qaida; and – as the Arab Spring took hold – the disastrous war in Syria.

The White House's calculus was strategic, though there was an element of wishful thinking too. Between 2008 and 2012, Dmitry Medvedev – an ex-lawyer who grew up in the 1970s and was a fan of the British rock group Deep Purple – was Russia's titular president. Leaked US diplomatic cables show that the US was keen to treat the liberal-seeming Medvevev as a genuine interlocutor. In reality, it was the hawkish Putin who pulled the strings.

When Browder turned up in Washington it was unsurprising that the state department responded coolly to his plan to punish Magnitsky's killers. Browder was seeking to use an obscure law passed by President Bush in 2004 that allows the US to impose visa sanctions on corrupt foreign officials. He lobbied senators, journalists and anybody who would listen to him. His aim was to pass into law a Magnitsky act. The act would freeze the assets of those involved in his lawyer's death.

Browder had found Putin and co.'s Achilles heel. In Soviet times, the politburo lived quite a bit better than the average Soviet citizen. It had special shops and holidays on the Black Sea. In Putin's Russia, however, the difference was vast. Top bureaucrats, including the Klyuyev gang, were worth millions. They enjoyed international lifestyles. What was the point of stealing all that money if you could only spend it in Sochi, with its scruffy pebbly beach?

In December 2012, weeks after Perepilichnyy's death, Congress passed a landmark Magnitsky law. It blocked eighteen Russian officials from entering America. Most importantly, the law denied them access to US banking facilities.

The law drew an apoplectic, asymmetric response from Putin. He ended the adoption of Russian babies by American couples. And, in a twist that might have been written by Gogol, the Kremlin put Magnitsky on trial. That he was already dead was apparently not an obstacle. In summer 2013, a judge convicted him of tax evasion, announcing a surreal verdict to an empty barred cage.

Britain's David Cameron once took a tough stance on the Kremlin. In 2008, as Russian troops overran Georgia, Cameron flew to the capital Tbilisi to show solidarity with Saakashvili. At the time, Cameron was leader of the opposition Conservatives. It was a piece of opportunism that embarrassed the UK's then prime minister Gordon Brown. Cameron called for Russia's suspension from the G8 and offered a memorable line: 'Russian armies can't march into other countries while Russian shoppers carry on marching into Selfridges.'

After entering Downing Street in 2010, Cameron's attitude towards the Russian government softened. Brown had refused to meet with Putin following Litvinenko's murder. Cameron, by contrast, appeared keen to move on from the polonium episode. Britain still sought the extradition of Lugovoi and Kovtun, of course. But, Cameron indicated, these bilateral differences could be 'negotiated around' and shouldn't prevent cooperation in other areas, especially trade.

In foreign affairs there is always a balance to be struck between national self-interest and values. There is *Realpolitik* versus *Moralpolitik*, with foreign-policy realists pitted against liberals who believe in universal rights.

Under Cameron's Conservative-led coalition, the UK's foreign policy moved decisively towards the first camp. It showed new understanding towards regimes that had scant regard for human rights.

In theory, of course, London still believed in principles. The BBC's political comedy *Yes Minister* expressed the gap between political reality and lofty aspiration well. The much-loved series features Jim Hacker as the well-meaning but inept prime minister and his Machiavellian cabinet secretary Sir Humphrey Appleby.

One exchange springs to mind:

JIM HACKER: Humphrey, are you saying that Britain should not support law and justice?

SIR HUMPHREY APPLEBY: Of course we should, prime minister. We just shouldn't let it affect our foreign policy.

Twenty-first-century Britain was a post-imperial, post-industrial island of middling importance. Its role in the world was ... what exactly? Unlike the US, it was no longer a superpower, though its government still nurtured the fantasy that Britain punched above its weight on the world stage. American observers noted that the UK was becoming increasingly parochial, and in many international questions looked mostly irrelevant.

Cameron's foreign policy objective, meanwhile, was quite simple: to sell stuff to foreigners.

The large influx of Russians to Britain was good for business, the prime minister appears to have concluded.

Wealthy Russians buy property in London and the Home Counties, send their children to British private schools, and go shopping in Harrods (and Selfridges). Increasingly, Russians come to the UK to settle their legal disputes, commercial and matrimonial. All this is a boon to headmasters, divorce lawyers, estate agents and purveyors of sushi.

Domestic political calculations explained Britain's attempt at a US-style 'reset' with Moscow. Russian investment helped the UK economy. A strong economy in turn helped deliver the Conservatives' election victory in 2015, after their failure in 2010 to win an outright majority. There were ideological commonalities, too. The right wing of the Tory party is Eurosceptic and wants Britain to exit the EU. The Kremlin is keen to torpedo EU power; it prefers to negotiate with weaker sovereign states.

In 2011, Cameron flew to Moscow. He met Medvedev and Putin. Then in summer 2012 – after Putin became president for the third time – Cameron hosted him in Downing Street and at the London Olympics. It was Putin's first trip to the UK since 2005 and Litvinenko's radioactive murder. They watched the judo, Putin's favourite sport. The two leaders sat together, somewhat awkwardly, as contestants from Holland and the Czech Republic rolled around on a yellow mat.

The same month, guests attended a launch party in Kensington, west London, for a new organisation, the Conservative Friends of Russia. Some 250 guests gathered in the garden of the Russian ambassador, Alexander Yakovenko. They included Tory MPs, peers and Russian diplomats. The event featured a barbecue, drinks and a raffle, with prizes of vodka, champagne and a biography of Putin. The group was apparently the brainchild of a PR consultant, Richard Royal; its stated goal to boost UK–Russian dialogue.

Behind the scenes, the Russian embassy itself was pulling the strings on this curious new body. The diplomat in charge, Sergei Nalobin, has close links with Russian intelligence. His father, Nikolai Nalobin, was a KGB general. According to Marina Litvinenko, Nikolai Nalobin was Litvinenko's former boss in the FSB. Nalobin Jnr's brother worked as an FSB agent. Nalobin's CV includes a stint in the ministry of foreign affairs. He described himself on his Twitter feed as a 'brutal agent of the Putin dictatorship :)'.

Leaked emails from Nalobin suggest Moscow's goals went beyond mere cultural understanding. The Kremlin was keen to rebuild ties with Britain post-Litvinenko and to mute criticism of Russia's human-rights record. It also wanted to deepen an alliance with the Conservatives, who sit with Putin's ruling United Russia party in the Council of Europe. Most of all, the Russian government was desperate to stop top officials from being denied entry to the UK, as part of a US-style 'Magnitsky list'.

Critics pointed out that the timing of the organisation's launch was dreadful. Days earlier, three members of the feminist collective Pussy Riot were jailed following an anti-Putin punk protest in Moscow's Christ the Saviour cathedral. The former Labour Europe minister Denis MacShane noted: 'Friendship groups with Russia used to be a speciality of the left in the days of communism. Now we have Putinism, it is the Tory party that is creating a pro-Russian group of fellow travellers. It reflects the shambolic incoherence of Tory networking.'

Sir Malcolm Rifkind, the group's honorary president, took a different view, arguing that there was nothing wrong with engagement. 'It would be silly to boycott everything Russian. Even during the Cold War, as a British foreign office minister, I had lunch with the Soviet ambassador in his residence. The worst thing is to have no contact.' Three months later, however, Rifkind quit the group after its apparent links with Russian spies were uncovered by my exposé in the *Guardian*. The organisation collapsed, to be rebranded in 2013 as the Westminster Russia Forum.

Russia's soft-power initiatives, which included hiring lobbyists in Washington, London and Brussels, may have seemed clumsy. In fact, they showed strategic ambition. From at least 2009, the Kremlin actively cultivated ties with the far right in eastern Europe. It established links with Hungary's Jobbik, Slovakia's People's Party and Bulgaria's nationalist, anti-EU Attack movement. The Kremlin wooed the far right in Western Europe too, loaning €9.4 million via a Moscow bank to France's Front National.

It also attracted support from Europe's far left. In Soviet times, the KGB used 'active measures' to sponsor front organisations in the west, including pro-Moscow communist parties. Radical left-wing coalitions such as Greece's Syriza expressed solidarity with Moscow. So did

Jeremy Corbyn, a backbencher and veteran anti-impe-
rialist who in 2015 would go on to become leader of
the opposition Labour Party. (The Russian embassy in
London greeted the election of the anti-Nato Corbyn
with an ecstatic press release.)

The Kremlin didn't invent the European far right or
British Euroscepticism or Corbyn. But in an analogous
way Moscow was lending these parties and individuals
support, political and sometimes financial. Moscow's
goal was to promote its economic and political interests
– and in particular to ensure that the EU remains heavily
dependent on Russian gas. The tactic was clever: to
exploit popular dissent against the EU, fuelled by immigration and austerity.

Marina Litvinenko had always believed in British justice.
The men who murdered her husband were beyond the
reach of UK law enforcement and safely in Russia. But
surely the legal system in London would afford her some
kind of closure – a full, fair and transparent explanation
of how her husband died and who might have killed him?
It had been a long wait. Six years on, her private tragedy
had become a public quest for some answers.

The most obvious vehicle for inquiry was an inquest.
The inquest had been delayed in the hope that Moscow
might give up Lugovoi and Kovtun. It was now evident
there was no realistic prospect of a criminal trial. In
autumn 2011, Marina Litvinenko moved to have the
inquest – stalled since 2006 – reopened. In 2012, Sir
Robert Owen, a High Court judge acting as assistant

deputy coroner, convened a series of pre-inquest hearings in London. He began by apologising for the delay: 'It's manifestly in the interests of his widow Marina and his son, Anatoly ... and in the wider public interest that [this] is brought to a conclusion.'

Owen promised an 'open and fearless' investigation. He said that he would examine the theory that 'Russian state agents' were behind the murder. He identified various 'interested parties' including Marina and Anatoly Litvinenko; the two alleged Russian killers; the UK Home Office; and the investigative committee of the Russian Federation. They would be given Scotland Yard's previously restricted forensic report on the case, and much other evidence.

There was discussion of the inquest's scope. Two issues were central. One was the question of Kremlin culpability. There was, Owen said, a '*prima facie*' case of the Russian state's involvement. The other was whether the British government could have prevented Litvinenko's killing.

All of this seemed reasonable. However, by 2013, the hearings had turned into a tug of war. On one side was Marina Litvinenko and her counsel, Ben Emmerson QC. On the other a government apparently unwilling to annoy Putin and fearful that British investors in Russia might suffer reprisals. The foreign secretary William Hague submitted something called a public interest immunity or PII certificate. This meant that the government's classified files on Litvinenko wouldn't be made public. Crucially, it meant that the inquest wouldn't be able to consider whether the Russian state had murdered Litvinenko.

Hague justified this drastic move on the grounds that openness would cause 'serious harm to national security and/or international relations'. The reasoning was bizarre. As the *Observer* columnist Nick Cohen pointed out, which one was it? The submission was at odds with several centuries of jurisprudence and principles laid down by the late Law Lord Thomas Bingham.

Emmerson accused Cameron and Hague of cover-up. He added that they were 'dancing to the Russian tarantella' – an image that didn't improve the more you thought about it – with Owen 'steamrollered by two states acting in collaboration with each other'. I attended the High Court hearing. Whenever the colourful Emmerson spoke, the journalists picked up their pens. The lawyer said: 'The British government, like the Russian government, is conspiring to get the inquest closed down in exchange for substantial trade interests which we know Mr Cameron is pursuing.'

The accusation was well grounded. It was left to Goldfarb to summarise what was really going on. He told me in the corridor: 'HMG is worried about fallout with Putin; MI6 is worried about its agent being killed by polonium; the Russians are worried about being caught red-handed; Putin is concerned about being called a mafia boss.'

The same month Cameron flew to Sochi for talks with Putin. It was a friendly encounter; the pair discussed Syria; there was no mention by the British of the awkward subject of human rights. Putin must have been pleased.

In a concession, Cameron agreed that British intelligence would resume cooperation with the FSB for the first time since Litvinenko's death. It would work with its Russian counterpart to ensure the security of the Sochi Winter Olympics in 2014.

Cameron's blossoming friendship with Putin left the coroner in an invidious position. Reluctantly, he upheld in part the government's request to keep secret material out of court. Without MI6's files, the inquest would be a meaningless exercise. It would be unable to examine the question of Russian state guilt. In a further act of meanness, justice secretary Chris Grayling was refusing to pay Marina Litvinenko's legal costs.

Owen came up with a solution. He wrote to home secretary Theresa May requesting a public inquiry. 'I have formed the firm view that a public inquiry is necessary if Mr Litvinenko's death is to be properly investigated,' he told her. Owen offered himself as chairman.

The advantage of an inquiry, he argued, was that the chairman could consider the secret material in closed hearings, an option not available to an inquest. This was a pragmatic way forward which balanced the government's security concerns with the need for open justice.

May, however, was having none of this. In a reply in June 2013, she rejected Owen's request. She offered six reasons for her refusal, including public expense. It was the sixth, however, which stuck out:

'It is true that international relations have been a factor in the Government's decision-making. An inquest managed and run by an independent coroner is more readily explainable to some of our foreign partners, and the integrity of the process more readily grasped, than an inquiry established by the government ... which has the power to see government material, potentially relevant to their interests, in secret.'

May's reasoning was legally dubious. That autumn, Marina Litvinenko filed a judicial review claim, asking the High Court to re-examine the government's decision. In February 2014, three High Court judges ruled unanimously in her favour. They described May's refusal as 'irrational' and 'legally erroneous'. They asked her to reconsider.

In its keenness to put trade above principle, the Conservative-led government had forgotten what the case was about.

Marina Litvinenko observed: 'I have never been able to see why the British government should want to protect the people in the Kremlin who ordered my husband's murder. This was the murder of a British citizen on the streets of London using radioactive poison. You would have thought that the government would want to get the bottom of who was behind it.'

The ball was back in May's court. Marina said: 'As one woman to another, I ask her to consider how she would feel in my position. If her husband had been murdered in this horrible way, wouldn't she want to get to the truth?'

In 2010, I had flown from Moscow to Italy. My destination was the seaside town of Senigallia on the Adriatic coast. Two years previously Walter Litvinenko and his wife

Lyuba had left Russia. After his son's death, the harassment Walter had already suffered from the authorities
continued. He joined his younger son Maxim – Litvinenko's half-brother – in Italy. Other family members
followed. They included Litvinenko's half-sister Tatiana,
her husband and their two kids.

By the time I caught up with them, the family were in
poor shape. They had opened a restaurant in the tourist
resort of Rimini. Maxim had been in Italy for nine years
and was a professional chef. The local police accused
them of operating illegally; during a late-night raid a
cop pushed Tatiana over so she banged her head on the
floor. The restaurant, La Terrazza, went bust. They were
forced to move into a cheaper flat down the coast.

Walter blamed their misfortunes in exile on Silvio
Berlusconi, Italy's prime minister, whose close friendship
with Putin was well known. The family's claim for asylum
was going nowhere. 'We have fallen victim to a political
game,' he told me. Walter blamed Putin for Alexander's
death, reasoning to me that – as in Stalin's times – only
Putin could have authorised the murder. 'I know it was
Putin who killed him. He's a sick person,' Walter said.

Tatiana, however, refused to impugn Russia's president. She bristled at the mention of Berezovsky. The
oligarch had initially supported the Litvinenkos in exile,
but had eventually stopped payments; his money had
run out. Tatiana and her husband had good careers
with the FSB in Nalchik, Litivnenko's home town; the
international scandal surrounding her brother had cost
them everything. 'He's clearly not interested in us,' she

said, of Berezovsky. 'I wouldn't stop to take money from him.'

The Litvinenkos – all eight of them, including two young children and Maxim's wife – were living in a small three-bedroom flat. They were broke. A local church was donating bread and apples; they ate pancakes and prawns salvaged from the freezer of their former restaurant. Walter and his wife were both over seventy. It was clearly too late for them to start a new life. On the wall was a map of Russia and several Orthodox icons; I spotted an Italian–Russian dictionary on a bookshelf.

Walter and I went for a walk outside. He put on the same flat cap he'd worn to his son's drizzly funeral at Highgate Cemetery in London back in December 2006. Since then he had urged the US congress to support a resolution that blamed the Russian government for Litvinenko's death. A public role didn't suit him. Walter was, it struck me, a broken figure – and a pitiful one. He was afraid. 'In Nalchik I didn't fear because I knew everybody's faces. Here it is different. At any moment a person could come up to you and that would be the end.'

In signed statements, Walter listed persecution in various forms by the Russian state. The police had beaten him up, he wrote, in an attempt to force him to incriminate his son. For five years he'd held one person responsible for these woes: Putin. In May 2011, Tatiana called me with further bad news. Lyuba had died. The Italian government was still refusing basic income support. Walter had moved out, into a one-bedroom flat.

He was too poor to pay the electricity, so would sit on his own in the dark.

Then, in 2012, something very odd happened. Walter gave a tearful interview from Italy to Russian state TV. He told the Russian public: 'Vladimir Vladimirovich, if you are watching this programme please forgive me for all the slander that I said and wrote about you.' Walter said that he had come to understand that his son was a traitor. He wanted to go back home to Russia.

Walter ascribed his radical change of heart to encounters with an Orthodox priest from Rimini. In an affidavit, sworn in September 2012 before Russian officials, he said he now believed Lugovoi was innocent, and that polonium had been 'skillfully placed' to incriminate him. The real murderer, he suggested, was Alex Goldfarb.

It wasn't difficult to piece together what lay behind Walter's stagey recantation. The death of his second wife had devastated him; he'd been very attached to her; now, in the final years of his life, he felt lonely and overwhelmingly homesick. Moreover, Walter wanted to help his surviving son Maxim. After Walter's TV confession, the family's business affairs were said to have suddenly improved.

Astonishingly, Walter said he wanted to contact Lugovoi in Russia. Goldfarb likened the encounter – between a father and his son's unrepentant killer – to a scene from Homer's *Iliad*. 'It has a proportion of drama akin to the Trojan War, with Priam and Achilles,' Goldfarb said.

Priam was king of Troy; his son Paris caused the Trojan War by abducting Helen from the Greeks. The

Greeks fought a war to get her back. Their best warrior Achilles kills another of Priam's sons, Hector. Achilles refuses to give back the body and so Priam goes to the Greek camp to plead with him for his dead son's return. He invokes memories of Achilles' own father and says: 'I kiss the hand of the man who killed my son.'

In Goldfarb's analogy, Walter is the ageing Priam, seeking out his son's killer, Achilles/Lugovoi, to make peace with him in return for personal favours. Marina Litvinenko said her father-in-law surprised and disappointed her. Contact between them stopped. 'I was very sad,' she said.

11

A Small Victorious War

Donbas, eastern Ukraine, Spring 2014

'We've come here to help'
RUSSIAN SOLDIER, SLAVYANSK, APRIL 2014

It was once the government building in Donetsk. But in spring 2014 the city's administrative HQ resembled a crazy Soviet theme park. Outside were barricades: a pile of tyres, razor wire and wooden crates. Stuck to them were banners with anti-western slogans. There were caricatures of Barack Obama. In one, Obama was dressed as Hitler, with a pencil moustache. In another, the US president was pictured next to Bonaparte and the Führer, and the words: 'They all thought their nations were superior.' In a third, Obama was a monkey.

Further inside, past a serpentine wall of debris, pro-Russian activist Vitaly Akulov stood under a Stalin flag. The Soviet leader had a Kalashnikov. He looked like a matinée idol. Wasn't Stalin responsible for the deaths of millions of Soviet citizens? 'Without a tough tsar who uses harsh methods you can't build an imperium,' Akulov replied. Other banners read: 'Fuck EU and USA', 'Donbas with Russia' and 'Russians should be together'.

That April, pro-Kremlin separatists seized the regional administration building in Donetsk, a city of one million people in eastern Ukraine. The activists hijacked a string of other buildings across the Donbas, Ukraine's traditional industrial heartland. They took over town halls and police stations. And proclaimed two new political entities: the Donetsk and Luhansk 'People's Republics'. The city of Luhansk – in the next-door region or *oblast*, with a population of 445,000 – was 20 miles (35 km) from the Russian border.

The rebels' Donetsk HQ was an improvised youth hostel and centre for revolutionary operations. The eleven-storey block overlooked Pushkin Boulevard. Inside, I found a group of teenagers in balaclavas, some just fifteen or sixteen, and bearded, newly important, middle-aged men in military jackets. The Donetsk People's Republic – or DNR – had taken over the top floor. To reach it you had to walk up a lot of stairs; the lifts didn't work. Its leader, or 'people's governor', was Denis Pushilin, a neatly dressed local businessman apparently picked by Moscow for the role.

The city police and security services had made little effort to stop this takeover. Indeed, they appeared to sympathise with it. A police car was parked outside; officers chatted happily to masked separatists. The separatists had commandeered another building opposite Donetsk's art gallery. (It housed a portrait by Leonid Pasternak, the father of Boris, author of *Doctor Zhivago*, alongside nineteenth-century works by the 'Wanderers', my favourite Russian artistic movement.)

Forty miles (65 km) up the road north of Donetsk were signs that Ukraine's sovereignty was fast disappearing. A pro-Russian militia unit had taken over the town of Slavyansk. They were equipped with Kalashnikovs – military-issue AK-74s – commando knives, flak jackets and walkie-talkies. They arrived in a green military truck. It bore no insignia. Who exactly were they? 'We're Cossacks,' one of the group explained, as he and his comrades – one in a traditional woolly Cossack hat – posed for photos outside Slavyansk's town hall. The commander declined to give his name.

Instead he offered me a quick history lesson, stretching back a thousand years, to when Slavic tribes banded together to form Kievan Rus – the dynasty that eventually flourished into modern-day Ukraine and its big neighbour Russia. 'We don't want Ukraine. Ukraine doesn't exist for us. There are no people called Ukrainians,' he declared. 'There are just Slav people who used to be in Kievan Rus, before Jews like Trotsky divided us. We should all be together again.'

The man – a middle-aged commando with a bushy beard – said he had come to Slavyansk 'to help'. He declined to say where he was from. 'It doesn't matter where we are from.' He didn't intend to kill anybody, he said. Producing a long knife, he said: 'I can't kill my brother Slavs.' The mysterious Cossacks had been visiting Crimea, where they had 'helped' with the peninsula's annexation. They disliked Jews but were now fighting 'fascism'.

Ukraine's new defence minister, Arsen Avakov, set a deadline for these enigmatic militia groups to give up their weapons. It came and went. On the road between Donetsk and Slavyansk, Ukraine's elusive army was nowhere to be seen. Poplars and colourful apricot trees with white blossom lined the highway; the route passed crumbling collective farms and old ladies selling local produce, including jars of birch juice and saplings.

Pro-Russian groups set up roadblocks heaped with black tyres. Masked youths, mostly armed with sticks, stopped and checked cars. Closer to Slavyansk the barricades got bigger. The route and main checkpoint led over a bridge. Halfway across was an extraordinary sight: a group of women, mostly elderly, stood in a line holding gold-framed icons, praying and bowing.

It was hard to tell whether the Cossacks were a serious military force or a sort of colourful grenade-wielding theatre troupe, made for Russian TV propaganda. The central government in Kiev responded by dispatching a convoy of six armoured personnel carriers (APCs). It turned up in Kramatorsk, 10 miles (16 km) south of Slavyansk. Other Ukrainian soldiers were holed up in a nearby aerodrome.

A crowd surrounded the column, then armed men in fatigues. Without firing a shot, they persuaded the terrified Ukrainian servicemen to yield their vehicles. The gunmen sat on top of them. Someone raised a Russian tricolour. Around 200 people cheered and took photos. The men drove off. The column rattled past Kramatorsk's train station and turned right over a steep dusty bridge, belching clouds of diesel smoke.

From close up, it was clear that these rebels were different from the amateur teenage volunteers camping out in Donetsk. They were professionals. They had

Kalashnikovs, flak jackets, ammunition. One even carried a green tube-shaped grenade-launcher. Where had they come from? Some hid their faces under black balaclavas. Others waved and smiled. All wore orange and black St George's ribbons – the symbol of the Soviet victory in the Second World War over Hitler and fascism.

The column disappeared. It was easy to follow. I got into my vehicle and pursued a line of fresh white tread tracks left in the tarmac. The column drove serenely into Slavyansk, past its checkpoints, and parked round the back of the occupied city hall, next to the White Nights café. Locals seemed mystified. 'I heard the sound of tanks approaching. I thought Ukrainian troops had arrived,' Vladimir Ivanovich said. So who were the soldiers in masks? 'I don't know,' he told me.

The mysterious armed men stood around in a small municipal park. It was sunny, a perfect spring morning. The captured APCs became the town's newest, most unexpected tourist attraction. Teenage girls posed with the masked gunmen. Small children lined up for photos as well. The atmosphere was calm, one of military order. The town hall had been meticulously sandbagged. Sniper points had sprung up on the roof.

I asked one of the masked men where his unit had come from.

He said: 'Crimea.'

Crimea was Ukraine's Black Sea peninsula, now under new Russian ownership. Vladimir Putin had annexed it the previous month. It had already been home to Russia's Black Sea fleet and to thousands of Russian military personnel. And it was several hundreds of miles away. It appeared the gunman and his unit had managed to infiltrate across the Russian–Ukrainian border. Now they were in Slavyansk.

How were things back in Crimea?

'*Zamechatelno*,' he replied in Russian – terrific, splendid. 'The old ladies are happy. Because of Russia their pensions have doubled.'

Where was he from originally? Ukraine? Somewhere else?

'I'm from Russia,' the soldier said.

Days later, the kidnappings and murders started. Those taken hostage included a group of international observers from the Organisation for Security and Cooperation in Europe; journalists, Ukrainian and western; and others suspected of pro-Kiev views. If Russia was a mafia state, the DNR, it appeared, was a mafia statelet.

A local councillor, Vladimir Rybak, confronted DNR supporters who had taken over the town hall in neighbouring Gorlovka. As he left the square, four men in masks and military fatigues grabbed him and bundled him into a Kia car. Three days later, his battered body was found in Slavyansk next to a river. He'd been tortured. There were stab marks on his stomach and bruising on his chest. His kidnappers had tied a sandbag to his body. While he was unconscious they drowned him.

The conflict that gripped Ukraine in 2014 wasn't, as Moscow would claim, a civil war. It was, in reality, a Frankenstein-like conflict, created by the Russian government artificially and given life by the brute external shock of military force and invasion.

Many of the themes that featured in Litvinenko's murder were here again, played out on a bigger and more terrible canvas. There was the use of violent methods to achieve political goals. As in his previous war in Chechnya, Russia's president seemed entirely indifferent to the cost in human lives. This was true both of Ukrainian civilians who were the war's main victims, and of Putin's own soldiers, whose deaths in conflict he refused to acknowledge.

The Kremlin had lied about Litvinenko's assassination; now it was lying about its role in a major war in Europe. The Russian military supplied the hardware used by the rebels: tanks, armoured vehicles, artillery pieces. Russian soldiers – sometimes repackaged as 'volunteers' – did much of the fighting. When it appeared the rebels were on the brink of defeat, Moscow used its regular units to crush Ukrainian forces.

Without Russia there wouldn't have been a war in 2014. There would undoubtedly have been tension between the central government in Kiev and its predominantly Russian eastern regions – a political dispute about autonomy, devolved powers, and the status of the Russian language. But Ukraine wouldn't have fallen apart. Fewer people would have died.

Months earlier, a pro-western revolution had taken place in the capital Kiev. It began as a spontaneous grass-roots movement. It sought to employ democratic methods and peaceful protest. It looked like other global uprisings in New York or Paris or London. There were tent encampments in the centre of Kiev, rallies, speeches and flags. It only turned violent following a brutal government clampdown.

The counter-revolution that took place in eastern Ukraine soon afterwards was different. For sure, it enjoyed some popular support. But this was in essence a top-down army and intelligence operation, coordinated from next door by Russia. It soon morphed into a full-scale covert Russian invasion. The first revolution happened by accident; its antithesis was the result of a carefully curated plan that might have come – and probably did come – from a KGB textbook.

In November 2013, a well-known Kiev journalist, Mustafa Nayem, posted a question on Facebook. Earlier that day, Ukraine's president Viktor Yanukovych had announced he was dumping his country's preparations to sign an association agreement with the European Union. The agreement had been long awaited. Instead, Yanukovych said he was turning to Russia. He said Moscow had offered Kiev a $15 billion loan.

Nayem – an investigative reporter born in Afghanistan – wrote on his Facebook page: was anyone planning to go to the Maidan? The Maidan is downtown Kiev's central square and the scene of Ukraine's 2004 Orange Revolution. 'In one hour my post had more than 1,000 "likes",' Nayem said. 'That night 400 people showed up. They stayed until 6 a.m. Most of them were my friends from Facebook. It was the so-called creative class,' he told me.

The demonstrators understood what Yanukovych's decision meant: that the president had abandoned the idea of closer integration with the west. Instead, Ukraine would remain part of Russian political and economic space – with key decisions over the country's future and foreign policy taken, in effect, by the Kremlin. Yanukovych would be Putin's provincial viceroy. The loan was a bribe.

For the opposition, this vision of Ukraine's future was unappealing. It came on top of four years of misrule, during which the president, his family and cronies had robbed the state. Corruption was nothing new in Ukraine; the country of 46 million had always had lousy leadership.

But after winning elections in 2010, Yanukovych divided the nation's assets among his immediate relatives. He built himself a palace on the outskirts of Kiev, Mezhyhirya, complete with a helipad, golf course, pirate-ship restaurant and a zoo. Sadly, his kangaroos failed to survive the Ukrainian winter.

Yanukovych also dismantled the democratic reforms carried out post-2004. He jailed his chief political rival Yulia Tymoshenko, whose chaotic term as prime minister contributed to Ukraine's economic and governance mess. Yanukovych suborned parliament and the courts. Political repression grew. He pursued a policy of Russification, which alienated many in the west of the country and fuelled the growth of radical Ukrainian nationalism.

Nayem's Maidan protest went through several iterations. For weeks it was peaceful. Then, the government used brutal force. This was counter-productive: the demonstrators grew. By February 2014, the mood in Kiev was angry and febrile. Prominent anti-government activists were disappearing; some turned up dead; others alive but showing signs of torture. *Titushki* – paid government thugs – roamed the streets, beating and killing. Crowds of protesters built barricades. The riot police fired teargas.

As the analyst Andrew Wilson put it, the uprising was a curious concoction of a revolution. It was the anti-Soviet rebellion that failed to happen when Ukraine got independence from the Soviet Union in 1991; a lot of Lenin statues were pulled down. It was also an Occupy-style protest and a Cossack rebellion. Much of it was strikingly retro. Protesters donned homemade shields and helmets. They hurled cobblestones and Molotov cocktails. There was a medieval-style catapult.

In the last hours of the regime, government snipers killed dozens. Video footage shows them firing on unarmed protesters trying to advance across open ground. Eleven police died too. Yanukovych was at his palace in the outskirts of Kiev. He was in no physical danger but chose to escape. He took $32 billion with him (having looted an estimated $100 billion in four years), leaving by helicopter and fleeing to Russia. Other members of his government ran away too, stuffing money and jewels in their hand luggage, like comedy gangsters.

Over the coming weeks and months, Putin would describe the uprising in Ukraine as a 'fascist coup'. According to the Kremlin, dark right-wing forces seized power in Kiev, with the support of the US and European governments. In turn, Putin said, Moscow was forced to 'protect' Ukraine's ethnic Russian minority from nationalist, 'neo-Nazi' attack.

As it turned out, the real coup took place not in Kiev but in Crimea. A week after Yanukovych's exit, masked gunmen seized the regional parliament building in Simferopol, Crimea's regional capital. Some of the gunmen were the same Berkut snipers responsible for shooting dead protesters on the streets of Kiev, now fleeing arrest. Others were Russian special forces. A vote of deputies took place while men with Kalashnikovs guarded the entrance. Sergey Aksyonov, a pro-Russian politician whose party won a paltry 4 per cent of the vote in 2010, became Crimea's PM.

Meanwhile, Russian troops seized key installations. They encircled garrisons of Ukrainian soldiers, leaving them little choice but to surrender. Putin initially denied that these mysterious armed individuals – nicknamed 'polite little green men' – were undercover Russian forces. He later admitted that he'd been lying to the international community all along. A hastily arranged 'referendum' confirmed Crimea's secession from Ukraine. In March, Putin annexed the territory.

The immediate big losers were Crimea's Tartars. The Tartars – whose claim to the peninsula long pre-dates Russia's – snubbed the referendum and supported Kiev. Russia's state media promptly cast them as pro-Ukrainian fifth columnists. The Kremlin banned the Tartar leader Mustafa Dzhemilev from Crimean territory; young Tartars began disappearing and turning up dead. It was depressing and familiar stuff: the modern persecution of an ethnic group deported by Stalin.

The threat to Crimea from 'neo-Nazis' was a Kremlin fiction, a rationale for a Crimea invasion plan cooked up long before. The far right did play a role in the Kiev uprising – but a minor one. The movement against Yanukovych was broad-based. It involved all sections of society. There were nationalists and liberals, socialists and libertarians, atheists and believers. There were workers from the provinces, as well as IT geeks from Kiev more at home with MacBooks than Molotovs.

The protesters who died were a diverse bunch. The first was an ethnic Armenian; another Russian. One was Joseph Schilling, a 61-year-old builder from western Ukraine, who was shot in the head by a sniper while standing beneath the neoclassical October Palace. Schilling was one of 102 civilians who perished. He was Jewish. The main synagogue in Kiev is a few hundred metres from the Maidan. It was untouched. Ukraine's chief rabbi, Moshe Reuven Azman, told me there was no evidence of an anti-Semitic backlash.

In the days after the revolution, the far right camped out at the bottom of the Maidan in the four-star Hotel Dnipro. This was the headquarters of Pravy Sektor. Pravy Sektor – 'Right Sector' – was an ultra-nationalist organisation. Its deputy leader, Andriy Tarasenko, refused to talk in Russian – universally understood in Ukraine. Speaking in Ukrainian, which I struggled to understand, he said his party didn't want to be involved in post-revolutionary parliamentary politics.

Was he a fascist? 'Putin is the fascist. He's the occupier,' he replied.

I arrived in Kiev as Russian troops swarmed over Crimea. I took a taxi out to the city's high-rise suburbs to meet Olexiy Haran, a professor of politics and a member of the Maidan's organising committee. Haran looked exhausted and strung out. He was a prominent opponent of the Yanukovych regime. It had been a scary few months. The professor took a hammer with him to protests on the Maidan, as well as an orange helmet and a gas mask.

A group of academics, including Haran, had signed a letter complaining of a 'dangerous tendency' to distort what happened during the revolution. Reports exaggerating the role of ultra-nationalist actors ended up serving 'Russian imperialism', they said. Haran expressed frustration that the Kremlin's 'fascist' trope had taken root in some western minds. 'I've had liberal Harvard professors asking me about this. We are talking traditional Russian propaganda,' he told me.

The fast-moving events of the previous three months had been about 'national liberation', he argued – a movement against corruption and in favour of decency and the rule of law. Those who took part formed a confusing mosaic. They had different backgrounds and motivations. The protesters turned violent only in response to increasing police ferocity and the radicalisation of Yanukovych's regime, the professor said.

In May 2014, Petro Poroshenko, a self-made businessman who owned a chocolate factory in Russia, won

Ukraine's presidential election. Poroshenko was an early Maidan supporter who stood on the barricades. Intelligent, decent, and with an increasingly haunted appearance in office, Poroshenko was probably the best candidate for the job. Pravy Sektor, meanwhile, failed to emerge as a serious political force. Its leader Dmytro Yarosh got 0.7 per cent of the vote.

There was a better critique of Ukraine's new pro-western leaders: that they came from the same political class that had failed Ukraine before. The oligarchs, the country's shadow rulers, still controlled huge chunks of the economy and its industrial assets. Meanwhile, the Russian-speaking east of the country – Yanukovych's heart-land – was under-represented. His former ruling Party of Regions disavowed its leader and went into opposition.

The mood in eastern Ukraine after the events on the Maidan was, broadly speaking, hostile to Kiev. As one protester told me: Yanukovych may have been a crook, but he was *our* crook. There was overwhelming support for greater autonomy. There was also backing for Russian to be given the status of an official state language. However, educated Ukrainians in Donetsk welcomed Yanukovych's demise. Opinion polls taken before the president's flight indicated that the separatists were a minority. Some 26 per cent in the east supported union with Russia.

In Donetsk's main square – its statue of Lenin a stroll away from a branch of McDonald's – the commu-nists held regular anti-Kiev rallies. Most communist supporters were pensioners. There were further pro-Russian demonstrations in the city's main boulevard. They ended in front of the now-occupied administration building, its balcony adorned with Russian and Donbas flags. A sound system pumped out a string of schmaltzy Russian disco numbers.

Those who took to the streets expressed frustration – at the new government in Kiev, which they believed to be illegal, and at the failures of the Ukrainian state since 1991. Most expressed nostalgia for the Soviet Union. Many were unemployed or in low-paid jobs, I discovered. There was admiration for Russia, which, judging from the shiny version presented by Russian state media, looked like a prosperous and well-run state. Several insisted that those who took part in the Maidan were drug addicts or CIA agents, a claim made repeatedly by Yanukovych's TV channels.

Still, this didn't quite feel like a revolution. The crowds outside the occupied Donetsk HQ were often sparse. There were counter-rallies by pro-Ukrainian groups waving blue and yellow flags. The city's football team, Shakhtar Donetsk, played in a stadium built for the Euro 2012 championship by the oligarch Rinat Akhmetov, a close ally of Yanukovych's. Shakhtar's hardcore supporters – ultras – opposed Russia. During the last match of the season several hundred of them jumped up and down in Ukrainian colours and sang: 'Putin is a prick.'

By April, however, outside forces were coordinating what Moscow dubbed 'the Russian spring'.

Previously, separatism had attracted little electoral support here. Now, it got a pseudo-historical makeover. Putin made reference to Novorossiya – or New Russia – a 'country' encompassing Ukraine's eight Russian-speaking regions or *oblasts*, stretching in a southern and eastern arc as far as Odessa and the breakaway Moldovan territory of Transnistria. Novorossiya was a made-up entity. Nevertheless, the flag of 'Novorossiya' soon hung from rebel buildings.

The new government's control over events was slipping away. I watched as a crowd of 300 pro-Russian activists marched through Donetsk, ripping down Ukrainian flags. They seized the city's TV station, a neo-classical Stalinist building in the east of the city. Masked youths armed with baseball bats ran up the DNR flag from the roof; three men in balaclavas and armed with Kalashnikovs supervised.

The station's director, Oleg Dzholos, emerged from the building, shaken. He said the separatists had brought with them a technician from Moscow. The technician switched off Ukrainian broadcasts and replaced them with Rossiya 24. The Russian state channel frequently denounces Ukraine's leaders as 'fascists' and runs montages of them with the Nazis. The capture of the TV tower was part of an unfolding plan: to shut out information critical of Moscow and to replace it with Kremlin propaganda.

The suspicion was that the Kremlin – and in particular its main military intelligence directorate, the GRU – was choreographing the takeover of eastern Ukraine. It was making use of three groups: veterans with military experience of the Soviet war in Afghanistan; members of sports clubs; and local mafia networks. Pro-Ukrainian activists said that Russia had recruited numerous agents inside the local police and security forces.

The DNR's new 'defence minister' was Igor Strelkov, a Russian citizen and GRU colonel. His real family name was Girkin. Strelkov was a veteran of conflicts in Chechnya, Bosnia and Transnistria who would become a cult figure in Russia. In Crimea, he supervised the Russian military invasion. He advised Aksyonov, the Moscow-appointed PM. In early April, Strelkov left Crimea for Donbas. He was going to start a war.

Strelkov later told Russian media he crossed the Russian–Ukrainian border with a squad of Russian special forces officers. His group included fifty-two undercover soldiers. They seized Slavyansk and in the days that followed kick-started the occupations of municipal buildings. 'It was me who pulled the trigger of war,' Strelkov told the *Zavtra* newspaper. Strelkov said that without his 'decisive' contribution the pro-Russian uprising in Donetsk would have fizzled out – as it did in the cities of Kharkiv and Odessa.

The response from Europe to the major crisis unfolding on its eastern border was feeble and unconvincing. Putin's land grab in Crimea was the first formal annexation of territory in Europe since 1945. By spring 2014 it was clear that Russia was laying the ground for a full-scale military conflict in Donetsk and Luhansk. Money, heavy weaponry, intelligence, political support and soldiers – some disguised as 'volunteers', some from regular Russian army units – were flowing into the new DNR and LNR.

There were two possible scenarios. One, the Kremlin might seek to annex these regions, as with Crimea. Two, it might establish puppet enclaves, controlled by Moscow. These pseudo-statelets would be similar to other disputed regions already occupied by Russian forces. They included Transnistria, where Russian troops had been stationed since the 1990s, and the breakaway Georgian micro-territories of South Ossetia and Abkhazia.

Putin's aims were uncertain. Perhaps the president didn't know himself. They went beyond territorial gain. They must have included undermining the pro-western government in Kiev and embroiling it in a debilitating on-off war. Analysts used the term 'frozen' to describe unresolved post-Soviet conflicts. But frozen wasn't the right word here. Rather, Moscow could turn the temperature up or down in the Donbas, depending on political need. There could be diplomacy and ceasefires; military offensives and covert actions; or both at the same time.

The crisis was a fundamental challenge to Europe's security order. This system – with the exception of the war in former Yugoslavia – had kept the peace for almost seventy years. Its principles were partnership and international law. In 1994, the US, UK and Russia had guaranteed Ukraine's international borders. All parties signed a treaty, the Budapest Memorandum. Ukraine agreed to give up its stockpile of nuclear weapons, at the time the world's third largest. In exchange it got security assurances, worthless ones.

Russia was turning the clock back – to an era of great powers and spheres of influence. Its foreign-policy officials floated the idea of holding a second Congress of Vienna – in effect, a new carve-up of Europe. (At the first one, back in 1815, Europe's victorious nations met to decide the fate of the continent following the defeat of Napoleonic France.)

This plan built on Medvedev's 2008 comments that Russia had 'privileged interests' in its post-Soviet 'near abroad'. In effect, this meant that Moscow believed it had the right to veto the security and foreign policy of neighbouring states. In particular, it was entitled to prevent them from joining Nato. The Russian government viewed Nato as an implacably hostile and encircling force.

Putin had never thought much of Ukraine's sovereignty. According to Poland's former foreign minister Radoslaw Sikorski, cited in leaked US diplomatic cables, Russia's president described Ukraine as a 'cobbled together country' with 6 million Russians in it. Now, it appeared, Moscow regarded its neighbour as sub-sovereign. It was to be treated as a rebellious colony or misbehaving province – like Hungary in 1956 or Czechoslovakia in 1968, where tanks met anti-Soviet uprisings.

According to Putin's new Crimea doctrine, Russia was entitled to 'protect' ethnic Russians wherever they were. The collapse of the Soviet Union had stranded large numbers of them outside the formal boundaries of the Russian Federation – in the Baltic states, Ukraine, Moldova and northern Kazakhstan. Putin wasn't Hitler, whatever cartoons on the Maidan might say. But his apparent project to redeem left-behind Russians was reminiscent of Adolf's own 'co-ethnic' policy, used to justify Germany's *Anschluss* of Austria and seizure of the Sudetenland.

The doctrine raised the question: where next?

The answer came in autumn 2015 when Moscow launched a series of air strikes in Syria. The ostensible target was Islamic State terrorists. In reality, those bombed were less extreme groups fighting against Bashar al-Assad's regime.

This was the first time the Kremlin had launched a major military action outside the borders of the former Soviet Union since the end of the Cold War. Putin's objectives here were several. They included bolstering Assad, securing Russia's air and naval bases on Syria's coast, and – of course – rubbing Obama's nose in it. In contrast to the US's confused Syria strategy, Putin was showing decisive global leadership.

The EU's response to Russian aggression in Ukraine was insipid, to say the least. As Putin had calculated, neither Washington nor Brussels was prepared to answer Russian hard power with analogous military force. There would be no weapons sent to Kiev. Lethal aid was ruled out.

Instead, western leaders offered … expressions of grave concern. Ukrainians who had stood on the Maidan in sub-zero temperatures, declaring their basic rights, were unimpressed. Vendors in Kiev began selling T-shirts to disillusioned Europhiles with the slogan: 'Fuck your grave concern'.

This left sanctions – the lever pulled by the US and its allies in the months to come. European governments were less willing to impose sweeping sanctions on Moscow than the White House was. The EU imported a third of its oil from Russia. It would suffer more pain than America, which was not dependent on Russian energy and did less trade. There was also the certainty that the Kremlin would respond with counter-sanctions.

The first EU sanctions list identified twenty-one individuals. All were accused of undermining Ukraine's sovereignty and territorial integrity. They included Aksyonov and Russian parliamentarians. One was Leonid Slutsky, a leading member of the ultra-nationalist Liberal-Democrats. Andrei Lugovoi was Slutsky's party colleague in the Duma. Most of those on the list were small fish – minor functionaries in the new Crimean ascendancy.

The US lists went further. They included Putin's closest political friends and cronies. Moreover, they sent a not-so-subtle message to Moscow: that America had identified Putin's personal financial interests and was prepared to target them.

Putin's wealth is a mystery. Officially, he lives the modest life of an ordinary citizen. In 2007, leaks from inside his presidential administration suggested he was worth $40 billion via undisclosed interests in oil and gas companies. Putin denies this. But the subject of the boss's wealth is something the Kremlin is reluctant to discuss.

According to leaked US State Department cables, members of Putin's inner circle acted as 'proxies' for his secret assets abroad. Formally, Putin owned nothing.

Informally, he controlled many billions of dollars, which belonged to his team, most of them close allies and friends from his early career in East Germany and St Petersburg and now elevated to high offices of state.

The US list included Viktor Ivanov, the former career KGB officer who was the subject of Litvinenko's explosive report. What – if anything – did US intelligence know of Ivanov's possible involvement in Litvinenko's assassination? Alongside his job as head of the federal drugs agency, Ivanov sat on Russia's security council. It also included Sergei Ivanov, Russia's hawkish deputy prime minister, once seen as a possible presidential successor, who knew Putin from the 1970s and Leningrad's KGB.

Then there was Gennady Timchenko, another long-term Putin associate, whose Swiss-based company Gunvor exported a third of Russia's seaborne oil. Gunvor rejects claims that Putin is a Gunvor beneficiary. The US Treasury Department was unconvinced by these denials and said: 'Putin has investments in Gunvor and may have access to Gunvor funds.'

The department said it was imposing asset freezes and visa bans on the Russian leadership's 'inner circle'. It threatened 'increasing costs' for Russia if it carried on with its 'provocative actions' and its efforts to destabilise Ukraine.

Many of those on the list were members of Putin's *ozero* dacha cooperative near St Petersburg. The president's friends and former neighbours formed a new oligarchic class, and in many cases were richer than some of the original oligarchs they replaced. There was Yuri

Kovalchuk, the head of Bank Rossiya – a 'personal bank for senior officials of the Russian Federation', according to the US. Also Vladimir Yakunin, the head of Russian Railways, a prominent conservative and former diplomat to the UN with alleged KGB connections. And Arkady and Boris Rotenberg, Putin's former St Petersburg judo partners. The treasury alleged the pair had 'made billions' from contracts awarded by Putin for Gazprom and the 2014 Sochi winter Olympics.

This was, in short, Litvinenko's mafia state.

By summer 2014, Donbas had become a full-blown war-zone. The regional governor – billionaire industrialist Sergei Taruta – fled Donetsk with his advisers. He escaped just in time. A group of Chechen gunmen turned up at his HQ, the city's multi-storey Hotel Victoria, shouting: 'Where is the fucking paedophile?' Fighting broke out around Donetsk Airport. Rebels held the approach road; the Ukrainian army the terminal. There were clashes further east near Luhansk. Ukrainian soldiers were in the airport there and villages to the north.

The separatists were losing ground. Ukrainian forces had one substantial advantage: air power. When pro-Russian fighters seized the airport terminal building, Kiev responded with airstrikes; two lorries transporting wounded were hit, most of the Chechen 'volunteers' wiped out. Units from Ukraine's national guard besieged Slavyansk, where Colonel Strelkov commanded a force of around 1,000 fighters. The rebels had mortars, small arms and a couple of armoured personnel carriers and infantry fighting vehicles. They were running low on ammunition and were outgunned.

In early July, the rebels broke out. Strelkov retreated south to Donetsk; others from his group headed south-east to the town of Gorlovka, where 350–400 separatist fighters were based. With the Donetsk People's Republic facing extinction, Russia moved to tip the balance in the rebels' favour. It supplied them with heavy weapons, smuggled across the border. They included Grad multiple rocket launchers and self-propelled artillery pieces.

Suddenly, Ukrainian military aircraft were being shot out of the sky. An Ilyushin was downed as it came in to land at Luhansk Airport. All forty-nine soldiers on board were killed. Russian agencies reported that the rebel 'people's republic' had got hold of the Buk, a sophisti-cated surface-to-air missile launcher. The Buk could fire missiles up to an altitude of 22,000 metres. The DNR tweeted news of its new weapon. In mid-July, two more Ukrainian planes were shot down: an An-26 military transport plane and a Sukhoi jet.

On 17 July, an Associated Press reporter spotted the Buk missile system in the town of Snizhne. He observed seven rebel-owned tanks parked at a gas station. Other witnesses told the BBC they saw the missile-launcher roll off a low-loader around 1.30 p.m. local time. 'We just saw it being offloaded and when the Buk started its engine the exhaust smoke filled the whole town square,' the witness said. The crew, he added, appeared to be Russian soldiers. They had pure Russian accents and said the letter 'g' differently from Ukrainians.

The Buk was photographed parked in a residential street in Snizhne. It's seen next to a shop, 'Olimpstroi'. Video captures it on the move too, transported on a lorry with a white cab, and rolling past a billboard. The missiles are clearly visible. The body is painted green, the arrow-shaped tips creamy white. As it drives past, a wood pigeon flaps from a hedge across the road.

According to Bellingcat, a team of investigative journalists, the Buk began its journey in Russia. It was part of a convoy that set off in late June from the Kremlin's 53rd anti-aircraft missile brigade in the city of Kursk. Social media postings by Russian soldiers chart its progress towards the Ukrainian border. By the afternoon of 17 July it was in separatist hands.

At 5.50 p.m. Moscow time, Strelkov sent out a tweet. It was headlined: 'Message from the militia'. The message's tone was self-congratulatory: the rebels, Strelkov said, had shot down another Ukrainian transport aircraft. Posted on Vkontakte, the Russian social media site, it said:

We just downed a plane, an AN-26, in the vicinity of Torez. It's lying somewhere near the 'Progress' mine.
We warned them – don't fly in 'our sky'.
Here's video confirmation of the latest 'bird drop'.

Strelkov posted two videos confirming the crash – taken from a distance and showing a plume of thick black smoke. He described the plane as a 'bird'. It had fallen, he wrote, on a slag-heap, far away from any residential areas. 'Innocent people weren't hurt,' he added.

[323]

Forty minutes later, Strelkov deleted the tweet. Rebels arriving at the crash site, 9 miles (15 km) from Snizhne, discovered a scene of utter horror: wreckage, bodies, plane seats. There were dead women. Dead children. They found passports – one belonging to an Indonesian student. The debris included clothes, toys, luggage. The signage from the plane said: 'Malaysian Airlines'.

Audio intercepts, released by Ukraine's intelligence agencies, show Igor Bezler, a DNR commander, discussing what happened with Vasili Geranin, a Russian colonel from GRU military intelligence. Bezler tells Geranin: 'We just shot down a plane.' Bezler explains that the plane was civilian, not military. There is incredulity. And then self-justification: what was a commercial plane doing above a war zone? Were there spies on board?

Strelkov's 'bird' was Malaysian Airlines MH17. The Boeing 777 had taken off from Schipol Airport in Amsterdam. It was flying to Kuala Lumpar. There were 298 people on board including fifteen Malaysian crew. Two-thirds of the passengers were Dutch; the others from Australia, Malaysia, Indonesia, UK, Germany, Belgium, the Philippines, Canada and New Zealand. MH17 had been at 33,000 feet. Some airlines had ceased flying over Ukraine because of the conflict, others hadn't. Wreckage from the plane covered 50 square kilometres. Contrary to Strelkov's assertion, debris did land on houses. Some bodies fell in gardens. Others in cornfields.

The rebels shot MH17 down in error. They believed it to be a military target. It was a terrible mistake, but one that flowed directly from Putin's very poisonous contempt for Ukraine's sovereignty and his decision to reshape Europe's borders.

Two days later, amid international outrage over MH17, and with evidence pointing strongly to Kremlin complicity, the Home Office in London made an announcement.

There would be a public inquiry into the murder of Alexander Litvinenko.

12

The Inquiry

Court 73, Royal Courts of Justice,
the Strand, London, January–July 2015

'Vladimir Putin is nothing more than a common
criminal dressed up as a head of state'
BEN EMMERSON QC, JANUARY 2015

It looked very much like a murder trial. Seated in the middle of the court was a judge, Sir Robert Owen. In front of him were lawyers. One of them was Ben Emmerson QC, the celebrated human-rights advocate. Owen and Emmerson were familiar figures from the pre-inquest two years earlier. To Owen's right was another barrister, Robin Tam QC, who assisted the judge. Next to Emmerson was Marina Litvinenko, dressed in black, with her student son, Anatoly. In the corner a witness box. There were shorthand clerks, solicitors, paralegals and ushers padding softly in and out.

At the back of the court was space for the media and public, and video screens for following the evidence. The walls were painted a classic shade of magnolia. From an open window you could hear the sounds of urban life penetrating from one of the world's great capitals outside: a seagull, a helicopter flying overhead, the whine of police sirens. Outside the grand Gothic entrance there was a row of TV cameras.

There was only one thing missing from room 73 in the east wing of London's Royal Courts of Justice – defendants. There weren't any.

In fact, the two men accused of murdering Litvinenko were about 1,500 miles away in Russia. More than eight years after Litvinenko's poisoning, his assassins – Andrei Lugovoi and Dmitry Kovtun – were still enjoying the favour of the Russian state. There was no prospect of their being extradited. And unless the Putin regime collapsed – an event that few believed would be happening any time soon – neither Kovtun nor Lugovoi would stand trial in Britain.

The date was Tuesday, 27 January 2015. After years of delay, legal challenge and obfuscation, by governments in London and Moscow, a public inquiry was being held into Litvinenko's murder. The visual grammar inside the court was misleading. This wasn't a pseudo-trial. Nor was it a court process in which the accused would be convicted and sentenced *in absentia*. There would be no finding of criminal liability.

Rather, the inquiry was a dispassionate exercise in truth-telling. It was methodical and thorough; inquisitorial rather than adversarial. For the first time, the evidence painstakingly collected by the Metropolitan Police in Operation Whimbrel – its codename for the Litvinenko investigation – would be made public. Participants got 16,000 pages.

More than sixty witnesses testified. Some played a direct role in the events surrounding Litvinenko's death.

Others were professional experts: scientists, doctors, pathologists, historians. A few, like Berezovsky and Patarkatsishvili, were dead, their police statements read from beyond the grave.

During Putin's presidency, numerous Kremlin critics met mysterious and violent ends. Twenty-three investigative journalists were murdered, together with other political activists. Invariably nobody got caught for these crimes. There was an investigation of sorts, maybe even a few arrests. But those in Russia who ordered up these killings were never identified.

What made Litvinenko's murder special was its extra-territorial location – London. The subsequent British police inquiry into his assassination took place free from political pressure. Detectives were able to follow leads, collect evidence, put together a case. These carefully assembled facts pointed in one direction: to Lugovoi and Kovtun's guilt.

Over six months, Owen – acting as chairman rather than as a judge – listened to all this evidence.

This was truly a strange British legal affair. A few witnesses gave evidence anonymously. Whenever this happened the room was cleared with the media turfed into a downstairs annex. From here, you could watch proceedings on a video feed. And tweet, which was impermissible in the main court. (The camera was turned away from the witness.) The video ran with a five-minute delay, just in case a secret was revealed by mistake.

The effect was to stimulate your imagination and to make you wonder what the witness might look like. Clues were scarce. Scientist A1, for example, who gave expert evidence on polonium, was a woman with a northern accent. That was it. C2, the cook, sounded Albanian but since he was speaking German, could anyone be sure? These participants in disguise were identified by letters and numbers.

Such measures were understandable. D3 had told German police he was afraid of being killed. Despite the inquiry's best efforts, he declined to give evidence. Kovtun's ex-wife and her mother – Marina and Eleanora Wall – refused to cooperate. Letters inviting them to turn up went unanswered.

Still, there was a wealth of material. And once the public hearings ended, the tribunal continued in secret session. Inside these closed hearings Owen examined a significant amount of classified material from the UK government and its various spy agencies including MI6, Litvinenko's old employer.

Nobody beyond a small circle of spooks, ministers and top civil servants knows what is inside MI6's files. Even in less sensitive cases, the agency argues that disclosure might threaten its sources. None of MI6's records have been made public since it was founded in 1909.

Goldfarb believes the Litvinenko files contain a well-grounded conclusion that Putin is a front for organised crime and that Litvinenko was murdered because he's key to that understanding. We can assume the documents include MI6's Litvinenko dossier. And its internal assessment – written in 2007 – as to who may have ordered his execution.

There may also be transcripts of intercepted phone calls made by Lugovoi, Kovtun and possible unknown third parties in London, Moscow and elsewhere. And email traffic. That the UK, US and others have the ability to eavesdrop on phone calls was well known, even before the US whistleblower Edward Snowden revealed the extent of this surveillance in 2013. Officially, this power isn't acknowledged. In addition, there may be human intelligence from agents in the field. London says covert work and the effective operation of its intelligence agencies requires secrecy.

At the heart of the inquiry were two simple questions.

The first: why was Litvinenko killed?

The second: was the Russian state responsible for his murder?

In previous hearings, Owen had indicated that there was a *prima facie* case against the Russian state. But did that mean that Putin – or those around him – had ordered Litvinenko's liquidation? How much was known? What could be inferred? The judge ruled there were no grounds for saying that the British state had failed to take 'reasonable steps' to protect Litvinenko. In short, the UK authorities couldn't have anticipated a Russian death squad.

Efforts were made to involve Lugovoi and Kovtun. They were invited to give evidence by video-link from Moscow. The investigative committee of the Russian Federation chose not to participate. That left four 'core participants': Marina and Anatoly Litvinenko; the Metropolitan Police; the UK home secretary; and the Atomic

Weapons Establishment. Each had solicitors and lawyers. And access to evidence – excluding the classified stuff.

Owen was seventy years old, had been a judge for more than two decades and was a popular figure on the legal circuit. He originally came from Wales. His appearance was that of a classic member of the British ruling class – his suits conservative, his white hair neatly combed, top button never undone.

As it turned out, Owen was 'a pretty cool judge', in Emmerson's words, and not as strait-laced as he seemed at first glance. 'He handles it with masterful calm and good judgecraft. He decides as little as he has to,' Emmerson said. 'He's run these proceedings impeccably. Nobody could challenge his integrity or impartiality.'

Owen had something of a puckish sense of humour. Most of the time he listened. When he did intervene in proceedings his comments could be droll; here was a playful intelligence. One witness told the inquiry that a group of powerful individuals in Russia sought to control the president. Owen responded drily: 'Some might say the British equivalent is the establishment.'

At 10.30 a.m., the chairman began by setting out the basic facts: that Litvinenko had died on 23 November 2006 after 'ingesting a fatal dose of the radionuclide polonium-210, a radioactive material'. His murder raised issues of the 'utmost gravity'. It had attracted 'worldwide interest and concern', he said. Owen then explained why it had taken so long for the circumstances of his death to be examined – a saga of delay. He promised his inquiry would be full and independent.

Litvinenko's death triggered many theories as to who might have murdered him. Tam, counsel to the inquiry, said all of these would be considered. For some there was considerable evidence, for others none. There were numerous versions besides the one Litvinenko himself believed – that the Russian authorities were to blame. They included: Litvinenko accidentally poisoned himself; Berezovsky killed him; British government agencies were responsible; the mafia did it.

For those of us watching from the public gallery there were early revelations. Tam set out in broad terms the evidence against Kovtun and Lugovoi. They had tried, he said, to poison Litvinenko twice, the first time unsuccessfully. Then there was the German restaurant manager D3, to whom Kovtun confessed he was carrying 'a very expensive poison'. Since Kovtun and Lugovoi apparently had no personal grudge against Litvinenko, they were acting on orders. But whose?

Tam described the question of state responsibility as 'multi-faceted' and said: 'Which elements of the Russian state might have had the motive, the resources and, quite frankly, the daring to carry out the killing of a British citizen on British soil? At what level would such an operation have been authorised? Is it possible that an operation of this nature would have been undertaken without the knowledge, without the express authorisation, of those at the highest levels?'

Furthermore, what was the motive? Did Litvinenko betray Russian secrets while allegedly working for the British and Spanish spy agencies? Or was the Ivanov report he compiled with Yuri Shvets the key to his grue-some murder?

On day one of the hearing I was just outside the court-room when I received an email from Emmerson. There was an attachment. It was an embargoed copy of the opening speech he would deliver on behalf of Marina Litvinenko a few hours later. I read with excitement. It was gloriously trenchant. It referenced my book, *Mafia State*, published in 2011 after my forced exit from Russia.

The speech was an unsparing anatomy of twenty-first-century Russian power – an indictment of a crim-inal regime prepared to murder its enemies, as its Soviet predecessor had done, using inventive methods. And led by a president who, when stripped down, is a mafia boss straight from a Mario Puzo bestseller.

Emmerson is a formidable lawyer. He is known for championing unpopular clients, and for offending governments and the powerful. He is a founder member of the left-wing Matrix chambers. He specialises in inter-national and domestic human rights and appears regularly before the International and European Courts of Justice, and the European Court of Human Rights. 'I'm driven by a passion for open truth and justice,' he told me.

In the words of Louis Blom-Cooper, a veteran lawyer of progressive views: 'Ben is a very clever man. Highly intelligent. A very good advocate. One of the leading public lawyers.'

Close up, it was easy to see why Emmerson is regarded as one of the best courtroom performers of his generation. Whenever present, he was the tribunal's irresistible mid-point, it struck me. There was the booming voice, of course. And the phenomenal work rate. There was a remorseless logic to his questions, too: any witness who lied or equivocated got crushed, as if by a mallet. In person, he looks a bit of a bruiser: broad shoulders, large head, black glasses, closely cropped hair.

Emmerson's preeminent gift is that he can render a complex legal argument in compelling and intelligible phrases, a process of rapid disassembly. Journalists don't need to think of a headline: he writes one for you.

At 2.50 p.m., Emmerson delivered his opening statement – a zinger. The barrister began by paying tribute to Marina Litvinenko, and her long, hard campaign for justice. The significance of her search involved broader national and international interests, in that it exposed 'unlawfulness and criminality at the heart of the Russian state'.

This wasn't about one murder, Emmerson said, rather about a government that had succumbed to a terrible criminal cancer:

'The intimate relationship that will be proved to exist between the Kremlin and Russian organised crime syndicates around the world are so close as to make the two virtually indistinguishable. The startling truth, which is going to be revealed in public by the evidence in this inquiry, is that a significant part of Russian organised crime around the world is organised directly from the offices of the Kremlin. Vladimir Putin's Russia is a mafia state.'

Next, he addressed motive. Litvinenko was liquidated 'partly as an act of political revenge for speaking out, partly as a message of lethal deterrence to others, and partly in order to prevent him giving evidence as a witness in a criminal prosecution in Spain'.

Litvinenko was about to expose the 'odious and deadly corruption among the cabal surrounding President Putin'. He had given information to Spanish and Italian officials about links between Russian organised crime groups and the Kremlin. Therefore: 'He had to be eliminated, not because he was an enemy of the Russian people, but because he had become an enemy of the close-knit group of criminals who surrounded and still surround Vladimir Putin and keep his corrupt regime in power.'

Litvinenko's killing, it appeared, wasn't about ideology, as in Soviet times. Moscow spymasters used to believe that the murder of enemies – both domestic and foreign – could be justified on the grounds that the Soviet Union was waging a life-and-death struggle to defend communism, a noble experiment. And that they were surrounded by hostile forces: Hitler, the west, etc.

Here, there could be no appeal to what you might term Leninist ethics. Communism was gone. Rather, Litvinenko's modern assassination was about money. He threatened the revenue streams of some very powerful people. So they killed him.

According to Emmerson, there was no doubt who gave the order – Russia's president. He dismissed alternative theories proposed by the Kremlin as outlandish and absurd. There wasn't the 'slightest doubt' that Lugovoi and Kovtun were the assassins. The forensic evidence confirmed this, Emmerson said. So did what had happened since 2006: Lugovoi's unexplained wealth and his successful career in Russian politics, none of which would have been possible without a Kremlin leg-up.

The 'cold, hard facts' said that Litvinenko's murder was a political crime. It bore all the hallmarks of a state-sponsored assassination, the QC asserted.

The polonium used to murder him came to London from Russia. It was very expensive, Emmerson said. 'The scientific evidence shows that the quantity of polonium of the purity used in the assassination of Mr Litvinenko would have cost tens of millions of dollars if it was purchased by end users on the commercial market. Just the amount that was used for the assassination. Well, obviously, a commercial transaction of that magnitude ... would have to be recorded, and if it had happened, the authorities would know about it. It is, we say, moreover, unlikely in the extreme that any private individual or purely criminal enterprise, a pure bunch of hoodlums involved in an organised crime gang, why on earth would they choose such a costly method of assassination, tens of millions of dollars, when they could simply put a bullet in someone's head?'

For the Russian state, on the other hand, the costs were by no means prohibitive. It just had to divert some of the material it was producing already. Polonium was selected 'in order to leave no clear trace as to how death was sustained'. It very nearly worked.

Emmerson's conclusions were blunt, and framed in highly personal terms: 'We say, sir, that when all of the open and closed evidence is considered together,

Mr Litvinenko's dying declaration will be borne out as true: that the trail of polonium traces leads not just from London to Moscow but directly to the door of Vladimir Putin's office and that Mr Putin should be unmasked by this inquiry as nothing more than a common criminal dressed up as a head of state.'

The barrister's opening statement was bold and provocative – an accusation against a major world leader expressed in language not usually heard in a court.

The Russian government had ostensibly paid little attention to the inquiry, viewing it as biased, unreliable and the latest manifestation of an anti-Russian campaign waged by the west and its puppet media. From Moscow, Lugovoi dismissed it as a 'judicial farce'. Traditionally, Russian officials were insouciant in the face of what they dubbed 'provocations'.

On this occasion, though, someone was watching. That someone was irritated.

Two days after the inquiry began, RAF controllers noticed two dots moving at high speed towards the south coast of Britain. The dots kept going. These were Russian Tupolev Bear bombers – giant, lumbering, Soviet-era aircraft capable of carrying nuclear bombs on long-range missions, their bright red communist stars still visible on a gleaming silver fuselage. The Bear bombers were heading directly towards the Channel. Downing Street scrambled two RAF typhoons to intercept them.

Since the war in Ukraine, the Russian airforce had dispatched Bear bombers on similar probing missions to European countries and to the Pacific coast of the

US and Canada. They had buzzed military and civilian aircraft. There were repeated forays into the airspace of the Baltic republics. In one incident in April 2015, a Russian SU-27 fighter missed a US military jet flying above the Baltic Sea by a few metres.

These sorties were a crude expression of displeasure. And a reminder that the Russian government presides over a nuclear arsenal and isn't to be messed with. Even David Cameron, a prime minister who showed little interest in international affairs, got the memo. 'Russia is trying to send some kind of message,' he said.

In the weeks before the inquiry began, I met Anatoly Litvinenko at University College London. In the spring of 2015 he was a second-year student of politics and East European studies; his last piece of coursework an essay on Putin. His choice of university was a nod to his father, who died just across the road in University College Hospital.

Anatoly is quiet, low-key and speaks with a typical London student accent. He seems mature for a twenty-year-old – something his friends attribute to his close relationship with his mother, a loving and affectionate parent. 'I'm so glad we can still hug,' Marina told me. 'After it happened, I realised I couldn't just be strict. I remember Sasha saying: "Be soft on him." I try and tell him every time that I love him.'

The UCL café was crowded, so we descended past the stuffed body of the philosopher Jeremy Bentham to an empty basement bar. Anatoly was dressed in a quilted overcoat and wearing fashionable lightweight black specs, bought in Berlin when his last ones broke.

We talked about his expectations of the inquiry. 'I'm pretty sure there will be some kind of closure for me and my mum,' he said. What would it bring? 'Probably a chance for us to move on. To move on past the whole thing, which has been central to my life for eight years.' He paused. 'I want to remember him as Dad, to have a chance to grieve properly.'

Anatoly recalled visiting his father in hospital nearby, and his last words to him: 'If I do die from this, take care of your mum, look after yourself and study hard.' He said he didn't recognise his father at the end: 'It wasn't my dad at all.' Alexander's death put him in a strange place; he coped by immersing himself in schoolwork ('I got a bunch of stupidly good marks') and shutting out his grief. 'There was a huge media storm. For a while I was lost in the chaos,' he said.

Anatoly had brought along some old family photographs. One from 1997 shows a grinning, small Anatoly lying above Alexander on a sofa at their Moscow home. It's a happy symmetry. The photo was taken at his parents' apartment in the Moscow suburb of Chertanovo. Like many Russian kids, Anatoly spent the long summer vacation at a dacha 25 miles (40 km) outside Moscow that belonged to Marina's parents. There was a vegetable plot and a pagoda.

Anatoly's maternal grandparents were regular Soviet citizens. His grandfather, also named Anatoly, spent his life working in a components factory and lost two fingers in machines; his grandmother, Zinaida, always insisted young Anatoly finish his food. Anatoly Sr was highly intelligent, but at the age of twelve, with the Soviet Union fighting for its existence against the Wehrmacht, he was forced to leave school and find a job. He finally went to technical college in his thirties.

Anatoly was named after his grandfather, now aged eighty-three and still living in Moscow. He said they are similar in character. 'He's quiet and introverted. He loves chess and mental games. He was unbeatable at dominoes. His colleagues at the factory got angry because he won every single match. If he were born later, he'd have been an avid gamer.'

As a child in Russia, Anatoly thought his father worked in some kind of law enforcement. After he moved to England he told his schoolmates his dad was a journalist and a police officer. He remembered his father as the more indulgent parent. Marina was the strict one – a 'typical communist mum', as she put it to me. Father and son would play chess. Anatoly always won – Alexander was a lousy opponent.

'My dad loved England. He felt extremely safe here. He loved the freedom of expression, the fact that people could vote for whomever they liked,' Anatoly said. One photo shows a visit to Hyde Park. Alexander introduced Anatoly to Speakers' Corner; they posed together next to two London bobbies in uniform. Litvinenko is grinning and wearing a pair of knee-length khaki shorts. Alexander told his son that, unlike in Russia, you could trust British justice. You could stand up on a box and say anything.

Anatoly was aware his father was a personal enemy of Putin's. But, by 2006, Moscow felt like the past. 'It was over. We were having a quiet normal life,' he said. The family would go for pizza at La Porchetta, their favourite local Italian restaurant on Muswell High Street. Once a week the two of them went to Finsbury leisure centre. Anatoly had a taekwondo class; Alexander went for a 10-mile (15-km) run. Afterwards, Anatoly would splash in the kids' pool, while Alexander swam lengths of vigorous front crawl.

On the way home to Osier Crescent, Anatoly would make a short cut – taking the diagonal across a muddy park and crawling through a hole in the fence. Alexander would go on the path. He was, Anatoly said, reluctant to get mud on his trainers. Like other Russians who had grown up with very little, Alexander had something of a 'a post-Soviet rush' towards consumer stuff, he said.

Sometimes his father was away on business trips. 'When he was there, he was fun,' Anatoly said. 'He was quite relaxed, happy to joke around with me.' That summer of 2006, they watched the World Cup on a giant screen, cheering on England against Trinidad and Tobago. Alexander flew a Union flag from their balcony. When they first arrived in London, Anatoly asked Alexander which team he should support. His reply: not Chelsea, Abramovich's club. 'I picked Arsenal,' Anatoly said.

I had asked Anatoly if he might write something for the *Guardian*. We had discussed this during earlier conversations. He was considering becoming a journalist after university, maybe specialising in Russia. He handed me several handwritten pages of A4.

His piece was moving. One of the hardest aspect of losing his father, Anatoly wrote, was not having had the opportunity to become friends with him – as he had with Marina:

'As a kid, you tend to perceive adults, be it parents or anyone else, differently from how you would at age sixteen, eighteen or older. These days I'm able to joke around and have interesting conversations with my mother. We have discussions and arguments. I have gained a certain maturity that allows for mutual respect. And through this sort of relationship you are able to get an insight into the other person: how they think, what troubles them, what forms their views on life and so on. You get to understand what really makes the person.'

With his dad, Anatoly wrote, he was forced to recon-struct the person from what was left – from 'little titbits' here and there. 'From small things I remember. How I used to run to him if I did something wrong and was getting scolded by my mother, how I could run to him for sanctuary, or how incredibly proud he was of my smallest academic achievement.'

Alexander had loved rock music. Anatoly hadn't much liked it as a child, but now found himself as a young adult listening to the same bands as his father. 'But I can never share my opinions of the music with him,' he wrote.

He continued: 'This, perhaps, is why the inquiry is so important to me. When there is a story of a death so sensational, it's very easy to get lost in the events of the few days and weeks, those of November 2006, with facts, accusations and intrigue. For me personally, this isn't paramount. For me, it's important to understand what Alexander Litvinenko was like behind the scenes, beyond the press conferences and the polonium; to construct an image, even half a one, in order to have a role model to look up to.

'And most importantly perhaps, to always remember him as a person, a human being and my father, rather than just an aspect of political history.'

After coffee and croissants we set off together to visit his father's grave. Litvinenko is buried in Highgate West Cemetery in north London. We took the Northern line to Archway and then waited at a bus stop in the chill. 'That's about as weird as it gets,' Anatoly said, pointing to the electronic sign that tells us which bus is arriving when. One of the buses that go to the cemetery is the 210 – as in polonium-210. 'How crazy is that?' he smiled.

We got on another bus and walked up to the cemetery's imposing black gates. They are locked to visitors, but Anatoly was known here; a woman radioed her colleague inside: 'There's a grave-owner; can you let him in?' Anatoly, Marina and a few close friends visit every year to mark the anniversary of Litvinenko's death.

We walked up a small bucolic path. It's an incongruous resting place for a patriotic Russian officer. Litvinenko's grave is set among mid-Victorian tombstones and fluted funerary columns. There are squirrels and magpies in a tranquil clearing; opposite lies an admiral whose family vault resembles a grand naval warship.

The conversation returned to the question of Putin's guilt. 'You have to ask yourself, which countries have the capability to produce polonium? Which country did my dad have a problem with? It's simple,' he said. And added: 'There was a radioactive trail that leads back to Lugovoi. You can't make that up.' Of Putin, he said: 'Dad used to get irritated about how many people in the west trusted Putin. The reality is: he's dangerous. He shouldn't be appeased.'

After Emmerson's opening statement, Marina and Anatoly Litvinenko gave evidence from the witness box. It must have been harrowing for Marina to relive it all again. Over two days she told the story of her husband's life and death.

There was also testimony from Dr Nathaniel Cary, the consultant forensic pathologist who examined Litvinenko's body. The scene in University College Hospital was extraordinary, like something from a horror movie. Cary said that he and other officials examining the corpse wore two protective suits, two pairs of gloves taped at the wrists and large battery-operated plastic hoods into which filtered air was piped.

Cary said that medical staff left Litvinenko's radioactive corpse *in situ* for two days. It fell to him to remove drips and disconnect tubes. He took a small sample of muscle from the right thigh to test for polonium. He then put the corpse in two body bags. Following this 'very hazardous' recovery operation, Cary said he conducted a post-mortem on 1 December 2006, together with a full team wearing protective gear.

In a long career, Cary had examined murdered children and victims of other gruesome crimes – but not this. 'It's been described as the most dangerous post-mortem undertaken … I think that's right,' he said. The case was unique. It was the first known example of acute polonium poisoning anywhere in the world.

Slowly, a picture was forming – of mediocre assassins who left behind clues. As Emmerson put it, the nuclear trail was 'almost as sure as the path of breadcrumbs left by Hansel and Gretel'. A senior scientist explained radioactive readings taken from a range of sites associated with Lugovoi and Kovtun. Litvinenko's deathbed interviews with police were made public. So was the last photo taken of him alive. There was discussion of Litvinenko's corporate security and investigation work. To what extent might this explain his murder?

For those following the inquiry, this new evidence was fascinating and multi-layered. For the first time, the public could see CCTV footage of Litvinenko arriving at the Millennium Hotel and of his shifty-looking killers in the minutes before he was poisoned. Other guests had their identities blurred out: they looked like surging blobs. There were surprises. Who knew that British spies use Waterstone's bookshop as a meeting place? Or that Litvinenko's anonymous monthly payments from MI6 were listed on his bank statement next to a meal from Nando's in Finchley?

Every evening the new evidence was posted to the inquiry's website, www.litvinenkoinquiry.org. Sometimes the court official responsible – a pleasant New

Zealander called Mike Wicksteed – didn't finish work until midnight. There were witness statements, newspaper articles, transcripts of interviews from Moscow with the two murderers, telephone schedules, forensic contamination reports. The contamination schedule listed every location where polonium was discovered. It ran to an impressive 265 pages.

At lunchtimes, Marina Litvinenko would head over the road from the white neo-Gothic court building to Apostrophe, a sandwich bar. Over soup and green tea, she would discuss the case with her legal team: Emmerson, junior counsel Adam Straw and her solicitor Elena Tsirlina. Sometimes I would join them. Our mood was more cheerful than gloomy. Marina would greet witnesses, kiss old friends on the cheek; her fortitude was amazing.

Back in the courtroom, there were entertaining moments. In April 2012, Andrei Lugovoi took – and apparently passed – a lie detector test in Moscow. A Russian TV documentary producer named Alexander Korobko arranged it. In the wake of the result and with pompous fanfare Russia's state media announced that Lugovoi's innocence had been conclusively demonstrated. 'We did the test because Andrei was so passionate about his innocence,' Korobko told RT, the Kremlin's English-language propaganda channel.

To give the test added credibility, Korobko got a British member of the Polygraph Association, Bruce Burgess, to conduct it. Burgess had embarked on a career in lie detection after doing other jobs including working as an apprentice ladies' hairdresser. He trained in the US at the Backster School of Lie Detection in San Diego. In the noughties he appeared on various UK daytime TV shows, including *Trisha* and *Jeremy Kyle*. He would carry out tests on individuals accused of marital infidelity; the parties would get the result – usually showing one of them had been unfaithful – live on air in the studio.

Korobko made Burgess an offer: an all-expenses-paid trip to Moscow, plus a £5,100 fee. The producer was enigmatic about who would be taking the test. He merely told Burgess the subject was a 'celebrity'. Burgess flew to the Russian capital with his son Tristam. There they were introduced to Lugovoi. The Burgesses performed the test, recorded on video, in Moscow's Radisson Slavyanskaya Hotel.

Nearly three years later, the inquiry summoned Burgess to give an account of what transpired. Aged seventy, with shoulder-length white hair and beard, Burgess looked like a 1970s rock star gone to seed. He admitted to feeling uncomfortable after discovering in Moscow that Lugovoi was accused of murder. After discussions, Burgess said he came up with three questions. The two main ones were: 'Did you do anything to cause the death of Alexander Litvinenko?' and 'Have you ever handled polonium?'

The inquiry was shown video footage from the encounter. Lugovoi sits in a leather armchair in the middle of a business suite, legs spread. Seated at a table behind him are an interpreter and the Burgesses. Their subject is hooked up to a polygraph, which measures breathing rate, pulse, and sweating. When asked the two key questions, Lugovoi replies: '*Nyet.*'

Afterwards, Lugovoi admits to feeling some 'internal tension'. Burgess says: 'Have faith in me.' Minutes later he delivers Lugovoi the result. 'You were telling the truth. No deception indicated,' he says. The next day Lugovoi invited father and son to breakfast at his daughter's upscale Moscow restaurant. The bill was on the house.

The inquiry adjourned for lunch. Emmerson whispered to me: 'Big bang coming up.'

At 2 p.m., Emmerson examined Burgess. It was a masterclass in how to eviscerate a witness, like watching a tiger play with a small, whiskery rodent. He asked if Burgess considered himself a 'reliable evaluator of whether someone is telling the truth'. Burgess mumbled: 'No, not really.' This was an odd reply. Its reason became apparent.

The barrister asked: 'What about yourself, Mr Burgess, do you consider yourself to be an experienced liar?'

In December 2009, Emmerson revealed, Burgess had been convicted of perverting the course of justice and sentenced to twenty-four weeks in jail, suspended for two years. He'd been caught speeding. He told police a fictitious 'friend' was behind the wheel. Burgess resigned from the Polygraph Association; the invitation to travel to Moscow came at a time when he was broke and somewhat demoralised. Korobko knew of Burgess's criminal record: this, it appears, is why he hired him. By way of justification Burgess said: 'We all lie at one point or another.'

There was more – the test results indicated that Lugovoi had actually failed the second question: 'Have you handled polonium?' The inquiry heard it was 'quite easy' to dupe a lie detector test – especially if you were a trained spy or intelligence agent. Countermeasures might be physical or mental. Techniques included counting backwards from 100, imagining that you are walking your dog on a promising spring morning, or thinking of an erotic situation. Even with likely coaching from the FSB, Lugovoi flunked it.

This was gripping courtroom theatre. Owen was on form, too. He observed: 'I'm amused to see that walking the dog on a promising spring morning is compared with thinking of a sexually arousing scene.'

There were more signs that the Kremlin was following events in London closely – and not in a happy way. In an interview with RT, Viktor Ivanov described the inquiry as 'a spectacle, a farce, a knockabout act'. The allegations against him were, he said, a conspiracy by Britain and its intelligence agencies. Ivanov also expressed bafflement as to why the US had sanctioned him.

The same day Burgess sagged in the witness box, the Moscow agency RIA Novosti put out a short news story. It said President Putin had handed out a state honour. The award was for services to the fatherland, second-class. Its recipient: Andrei Konstantinovich Lugovoi. The presidential citation said the honour was bestowed in recognition of his contribution to Russia's parliament and to law-making.

Lugovoi was deputy chairman of the Duma committee for security and fighting corruption, the agency noted. The committee wrote legislation for Russia's spy agencies.

In late 2013, Lugovoi had proposed a blacklist of leading opposition news websites. They included a blog written by the anti-corruption campaigner Alexei Navalny and a news portal run by Garry Kasparov, the former chess champion, Kasparov.ru. Putin approved Lugovoi's suggestion. It was part of a wider crackdown on internet freedoms, justified in the wake of Snowden's revelations on the grounds of 'digital sovereignty'.

Lugovoi's law-making efforts were clearly helpful to the Kremlin. But this state honour looked like a reward for something else, namely murder. And a sign of high-level political approval. Surely it was no accident?

As Emmerson remarked: 'Whatever the pretextual justification for that award, its timing on day twenty-two of this inquiry, after a substantial amount of evidence has been called establishing Mr Lugovoi's involvement in the murder of Mr Litvinenko, is clearly both a provocation by President Putin and the clearest possible message that he identifies himself with Mr Lugovoi.'

The award was probative, the barrister said. In other words it should be added to the evidence that Owen would consider before writing his report, due by Christmas 2015.

After a month of hearings it was clear that Scotland Yard had garnered more than enough material to convict Lugovoi and Kovtun, were they to stand trial. But the question of Putin's personal culpability was more complex, and harder to answer. Several factors had to be considered: the nature of the Russian state, past and present; the interplay between Putin and his spy agencies; and whether

Putin micro-managed security operations or merely set broad policy parameters. Plus, what might be read from previous political killings, of which there were quite a few.

To examine all this, the inquiry turned to Robert Service, professor of Russian history at Oxford University and a distinguished writer and scholar on modern Russia. Service had previously been commissioned to write an expert report for the *Berezovsky vs Abramovich* case, offering guidance on Russian high politics and big business. He had published full-scale biographies of Lenin, Stalin and Trotsky. These were model studies: lucid, elegant and readable.

Service was asked to provide information in key areas. The first was to explain internal power structures in Russia, and to say if it was possible for 'the Russian state' to order the assassination of a critic. Next, he was to give his expert opinion as to what extent it could be credibly said Putin might commission any such killing, or for it to be carried out with his knowledge or approval. Further questions: did Putin and other senior individuals have links to mafia gangs? Could the state kill someone at the behest of such groups? And what was the Russian administration's attitude to the 'rule of law'?

Service's 2015 report was a highly nuanced document. It made clear what was known, and evidentially based, and what was speculation. It avoided simplification or what Service termed 'unidimensional' answers.

Analysing Russia was much tougher than it had been twenty-five years ago, he began. During glasnost and the Yeltsin era there was real information about disagreements at the top of Russian politics. High-ranking insiders, including Yeltsin, wrote revealing memoirs. But with Putin's rise to power in 2000, access to information in Russia underwent a 'severe constriction'.

Top-level secrecy came back; the country reverted to a pre-1985 Kremlinology – when observers tried to decipher what might be going on by watching who stood next to whom on Lenin's Red Square tomb. The impenetrable nature of contemporary Russian power diminished what could be said with confidence.

Service took issue with the way some commentators depicted Putin – 'as the evil dwarf who operates from his secret cave and controls every minute step taken by his robotic minions'. He argued that there were two flaws to this negative school. First, it didn't give credit to Putin for anything. Second, Russia from the time of Nicholas II onwards has always been a tricky country to rule. Service argued that Russia's power vertical – its centralised political hierarchy – was in reality 'patchily organised'. And, he said, even dictators had less power than they might wish for, and couldn't ignore popular pressures or demands from Russian society.

Another known unknown was Putin's relationship with Nikolai Patrushev, the head of the FSB at the time of Litvinenko's murder. Putin's backstory was understood; Patrushev was an old KGB associate of his from Leningrad. But it was unclear whether Patrushev secured Putin's permission for operations in advance.

Service pointed to one piece of evidence – a memoir by Mikhail Kasyanov, Russia's former prime minister. Putin offered Kasyanov the job in 2000. There was a condition: that Kasyanov didn't meddle in Russia's 'coercive structures' – the FSB and other security organs – which Putin considered his exclusive 'turf'. Kasyanov stuck to the deal. Putin fired him anyway in 2004. He joined the opposition.

Kasyanov survived, but many other prominent Putin critics wound up dead. Service cautioned that it was difficult to prove the administration's complicity in these crimes. Putin's public response to Litvinenko's killing illustrated 'a verbal levity that borders on the macabre', the professor observed. (Putin mocked Litvinenko's letter of accusation and said there was no indication he'd suffered a 'violent death'. 'The people who have done this are not God, and Mr Litvinenko, unfortunately, is not Lazarus.')

Putin's own guilt was unproven. 'But there can be little doubt about where his feelings lie,' Service said.

Despite all of these caveats, Service's conclusions were unambiguous: that Russia's president set 'a political climate of tolerance' in which his agencies could go about their 'repressive business' without hindrance.

He went on: 'The Putin administration has always been demonstrably secretive, manipulative and authoritarian with a ruthless commitment to protecting its interests at home and abroad … It appears to me unlikely that Putin did not exercise – at the very least – some oversight of Patrushev's activities.'

Speaking from the witness box, Service said his findings might be 'inscribed on my tombstone'. As befits an Oxford don, he employed a sparkling vocabulary.

There was a rare outing for the word 'desuetude'. (Service complained that the tradition of looking at the big picture had fallen away, replaced by compartmental-ised scholarship.) The professor also talked about how Russia's post-1991 market economy had 'immiserated' large sections of the country's population.

In a supplemental report, Service further considered whether Putin's Russia could be called – as Litvinenko originally hypothesised – a mafia state. The inquiry wanted to know the answer. Did Putin and senior figures in the Russian government have links with St Peters-burg's Tambov-Malyshev crime gang? Or with members of Russian organised-crime groups in Spain? And what about Litvinenko's claim that Putin had good relations in the 1990s with the mobster Semion Mogilevich?

Mogilevich is an almost mythical Ukrainian-Russian mafia don who features on the FBI's list of ten most wanted. The US accuses him of running a trans-national crime empire. It deals in weapons, contract murders, extortion, drug trafficking and prostitution. And oper-ates in America. According to Litvinenko, Putin met Mogilevich and gave him a *krysha*, or protection. Mogi-levich lives in Moscow, shielded by the FSB and beyond the reach of US law enforcement. (Some sources say Mogilevich is now in Hungary.)

Mogilevich crops up in the leaked conversations from 2000 between Ukraine's president Leonid Kuchma and his intelligence chief Leonid Derkach. Derkach says the mafia boss is on his way to Kiev to sort out various disputes, and adds: 'He's on good terms with Putin. He and Putin have been in contact since Putin was still in Leningrad.' Was this in any way proof?

Service answered that such matters were 'highly contentious'. There were few reliable sources. And the phenomenon wasn't new. Organised crime had rooted itself in the USSR after Stalin's death. It had truly flourished under perestroika, and had grown exponentially under post-communist conditions. The 'corruption of the political process' visible with Yeltsin had continued under Putin, Service said.

Russia, of course, wasn't the only country with criminality at its core. Organised crime has penetrated practically every state in Latin America. Likewise Africa. And the state is geographically more extensive than just the capital. In Mexico, for example, criminal gangs have subverted entire regional administrations.

There was crime in other parts of Europe, too. Italy under the Christian Democrats harboured a huge mafia problem in the south – and in the north as well. In Italy, though, mafia interests never wholly predetermined public policy.

Service offered his own taxonomy as to what 'mafia state' meant. He gave ten definitions. He agreed that the ninth offered the best fit when talking about contemporary Russia: 'a state in which criminal methods and organised crime play a substantial part but which also has countervailing features'. Undoubtedly, ministers and other top Russian officials were keen to enrich themselves. At the same time, Service told the tribunal, 'not everything that happens in the Putin administration is unconstitutional and illegal and run for criminal purposes'.

It was illuminating. At times the conversation between Emmerson and Service took on the quality of a highbrow BBC or NPR discussion. Putin wasn't Stalin; his popularity was, 'alas, real'; like interwar Germany, post-1991 Russia was tempted towards extremism after economic depression and military defeat. Service said he didn't see many positive sides to Putin. He was bad enough without the overdrawn comparisons made by some Russian democrats to Hitler. And he was the 'luckiest ruler of the twentieth century', who had benefited from a steeply ascending oil price.

There was some disagreement on method. Service took the long view: that the truth about Putin would emerge but that we'd have to wait. 'It will be knowable eventually. It always is. We now know a lot of what we needed to know for decades about even Joseph Stalin. So I am confident that one day we will know about Putin, but it will be too late then. It will just be a matter for historians and not for people engaged in public affairs.'

Other witnesses took a less detached view. Litvinenko's co-author Yuri Shvets, the former KGB agent, pointed out that 'active measures' – such as state assassinations – were always authorised at the highest political levels. This was, Shvets said, one of the KGB's main traditions. It would be unthinkable for an FSB general, whether Viktor Ivanov or anybody else, to murder a political dissident without Putin's express approval.

Speaking by video-link from the US, Shvets said that KGB 'rule number one' was to cover your back. That meant getting permission from your superior; in Russia the most important decisions were made by just one person. 'I rule out the possibility that a decision to assassinate Sasha [Litvinenko] or anybody else outside of Russia would have been made without approval of the top authority of Russia, which is Vladimir Putin,' Shvets told the inquiry.

In Litvinenko's case, there were special factors as well. As Goldfarb put it, Putin's conflict with Berezovsky and Litvinenko was deep-rooted and highly personal. 'Nobody in his right mind, knowing how things run there [Russia], would authorise such an operation when one could be sure that Mr Putin would take a very close look at it after the fact,' Goldfarb said. He characterised Litvinenko's killing as not just a crime of politics but an emotional act – a work on Putin's part of 'passion'.

There were other good reasons to believe that Putin authorised the operation, Goldfarb added. One was polonium – non-state players couldn't get hold of it. Russia's atomic industry ministry would give it to the FSB only with presidential permission. Goldfarb cited a lengthy interview Putin gave state TV on the annexation of Crimea. The president boasted the operation had worked so smoothly because 'I personally micro-managed it.'

There were few leaks from inside Putin's Kremlin. What happened in its corridors was an enigma.

What there is is a literature from earlier times: a previous generation of Soviet spies had given details of Litvinenko-like operations. Goldfarb mentioned Sudoplatov, the Soviet intelligence chief whose department, the Administration for Special Tasks, was responsible for sabotage, kidnapping and assassination of enemies abroad. Sudoplatov's book corroborated rumours that the KGB had a poisons institute – Lab X – set up by order of Lenin. It functioned throughout the Soviet period. 'As to whether it still exists, I don't know,' Goldfarb said.

If Soviet practices were anything to go on, orders to murder political enemies were never written down. There was no documentation for missions of the highest secrecy – only an oral instruction. (In an interview with Nick Lazaredes in 2003, Litvinenko recalled how in December 1997 he was summoned to the Lubyanka, the KGB and FSB HQ. His deputy boss Alexander Kamishnikov berated him for arresting rather than 'removing' criminals, in other words, snuffing them out. He showed him a copy of Sudoplatov's memoir and said: 'That's what you should be doing.')

Conversations like this were usually phrased in an oblique way. Sudoplatov recalls how in 1937 Stalin summoned him to discuss the fate of Yevhen Konovalets, a Ukrainian nationalist sentenced *in absentia* to death. Stalin urged Sudoplatov to exploit Konovalets's personal weaknesses. Sudoplatov said that Konovalets liked chocolates. When the meeting broke up, Stalin asked him if he understood the political importance of his mission.

Six months later, Sudoplatov met Konavalets in Rotterdam and presented him with a box of chocolates containing a bomb. He walked away; it blew up soon afterwards; the target was killed. Stalin was pleased.

Sudoplatov also masterminded the operation to murder Leon Trotsky, carried out in Mexico in 1940 by a communist agent, Ramón Mercader, using a small, sharp mountain-climbing pickaxe concealed under a raincoat. The previous year Stalin had summoned Sudoplatov to the Kremlin and in the presence of Laventry Beria, head of the NKVD secret police, said that Trotsky should be eliminated. The plan was discussed in euphemistic terms. Sudoplatov writes: 'Stalin preferred indirect words like "action", noting that if the operation was successful the party would forever remember those who were involved and would look after not only them, but every member of their family.'

The spy chief carried out further operations against other Ukrainian nationalists, some of whom were executed by injections of poison, under the guise of medical treatment. These murders were made to look like natural deaths, Sudoplatov said. Assassinations continued after Stalin's death, always sanctioned at the highest level of the Communist Party.

According to Sudoplatov, the KGB's special toxicological department fascinated successive Soviet bosses, including Gorbachev. 'Our leaders were always interested in poisons; afterward the doctors who were involved in these experiments were purged,' he wrote.

Inevitably, Sudoplatov was himself arrested after Stalin's death. He spent fifteen years in jail before being released in 1968. At first, he had no doubts about the morality of killing Trotskyites and fascists – his country's enemies. Later, he regretted the way in which communism chewed up so many innocents, including those who fought bravely against the Nazis.

In Sudoplatov's view, Stalin and Beria were tragic and criminal figures – but also visionaries who played a constructive role in transforming the Soviet Union from a backward peasant state into an atomic superpower. 'Victorious Russian rulers always combined the qualities of statesmen and criminals,' the general observed.

Like Service, Sudoplatov believed the truth of any conspiracy would eventually emerge: 'History shows that no top-secret decisions, no secret crimes or terrorist plans can be concealed forever. This is one of the great lessons of the breakdown of the Soviet Union and Communist party rule. Once the dam is broken, the flood of secret information is uncontrollable.'

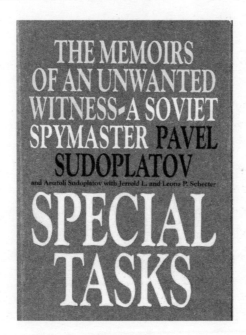

13

Leviathan

Bolshoi Moskvoretsky Bridge, Moscow,
27 February 2015

'He is a totally amoral human being.
Totally amoral. He is a Leviathan'

BORIS NEMTSOV ON VLADIMIR PUTIN, FEBRUARY 2015

Boris Nemtsov was in good spirits. It was February 2015 and Nemtsov – once Russia's deputy prime minister but for many years at odds with official power – was due to lead an anti-government rally. True, the authorities had banished the protesters to Marino, a gritty suburb of Soviet high-rises in Moscow's distant south-east. And true, Russia's opposition was, generally speaking, in poor shape.

A few years earlier it was just about possible to fantasise that street power might drive Putin from office. His announcement that he was 'returning' to the presidency – after four years as prime minister – triggered the biggest demonstrations since the end of the Soviet Union. But the euphoric rebel mood of 2011–12 was gone. People had been arrested and given lengthy jail terms; Putin had enacted the worst human-rights crackdown for decades; human-rights groups were being forced to register themselves as 'foreign agents'.

The Putin era looked interminable. Brezhnev did eighteen years as general secretary of the Communist Party, his rule associated with stagnation. Putin – on fifteen – seemed poised to overtake him. In 2017 Putin would likely stand again as president. Another seven years would take him to 2024.

And then there was the war in Ukraine. In the wake of Crimea's annexation, the president's ratings had skyrocketed. Many former liberals had embraced the new patriotism, cut dead their western acquaintances, and adopted the slogan *Krym Nash* – Crimea is ours! One morning a Dutch reporter in Moscow – married to a Russian woman and with a small child – found the words 'Nato out' written on his postbox in the stairwell of their communal apartment building. Nationalism – sullen and defiant – was everywhere.

Against this backdrop, Nemtsov knew that the numbers for the rally would be relatively modest. Even if the turnout were huge, the protest wouldn't feature on night-time TV. Nemtsov hadn't appeared on federal channels for eight years. The Kremlin had slowly strangled Russia's opposition, denying it finance, airtime and the ability to take part in elections. Those indomitable souls who kept going weren't activists but this century's dissidents, in the tradition of Sakharov and Bukovsky.

Since 2000, Russia had gone from a semi-democracy into something approaching a dictatorship. So why bother? Well, for one thing Nemtsov believed in democratic methods, even though democracy in Russia had practically disappeared. For another, there was Putin's covert invasion of Ukraine. According to Putin, Russian forces played no role in the conflict. The lie was so blatant, so ridiculous and so easily disprovable, it gifted fresh impetus to Russia's liberal intelligentsia, lifting them out of their low morale and disarray.

It was a Friday, 27 February. The march – dubbed 'Spring' – was due to take place on Sunday, 1 March. Nemtsov was sitting in the studio of Echo of Moscow, the independent radio station. Many opposition media outlets had closed since Putin resumed the presidency in 2012, for the third time. Somehow Echo of Moscow survived. Nemtsov was a frequent guest here. He was dressed casually, as always, in jeans and a turquoise jumper. Nemtsov was an alluring figure – fifty-five years old, good-looking, charismatic.

During his early political career, he had enjoyed high office. He came to prominence in the 1990s as the governor of Nizhny Novgorod. A reformist, a liberal and a supporter of Boris Yeltsin, he rose in 1997–8 to become deputy prime minister. He was talented and genuinely popular, with more than a sprinkling of stardust. Was he, as some thought, even a future president?

In fact, the new millennium belonged to Putin, an obscure and charmless KGB agent. Nemtsov started his own liberal party, the Union of Right Forces, which in the early stages of Putin's presidency was electorally competitive. Slowly, however, he was squeezed out – from the Duma, from TV, from public space. He carried on anyway – co-founding another democratic party,

Solidarity, in 2008, and standing to be mayor of Sochi, his home town, the following year.

I first met Nemtsov in 2009, on the campaign trail. We sat together in a rusty yellow minivan as it rattled up Sochi's steep hills. Nemtsov was bitterly critical of the forthcoming Sochi Olympics, a project mired in corruption and 'banditism'. He visited sanatoria and held meetings with local Sochi workers. He was a charming and persuasive candidate.

Terrified that their apparatchik candidate might lose, the local Sochi authorities banned Nemtsov from appearing on TV and in local newspapers. He faced dirty tricks and a pro-Kremlin activist chucked ammonia in his face. The Kremlin candidate won. Undeterred, in 2011 Nemtsov co-founded the Popular Freedom party – together with Mikhail Kasyanov, the former PM. Election officials refused to register it.

Even now, Nemtsov had not lost hope. During the interview with Echo of Moscow, Nemtsov came across as honest and cogent. He rubbished the Kremlin's mismanagement of Russia's economy and its 'dead-end domestic politics'. The current model, of giant state corporations run by incompetent bureaucrats, had failed, he said. Much of Russia was in a state of crumbling decay. He wanted an improved deal for the provinces, an end to rigged elections, better healthcare.

But his main preoccupation was Putin's Big Lie. Nemtsov had always seen his role as educational. He would explain to voters, argue with them, debate. At a time of blanket state propaganda this mission –

you could call it enlightenment – was more important than ever.

The interview lasted an hour. Nemtsov told the station's listeners that he had 'documentary proof' that undercover Russian soldiers were fighting and dying in eastern Ukraine. This was borne out by a steady flow of zinc coffins returning in the dead of night from the war zone in Donetsk and Luhansk – back to Russian cities like Pskov, Kostroma and Nizhny Novgorod, where Nemtsov was once governor. Putin wasn't just a liar – he was a specialist in lying, Nemtsov said. A 'pathological liar', in fact.

The interview went well. Nemtsov was optimistic that a well-attended march for peace might have a sobering effect on the Kremlin, and challenge the prevalent mood of ugly nationalism. That evening he had a late dinner with his girlfriend, Anna Duritskaya. She was Ukrainian and he'd collected her from the airport that morning. They ate at a café in GUM, the State Department Store, famous in Soviet times and now a capitalist shopping mall with worn marble stairs and ornate balconies off Red Square. Fairy lights outlined the nineteenth-century building. The café, Bosco, looked out onto Lenin's tomb.

Normally, Nemtsov would drive home in his Land Rover. He decided instead to walk. They took a scenic route south past the red walls of the Kremlin, the iconic Spassky tower, and the surrealistic domes of St Basil's cathedral.

This was Russia's most protected area. Wherever you looked there were CCTV cameras; unauthorised demonstrators who popped up here in the heart of political power were detained in a matter of seconds. The Kremlin even had its own powerful internal agency, the Federal Protection Service or FSO, with thousands of agents. It took care of security around state buildings.

Around 11.30 p.m., Nemtsov and Duritskaya started walking across Bolshoi Moskvoretsky Bridge. Beneath them was the Moskva river, cold, glittering, black.

The bridge offered a panoramic view of the city's illuminated skyline. Tourists come here to photograph St Basil's, dazzlingly floodlit at night and flanked by the white towers and golden domes of the Kremlin's churches and cathedrals. There were generous views along the river. The Gothic Kotelnicheskaya apartment building hulked imperiously over the water to the east, one of the capital's seven Stalin-era skyscrapers; in the opposite direction you could see the ivory edifice of Christ the Saviour cathedral – demolished by Stalin, rebuilt by Yeltsin – and the beginnings of Gorky Park.

Normally there was traffic. At this moment the bridge was oddly deserted. Only two vehicles were visible: a slow-moving municipal truck hugging the pavement and a white car. According to Duritskaya, someone emerged from immediately behind them. She didn't see his face. The assassin shot Nemtsov six times in the back. Four bullets hit him, one in the heart; he died instantly. The killer jumped into the car. It reversed back towards Nemtsov's body – seemingly to check if he was dead – and then shot off into the night.

The hitmen were evidently professionals. Their weapon was a Makarov pistol, a standard Russian and

Soviet police-issue semi-automatic. Six 9-mm cartridge cases were recovered.

Nemtsov was the victim not of a subtle poison but of old-school mafia methods. The location too told its own chilling and melodramatic story: an opponent of Putin lying dead in the street, under the implacable walls of Russian power, and next to St Basil's, the country's chocolate box landmark. The visual scene was perfect for TV. The first militia officers turned up. There was nothing to be done. They heaved Nemtsov's body into a black plastic bag.

It seemed extraordinary that a former vice premier could be murdered here, outside the Russian equivalent of the White House or the Houses of Parliament, with the shooter apparently able to simply drive off.

The murder of Boris Nemtsov was Russia's most high-profile political assassination for seventeen years. (In 1998 the liberal politician Galina Starovoytova – a notable opponent of the security services – was shot dead in the stairwell of her apartment building in St Petersburg.) Nemtsov's body had scarcely been loaded into an ambulance before the Kremlin responded. Dmitry Peskov, Putin's press spokesman, said that the president believed the murder was a 'provocation'.

'With all due respect to the memory of Boris Nemtsov, in political terms he did not pose any threat to the current Russian leadership or Vladimir Putin. If we compare popularity levels, Putin's and the government's ratings and so on, in general Boris Nemtsov was just a little bit more than an average citizen,' Peskov said. The rhetoric – insignificant, irrelevant, etc. – was reminiscent of Putin's response to the murders of Litvinenko and Politkovskaya.

The word 'provocation' carries its own special meaning in Russian. What Putin meant is that whoever murdered Nemtsov did so to discredit the state. Since the state was the primary victim here, the state couldn't be held responsible, this logic runs.

The office of Russia's prosecutor general offered an array of motives to explain Nemtsov's murder. None seemed convincing. It suggested his killing might be the work of Islamist extremists, radical Ukrainian factions, or the opposition itself, which could have used Nemtsov as a 'sacrificial victim'. Putin's ally Ramzan Kadyrov, the Chechen president, accused 'western spy agencies'. They were trying to 'destabilise Russia', he said. The muck-raking website LifeNews.ru, which has links with the FSB, pointed to Nemtsov's colourful love life and his relationship with Duritskaya, a 23-year-old model and Ukrainian citizen.

The investigative committee seemed to be moving in a predictable direction: towards an old-fashioned cover-up. Officials released one carefully curated CCTV film taken from far away. The municipal truck obscures the moment when Nemtsov is killed. The video offers few clues. There are no close-ups of the suspects. Three days after Nemtsov's death, officials told *Kommersant* newspaper that the Kremlin's CCTV cameras immediately next to the spot where he was shot 'weren't working'.

Like all high-profile critics, Nemtsov was under close FSB surveillance. The spy agency would have monitored Nemtsov carefully: it expends enormous efforts on keeping track of its targets. On this occasion, however, an organisation known for its resources and unlimited manpower seems to have lost him. Meanwhile, his killers appear to have had real-time intelligence concerning his movements.

The murder made headlines around the world. The Russian authorities avoided the one explanation that made sense: that Nemtsov was shot for his opposition activities. Specifically, for his public criticism of the war in Ukraine, in which – at the time of his death – at least 6,000 people had been killed and 2 million displaced.

In his last Echo of Moscow interview, Nemtsov had called Putin's intervention in Ukraine 'insane', and 'murderous' for Russia and its citizens. He described the takeover of Crimea as 'illegal', though he acknowledged it had the consent of many Crimeans.

At the time of his death, Nemtsov had been gathering material for a new report on Ukraine. Its contents were to have been explosive. Over the years he had written eight pamphlets on a variety of themes. One of them, *Putin: A Reckoning*, accused the president and his circle of massive personal corruption. It said that they had accumulated enormous personal wealth by pillaging oil revenues. Nemtsov shared Litvinenko's thesis that Russia had grown into a mafia state. He alleged Putin had links with the Tambov crime group.

Another Nemtsov booklet targeted Yuri Luzhkov, Moscow's mayor, and his billionaire wife Elena Baturina. (A year after it came out in 2009, Medvedev gave Luzhkov the boot.) There were further dossiers on the 2014 Sochi Olympics, where billions of dollars of public money had gone missing, and Gazprom.

According to his aide, Olga Shorina, Nemtsov came up with the idea of a Ukraine dossier in early 2015. It was to be called *Putin and the War*. It would reveal how Russian commanders had secretly smuggled servicemen into Ukraine to fight in the Donbas. His friend, the opposition leader Ilya Yashin, said that one morning Nemtsov turned up at his party HQ and announced triumphantly: 'I've thought what to do. We need to write a report, publish it with a massive circulation, and distribute it on the streets. We explain how Putin unleashed this war. Only that way can we beat the propaganda.'

Nemtsov believed that opposing the war was a patriotic act, Yashin said – and that by handing out the dossier outside metro stations he could punch through the wall of state disinformation. Putin's intervention in Ukraine was 'base and cynical'. It had led directly to sanctions, international isolation and the needless deaths of Russian citizens. The idea germinated in February, when relatives of servicemen killed in eastern Ukraine approached Nemtsov. The Russian ministry of defence was refusing to pay the families compensation – since the soldiers had, like so many ghosts, never officially been there.

Hours before his murder, Nemtsov wrote a note to Shorina. Scribbled in blue Biro, on a sheet of white A4, it said: 'Some paratroopers from Ivanovo have got in touch with me. 17 killed. They didn't give them their money, but for now they are frightened to talk.' Ivanovo was 185 miles (300 km) north-east of Moscow and home to the Russian army's 98th paratroop division. There were no other details.

As the authorities perfectly knew, Nemtsov's investigation was a bold challenge to Putin. From late 2013 onwards, the president had used his monopoly over state TV – watched by the overwhelming majority of Russians and the prime source of political information – to unleash a wave of nationalist hysteria and hatred. TV depicted the uprising in Ukraine as a 'fascist coup', backed by America. Ukraine's new provisional government was a 'fascist junta'.

According to this narrative, the rebellion in the east – actually choreographed by Moscow and its special services – was a continuation of the great patriotic war fought in 1941–5 by the Red Army against the Nazis.

The propaganda had little basis in reality. The far-right Pravy Sektor won less than 2 per cent of the vote in Ukrainian parliamentary elections in 2014 but was presented every evening as Ukraine's ruling political party. Some stories were wildly exaggerated. Others were made up. An eyewitness told Channel One she had watched Ukrainian Nazis crucify a six-year-old Russian boy in Slavyansk. The report was a lurid invention. However, the remorseless campaign worked. Most Russians believed that fascists were torturing and murdering their brother Slavs in eastern Ukraine; that the conflict next door was 'unfinished business'.

The prevailing ideas on Russian TV talk shows were familiar ones – victimhood; encirclement by the west; the evils of Nato; Russia's reemergence as a great power; the US's swooping plan for global hegemony.

At the same time, the propaganda had a dark internal message. The Kremlin branded those at home who opposed the war as fifth columnists. Russia's opposition supporters had grown used to the accusation that they were western stooges, paid by the US State Department, whose goal was to install a pro-US puppet government. A sign at one opposition rally joked: 'Hillary, I'm still waiting for my money.'

As the war intensified, the humour disappeared, and the accusations got nastier. Online lists began to circulate identifying 'national traitors'. The NTV channel ran a series of 'exposés' claiming links between anti-government activists and the CIA. It began planning a hatchet job on Nemtsov, entitled *Anatomy of a Protest*, to be broadcast on the day of the 1 March rally.

Nemtsov was aware that this swirling toxic climate made him vulnerable. As well as opposing the war in Ukraine, he had lobbied western leaders to impose sanctions on Russia, an action bound to infuriate the Kremlin elite. He was one of only two or three opposition leaders who could talk directly to Washington, Brussels and London. Sanctions – linked to Magnitsky or Ukraine – were a threat to the financial interests of Putin and his circle. And, from their point of view, treason – a betrayal every bit as great as Litvinenko's.

In an interview with the *Financial Times*, four days before he was gunned down, Nemtsov said Putin was distinctly capable of murder: 'He is a totally amoral human being. Totally amoral. He is a Leviathan.' He added: 'Putin is very dangerous. He is more dangerous than the Soviets were. In the Soviet Union, there was at least a system, and decisions were taken by the politburo. Decisions about war, decisions to kill people, were not taken by Brezhnev alone, or Andropov either. But that's how it works now.'

By 2015, Nemtsov was one of the few opposition leaders still based in Russia. Many had gone abroad. The former oligarch and prisoner Mikhail Khodorkovsky lived in Switzerland and the UK; Kasparov, the ex-chess champion turned Putin critic, was in self-exile in New York. The anti-Kremlin blogger Alexei Navalny remained in Moscow, though under house arrest. Prominent journalists and economists had departed too. Some moved to Paris or Chicago. Others went to London, following a well-trodden path taken by Litvinenko a decade and a half earlier – and by Lenin, a century before that.

The peace rally Nemtsov had been planning to lead turned into his funeral march. Fifty thousand mourners filled Moscow's embankment: a human mass dressed in thick hats and padded winter coats. They carried flowers, icons, Russian tricolours, homemade placards, and photos of Nemtsov with the words 'Boris' and 'I am not afraid', in black and white. Posters linked the four bullets that killed him to Russia's four federal TV channels. One read:

'Propaganda kills'. The spot on Bolshoi Moskvoretsky Bridge where he fell became a makeshift shrine, heaped with tulips and red carnations.

It was an icy day, with a grey sky; the queue to pay respects stretched around the Garden Ring road. Nemtsov's body was moved in a hearse and then lay in an open coffin for four hours, inside a museum dedicated to Sakharov, the nuclear scientist turned dissident. There were similar memorial meetings across Russia – in St Petersburg, Novosibirsk, Kaliningrad, Voronezh, Nizhny Novgorod – with smaller gatherings in European capitals. Neither Putin nor prime minister Dmitry Medvedev came. The chief mourner was Nemtsov's 88-year-old mother; the mood one of profound shock and gloom.

The Kremlin said it had nothing to do with the murder.

Nemtsov's friends found this denial unpersuasive. They believe that Putin may well have ordered his killing. Or that shadowy nationalist forces were allowed to eliminate someone routinely derided as a US spy. Either way, Putin deliberately fostered the atmosphere of hysteria and hatred that made Nemtsov's assassination possible; he was, therefore, morally responsible, they argue. As the journalist Ksenia Sobchak told the *Guardian*'s Moscow correspondent, Shaun Walker, it was somehow worse if Putin hadn't given the command to kill. That meant the president had constructed an 'appalling terminator' and 'lost control of it'.

Putin promised to take the investigation into Nemtsov's murder under his personal control. The statement didn't inspire confidence and led the satirical magazine *Private*

Eye to feature Putin on its cover with this remark. Putin is giving a large wink. Within days, the case resembled the unsatisfactory probes into earlier politically motivated killings in Russia. There were suspects – or, better, fall guys – but no real evidence, no motive, and a lingering sense that those who ordered the murder would escape justice once more.

Traditionally, the KGB and its successor the FSB had employed hitmen from the North Caucasus to carry out political killings. In his book *Blowing Up Russia*, Litvinenko recalled how the FSB used contract killers to liquidate a mafia boss in Yaroslavl. After doing the job, they abandoned their automatics at the scene together with the ID of a Chechen: 'The operation's Moscow controllers thought it would be a good idea to send the investigation off along the "Chechen trail",' Litvinenko wrote.

There were advantages to using outside killers. Any clues leading back to state organs were impossible to find. Such men were expendable.

What happened next was predictable and darkly ridiculous. Investigators arrested a Chechen, Zaur Dadayev, the deputy commander of the Chechen interior ministry's northern battalion. According to police, Dadayev confessed to shooting Nemtsov. Dadayev had close links with the Chechen leader Ramzan Kadyrov. Kadyrov duly provided a 'motive' to excuse the crime: Dadayev had been 'shocked' by Nemtsov's support for the *Charlie Hebdo* cartoonists gunned down in January in Paris by Islamist terrorists.

Four other Chechen suspects were rounded up. Another, Beslan Shavonov, allegedly 'blew himself up' when police tried to capture him in the Chechen capital Grozny, officials indicated. The suspects were paraded in front of journalists in Moscow. Dadayev, however, recanted his confession and said he'd been beaten in custody. Human rights observers recorded bruises and cuts on the arms and legs of the other accused.

Nemtsov had been one of the few politicians brave enough to criticise Kadyrov. He said openly what was well understood inside the Russian government: that Chechnya had become an out-of-control entity, corrupt, criminalised and increasingly dangerous. Formally it is part of the Russian Federation. In reality, it is an autonomous rogue fiefdom run by one psychotic strongman, to whom Moscow pays tribute in the form of large budget payments.

In January, Nemtsov had attacked Kadyrov on Facebook. Kadyrov had said that Khodorkovsky was an enemy of Putin's, an assertion that had chilling implications. Nemtsov re-posted a list of Kadyrov's alleged victims. It included Chechen émigrés gunned down in Dubai and Vienna. One was Umar Israilov, a 27-year-old former insurgent who filed a complaint to the European Court of Human Rights alleging that Kadyrov had personally tortured him in a secret prison. In 2006, emissaries from Kadyrov ambushed Israilov outside a supermarket in Vienna and shot him in the head.

Now Kadyrov was claiming that Nemtsov's murder was unrelated to internal Russian affairs. Rather, he was killed because he had offended Islam, Kadyrov proposed, with Dadayev acting from 'religious feelings'. The Nemtsov investigation looked like a carbon copy of the bungled case into the murder of Anna Politkovskaya, who had been shot dead just before Litvinenko was poisoned in October 2006. It was widely believed that Kadyrov had ordered the hit on the journalist. Several men from the North Caucasus were tried for her murder; I attended their first Moscow trial. But the mastermind and motive remained obscure.

The Kremlin's aim was to avoid an evidence-led inquiry into Nemtsov's assassination, it seemed, and to confuse the public mind. The numerous 'versions' of Nemtsov's murder – from love tiff to *Charlie Hebdo*-inspired Islamists to 'provocation' – were part of a sophisticated media strategy with its roots in KGB doctrine. As with Litvinenko, or MH17, there were multiple explanations. How was one supposed to know which one was actually true?

In fact, the aim is to blur what is true with what is not, to the point that the truth disappears altogether. By noisily asserting something that is false, you create a fake counter-reality. In time this constructed sovereign version of events becomes real – at least in the minds of those who are watching.

RT, the Kremlin's ambitious English-language propaganda channel, uses these same methods for western audiences. Its boss, Margarita Simonyan, argues that there is no such thing as truth, merely narrative. Russia's narrative is just as valid as the 'western narrative', she argues. In this cynical relativistic world of swirling rival versions, nothing is really true.

In a notable editorial after Nemtsov's murder, the *Guardian* described this approach as 'weaponised relativism':

'Like so much electronic chaff dropped out of the back of a Tupolev bomber to confuse an incoming missile, the idea that there are multiple interpretations of the truth has become the founding philosophy of state disinformation in Putin's Russia, designed to confuse those who would seek out the truth with multiple expressions of distracting PR chaff. The tactic is to create as many competing narratives as possible. And, amid all the resultant hermeneutic chaos, to quietly slip away undetected.'

The tactic, the editorial noted, wasn't new. It came 'straight out of Mr Putin's KGB playbook from the 1970s'.

In May 2015, Nemtsov's friends published the report he was unable to finish. After his death police seized his computer and hard drives. His friends – Olga Shorina, Ilya Yashin, Sergei Alexashenko, Oleg Kashin – made use of Nemtsov's jottings and notes. 'Our task: to tell the truth about Kremlin interference in Ukraine's politics, which has led to war between our peoples. Led to a war that must be quickly stopped,' they write in the introduction.

As with Nemtsov's previous reports, the sixty-five-page dossier is based on open sources. It includes interviews with Russian soldiers who had served in Crimea and the Donbas, photos, YouTube videos and social media posts.

Also featured are Nemtsov's letters to Alexander Bort-nikov, the FSB chief, and to Russia's prosecutor general. These reference Russian media articles which said that Russian troops had crossed into Ukraine, an illegal act. Alexashenko, a former deputy governor of Moscow's central bank, now based in the US, called the dossier a Wikipedia-style guide to the Crimean–Ukraine war.

According to Nemtsov, the Kremlin began secretly planning its Crimea operation in detail as far back as 2012. The goal was to improve the president's approval rating, which had sunk to 45 per cent (and by spring 2015 had shot up to 74 per cent). The FSB began actively recruiting generals and officers inside the Ukrainian army, funding pro-Russian groups and media, and offering credit to Crimean business. The revolution in Kiev offered the perfect moment for Putin to push the button on this military plan to seize the Black Sea peninsula.

As well as an invasion by 'little green men', state propaganda reached 'monstrous' levels, the report says. The Kremlin's earlier efforts at brainwashing seemed, by comparison, 'vegetarian'. Federal channels took anti-Americanism to new and extravagant levels. Putin's favourite TV host, Dmitry Kiselyov, told his viewers that Russia was the only country capable of 'turning the US into radioactive dust'; the idea of a nuclear first strike, by Moscow against the west, was discussed. The result: an 'atmosphere of continuous hate'.

In summer 2014, Putin categorically denied claims that serving Russian soldiers and military instructors were in Ukraine. This was, he said, an 'American lie'.

The report, however, says that Russian troops took part in the fighting and played a decisive role in the conflict. In August 2014, the Ukrainian army was advancing on all fronts. It had driven the rebels from Slavyansk back to Donetsk and had cut off the DNR and LNR from each other. Ukrainian troops were on the brink of seizing back the border with Russia – a move that would sever the rebels' supply lines.

The Kremlin responded with reinforcements, including heavy weaponry and some regular troops. Moscow sent across the border 120 armoured vehicles – including thirty tanks – and around 1,200 regular servicemen. The Russian counter-attack wiped out Ukrainian troops in and around the town of Ilovaisk. A similar offensive in February 2015 involving Russian tank units made possible the capture by rebels of the Ukrainian government-held city of Debaltseve, straightening a bulge on the map.

These Russian-aided offensives significantly expanded the territory under rebel control. But they came at a price. At least 220 Russian soldiers were killed fighting in eastern Ukraine, the report says. The figure included 150 killed during the battle for Ilovaisk and at least seventy in January and February 2015, as fighting intensified – including Nemtsov's seventeen paratroopers from Ivanovo. The figure was based on provable cases. The real death toll was likely much higher, the report adds.

In response to embarrassing evidence of Russian involvement in Ukraine, the Kremlin changed tactics. It 'fired' soldiers from the army before sending them as 'volunteers' across the Russo-Ukrainian border in small groups.

Other 'volunteers' were really mercenaries, recruited from veterans' organisations and centres inside Russia, and paid average salaries of $1,200 a month. The report estimates the bill to Russia for the first ten months of the conflict at $1 billion – for mercenaries, separatists and the upkeep of military hardware, supplied from Russia.

The DNR and LNR, meanwhile, are under the direct control of the Kremlin, the report says. The republics' chief political and military leaders are Russian citizens. Vladislav Surkov, Putin's aide and political spin-doctor, is in charge of the official structures in eastern Ukraine, the report adds. It quotes Andrei Borodai, the DNR's first 'prime minister', who in summer 2014 described Surkov as 'our man in the Kremlin'.

Nemtsov didn't live to see its publication. But his document was an important – and damning – piece of work. It features tragic photos: of young men, in their early twenties, wearing military berets and smiling with their girlfriends. And of a row of coffins, decorated in red satin, being unloaded from the back of a truck. And graves. Another photo, extensively examined and verified by the authors, shows a plume of smoke above the town of Torez. There is blue sky, cornfields, trees. The smoke comes from the rocket fired shortly before at Malaysian airlines MH17.

One of the mourners at Nemtsov's funeral was Vladimir Kara-Murza. Kara-Murza is thirty-three years old, a prominent opposition activist and a member of the board of Nemtsov's People's Progress Party. His father – Vladimir

Kara-Murza Sr – is a distinguished journalist with the same name. Kara-Murza Jr was closely involved in the publication of Nemtsov's report. He works for Open Russia, a pro-democracy organisation funded by Khodorkovsky, with offices in Moscow, London and Prague.

Kara-Murza was an outspoken anti-Putin critic who was well known on both sides of the Atlantic. He was educated in England (reading history at Trinity Hall, Cambridge, where contemporaries considered him brilliant) and had joint UK–Russian citizenship. There, he met Litvinenko and Bukovsky. He moved to the US and lived with his wife Evgenia and their three children near Washington DC. Latterly, he had gone back to Moscow.

Like Nemtsov, Kara-Murza badly annoyed the Kremlin. He played a key role in rallying support for a Magnitsky act and western sanctions against corrupt Russian officials; he lobbied on Capitol Hill and testified before Congress and European parliaments. He blogged for *World Affairs*, a US journal. Some wondered whether moving back to Russia was a good idea. Marina Litvinenko saw him in London in 2014. 'I asked him how he felt about going back to Moscow. He told me: "I believe it will be fine." I wasn't so sure,' she told me.

Nemtsov's murder badly shook Kara-Murza. He spoke at the funeral. 'A sense of political tragedy for Russia has been overshadowed by an irreplaceable personal loss,' he wrote, summing up the mood among Nemtsov's friends, and adding: 'Boris Nemtsov will not live to see the day Russia becomes a democratic country. But when that day comes, his contribution to it will be one of the greatest.'

LEVIATHAN

In April, Moscow police raided the offices of Open Russia. The NGO hadn't registered with the authorities in an attempt to avoid the fate of other human-rights groups which had been shut down. Police said they were looking for evidence of 'extremism'. Kara-Murza's latest project was a twenty-six-minute documentary film, *Family*. Its subject was Kadyrov. It alleged that the Chechen president is guilty of widespread human-rights abuses, presides over a personal army of 80,000 fighters, and skims off money from the federal budget.

Two days after a screening in Moscow, Kara-Murza collapsed in his office. He lost consciousness. His symptoms – a sudden incapacitating illness leading to immediate multiple organ failure – were troubling and strange. An ambulance took him to Moscow's First City Clinical Hospital. Doctors put him on life support. His condition was critical. As he hovered on the edge of death, Kara-Murza's father said his son was suffering from some kind of 'intoxication'. He believed he may have been poisoned.

Kara-Murza's illness remained undiagnosed and undetermined. Doctors appeared reluctant to give an explanation or to use the word poisoning. His family were circumspect. They seemed fearful that even in hospital Kara-Murza might not be safe.

Later he recovered. It appeared the FSB's poisons factory was still in business.

14

The Man Who Solved His Own Murder

Gray's Inn, South Square, London,
21 January 2016

'Hermione: Your honours all,
I do refer me to the oracle:
Apollo be my judge!'

THE WINTER'S TALE, ACT III SCENE 2, WILLIAM SHAKESPEARE

For the Fourth Estate it was an early start. Soon after
7 a.m., the first reporters began to arrive at Gray's Inn
in London, one of four ancient Inns of Court. The
entrance was a little hard to find, sandwiched between
the Cittie of Yorke pub and the stationers Ryman's. You
went through a narrow passage. A little further on was
a peaceful square. Here were Georgian buildings and a
statue of the inn's first senior member, going back in
time some five centuries, Francis Bacon. The reporters
filed through a doorway: the Benchers' entrance.

They had come for an event known in the news business
as a 'lock-in'. At 9.35 a.m., Sir Robert Owen's long-
awaited report into the death of Alexander Litvinenko
was due to be presented to parliament. What was in it?
Nobody knew. There'd been no leaks. Sixty media representatives – ranging from the *New York Review of Books*
to Germany's ARD channel – had been invited to an

embargoed preview, starting at 8 a.m. This was a sensible arrangement. It gave time to grasp the judge's conclusions – if not, perhaps, his fine argument.

An usher ticked the journalists off against a list. They climbed to the first floor, past an ante-chamber hung with lawyers' black cloaks, and up a grand oak staircase. Portraits of distinguished former members lined the walls. Here was Lord Burghley, Queen Elizabeth I's secretary of state, and a series of bewigged gentlemen. All electronic devices had to be left in the library, a condition of entry. Once inside the lock-in you couldn't leave. A bloke in uniform guarded the exit, just in case.

The mood was one of excitement. Over the previous half-year, Owen had privately sifted the evidence and cogitated. He then set down his independent conclusions. The media consensus was this: Owen would certainly rule that Kovtun and Lugovoi were murderers. After all, a fraction of the forensics available would have doomed them. His report, it was assumed, would find the Russian state guilty. Few expected him to point the finger directly at Putin.

Owen was the oracle. Now he was to deliver. Or, to use the language of Shakespeare, we were about to break up the seals and read.

The journalists filed into a red-carpeted space known as the Large Pension Room. Arrayed on a series of tables, and illuminated by chandeliers, were several copies of a chunky-looking booklet. It had a cerulean blue cover and was titled *The Litvinenko Inquiry: Report into the Death of Alexander Litvinenko*. There was a stuck-on note: 'Strictly embargoed'. We took our places. This felt a little gigglesome: here were a group of middle-aged professionals, sitting together as if on the cusp of a high school test. At 8 a.m. we picked up the report. We began reading.

The report was 328 pages long but it took mere seconds to locate the judge's stunning final ruling. On page 246 was a single sentence. It featured at the end of part ten, 'Summary of Conclusions'.

The sentence said:

'The FSB operation to kill Mr Litvinenko was probably approved by Mr Patrushev and also by President Putin.'

These eighteen words had an empirical solidity. They were hard judicial fact.

The sentences running up to this point were equally damning, and couched in psalm-like terms, with one striking repeated phrase: 'I am sure'. These words had an especial legal meaning. They meant Owen was satisfied his conclusions met a criminal standard of proof.

I am sure that Mr Lugovoi and Mr Kovtun placed the polonium-210 in the teapot of the Pine Bar on 1 November 2006. I am also sure that they did this with the intention of poisoning Mr Litvinenko.

I am sure that the two men had made an earlier attempt to poison Mr Litvinenko, also using polonium-210, at the Erinys meeting on 16 October 2006.

I am sure that Mr Lugovoi and Mr Kovtun knew that they were using a deadly poison (as opposed, for example, to a truth drug or sleeping draught), and that they intended to kill Mr Litvinenko. I do not believe, however, that they knew precisely what the chemical that they were handling was, or the nature of all of its properties.

I am sure that Mr Lugovoi and Mr Kovtun were acting on behalf of others when they poisoned Mr Litvinenko.

And:

When Mr Lugovoi poisoned Mr Litvinenko, it is probable that he did so under the direction of the FSB. I would add that I regard that as a strong probability. I have found that Mr Kovtun also took part in the poisoning. I conclude therefore that he was also acting under FSB direction, possibly indirectly through Mr Lugovoi but probably to his knowledge.

Then:

The FSB operation to kill Mr Litvinenko was probably approved by Mr Patrushev and also by President Putin.

Owen had gone further than anyone predicted. Though with a degree of caution, he had ruled that Russia's president was, in effect, a murderer who wiped out his personal enemies in spectacularly vindictive fashion. It was an unprecedented conclusion.

And one that raised a host of further questions. How had the judge arrived at this? What should the UK government do by way of response? And how should other world leaders behave the next time that Putin popped up among them? Could Barack and David really shake Vladimir warmly by the hand?

As Owen made clear, he had relied on two types of evidence. One was the public stuff laid out in open hearings during January, February, March and July 2015. This material alone, he wrote, established 'a strong circumstantial case that the Russian state was responsible for Mr Litvinenko's death'.

The judge's reasoning was set down in numbered paragraphs. He noted that the two Russian killers had 'no personal animus against Mr Litvinenko'. There was a 'possible relationship between Mr Lugovoi (who was clearly the leader of the two men) and the FSB in the years leading up to and including 2006'. Polonium was made in a nuclear reactor. Its use for the hit suggested the pair were 'acting for a state body' rather than, say, mafia interests.

On the logistics chain inside Russia, Owen noted: 'Although it cannot be said that the polonium with which Mr Litvinenko was poisoned <u>must</u> have come from the Avangard facility in Russia, it certainly <u>could</u> have come from there.'

There were, he added, 'powerful motives' for individuals and organisation inside Russia to take action against Litvinenko, 'including killing him'. They included – from the agency's point of view – his betrayal of the FSB.

Additionally, there was his work for British intelligence, his association with leading opponents of the Putin regime, his possible attempt to recruit Lugovoi for MI6, and his 'highly personal public criticism' of the president.

Owen was further persuaded by contextual evidence. It said that prior to Litvinenko's death the Russian state 'had been involved in the killing of a number of opponents of President Putin's administration'. The chairman observed: 'The pattern was of killings both inside and outside Russia. There was evidence of poisons, including radioactive poisons, being used in some cases.'

Then there was Putin's strange behaviour in the aftermath of the murder. Putin had 'supported and protected' Lugovoi, and latterly handed him an honour for 'services to the fatherland'. 'Whilst it does not follow that Mr Lugovoi must have been acting on behalf of the Russian State when he killed Mr Litvinenko, the way in which President Putin has treated Mr Lugovoi is certainly consistent with that hypothesis,' Owen found. 'Moreover, President Putin's conduct towards Mr Lugovoi suggests a level of approval for the killing of Mr Litvinenko.'

So far, so commonsensical. But the judge signposted that he had relied heavily in his conclusions on material presented in closed sessions – 'all the evidence and analysis available to me', as he put it. He had conducted what he termed a 'global analysis'. The most intriguing section of his report was part seven. It wasn't very long, just two pages. It dealt with material covered by restriction notices issued by the home secretary.

So just how much evidence had MI6 and GCHQ presented to Sir Robert? As it turned out, rather a lot: 'There is a considerable quantity of closed documentary evidence in this case. I have also received a number of closed witness statements, some of which are lengthy,' he admitted.

The details of these closed sessions had previously been fuzzy. Now, Sir Robert revealed, he'd held secret hearings 'over several days' in May 2015. They had taken place 'in a government building in London'. MI6's HQ overlooking the Thames? The Home Office? This was the private part of the public inquiry. Those present had included only Sir Robert, the counsel and solicitor to the inquiry, and home secretary Theresa May's legal team. Plus, of course, 'a number of witnesses' who were called to give evidence.

It's unclear who these anonymous witnesses were. But it's a fair guess they might have included 'Martin', Litvinenko's Russian-speaking MI6 contact. And 'Jorge', who performed the same role in Madrid. Senior figures from MI6 may have testified too. Almost certainly there was electronic intercept evidence: the report allows the inference that chatter might have been picked up between Lugovoi and his FSB bosses. Did this come from British spooks at GCHQ? Or from Washington via the NSA, the world's most potent government eavesdropping organisation?

The judge, then, had produced two versions of his report: a public version, and a closed version for a small official readership. Only those in government who had signed the Official Secrets Act got appendix twelve. This featured transcripts of the secret sessions, closed documents and witness statements. The restricted version dealt with two key themes: the nature and extent of Litvinenko's relationship with the UK's security and intelligence agencies; and the question of whether the Russian state murdered him.

Owen's closed findings remain unreleased. They include one 'recommendation', under the terms of the UK's 2005 Inquiries Act, so far mysterious. What is clear, however, is that this secret material played a crucial role in convincing the judge that Putin 'probably approved' Litvinenko's exotic, near bungled execution. Like an invisible springboard, it vaulted his understanding of what had gone on in the febrile months of October and November 2006 to another level.

Marina Litvinenko had seen the report twenty-four hours earlier. She and Anatoly, plus their legal team, paged through it in a secure room, on condition that they said nothing about its contents. At 9.35 a.m., the embargo was lifted. The excited journalists locked in at Gray's Inn promptly shared the findings around the world. I did the same, before running over to the next venue of interest, the High Court.

Events were moving at pace. At 10 a.m., Owen was due to read a short televised statement.

I arrived at Court 73. The public gallery was full. Some there knew that Owen was about to deliver his bombshell; others didn't. I spotted DI Craig Mascall and other Scotland Yard coppers. They were grinning. Litvinenko's surviving friends had come along: Zakayev, with his wife and wearing an astrakhan hat; Goldfarb; Dubov. Oxford historian Robert Service had dropped in. Owen, he would soon discover, had praised his 'impressive' expert evidence.

There were London-based Russian dissidents, and a reporter from *Novaya Gazeta*, who'd flown in from Moscow. There was a buzz of voices, speaking Russian and English. Marina Litvinenko and Anatoly sat at the front. She looked radiant; her son, understandably, somewhat wiped out and dazed.

Owen came in, made a nod, began. He explained why it had taken so long to get to this point – more than nine years – and stressed that he'd drawn on open and closed evidence for his findings of fact. The government hadn't influenced his conclusions, he said. He stressed: 'They are mine and mine alone.' Owen said the open scientific evidence had demonstrated conclusively Lugovoi and Kovtun's guilt. Then he got to the dramatic finale – Patrushev and Putin had 'probably approved' the FSB's London poisoning operation. From the public rows came cries of 'Yes!'

The judge thanked all of those who had assisted him. He praised the 'exemplary' job done by Scotland Yard and had kind words too for the lawyers and courtroom staff. It was made clear that Sir Robert wasn't giving interviews. He didn't need to. His report – completed on budget and done by English judicial standards with Usain Bolt-like speed – spoke for itself.

No one, it appeared, had quite seen this coming. 'I'm gobsmacked,' Service told me. 'It shows the autonomy of the judicial process from politics.' He added: 'Anglo-Russian relations are not going to be easy for the next few weeks, months or years.' Goldfarb was exultant. 'I didn't expect the role of Putin,' he said. 'Now it's become a legal fact.'

Marina Litvinenko gave her reaction outside the High Court:

'I am of course very pleased that the words my husband spoke on his deathbed when he accused Mr Putin have been proved true in an English court with the highest standards of independence and fairness.

'Now it is time for David Cameron [to act]. I am calling immediately for the expulsion from the UK of all Russian intelligence operatives, whether from the FSB (who murdered Sasha) or from other Russian agencies based in the London embassy.'

As well as a wholesale chuck-out of Russian spies, Marina called for the imposition of targeted economic sanctions and travel bans against named individuals, including the duo of Putin and Patrushev. 'I received a letter last night from the home secretary promising action. It is unthinkable that the prime minister would do nothing in the face of the damning findings of Sir Robert Owen,' she said.

In fact, the unthinkable was entirely thinkable. It soon became clear that the government's response was going to be – well, not much. Speaking in the House of Commons, May described Litvinenko's murder as a 'blatant and unacceptable breach of international law'. The probable involvement of Putin's Kremlin came as no surprise, she said. It was 'deeply disturbing'. Britain had no illusions about the state of Russia. The subtext: we know what's going on.

May, however, admitted she had little appetite for imposing punitive measures against Moscow. She told MPs there was a wider national security interest in retaining a guarded engagement, including working with Russia to bring about a peace settlement in Syria. More-over, it was impossible for Britain to impose a travel ban on a serving head of state, she claimed.

Over in Davos, where he was attending the World Economic Forum, Cameron made a similar point. Litvinenko's murder was a shocking event but, he indi-cated, it was necessary to keep working with the Kremlin: 'Do we at some level have to go on having some sort of relationship with them because we need a solution to the Syrian crisis? Yes, we do but we do it with clear eyes and a very cold heart.'

May announced one token reprisal: the treasury was freezing Kovtun and Lugovoi's UK assets. This didn't mean much. Back in 2006, Kovtun was so broke he didn't even own a credit card. He had to get his ex-wife's boyfriend, Radoslaw Pietras, to pay for his flight from Hamburg to London. It was a fair assumption that his and Lugovoi's seizable assets were zero.

Critics, led by Marina's counsel Ben Emmerson, argued that the UK government's response was weak, wrong-headed, and depressingly predictable. It was predicated on the make-believe that Putin's strategic and military goals in Syria were the same as Obama's and

Cameron's: the defeat of Islamic State. They weren't. Putin's objectives, instead, were focused on demonstrating Russia's status as an indispensable international power; shoring up the pro-Moscow regime of Bashar al-Assad; and protecting Russia's own naval and army assets in Syria's western Latakia province.

And, it might be argued, bombing previously peaceful areas held by Syria's moderate opposition in order to drive more refugees towards Germany and Europe. Crushing Isis, if it were on Putin's list, was somewhere at the bottom.

As some MPs had long argued, a proper response to the report would be to introduce the UK's own Magnitsky list. Like the US administration in 2012, Downing Street was perfectly capable of banning Russian officials and entities associated with Litvinenko's murder. Given that many of them had connections with London, this would be a powerful weapon.

Marina Litvinenko was proposing exactly that. As Owen's report went live, Marina sent a private letter to Downing Street, via the government's legal department. In it she called for a 'firm response'. This was needed, she argued, to 'secure accountability, to deter others from attempting something like this again, and to properly protect the British public'. She invited the prime minister to consider Ukraine-style sanctions against named Russian officials, with asset freezes and visa bans.

She had a list. It featured Putin, Patrushev and Ivanov. And those involved in the polonium chain, including companies: Rosatom, the state nuclear energy corporation; its head Sergei Kirienko; the boss of the Avangard laboratory, Radii Ilykaev; Tenex, Rosatom's export division; and Tenex's former CEO, Vladimir Smirnov. Plus an assortment of Russian politicians and prosecutors including prosecutor general Yuri Chaika (the man who in 2006 gave Scotland Yard detectives the run-around) and Alexander Bastrykin, investigative committee chairman.

From Russia, meanwhile, came a glacial response. Lugovoi told Interfax: 'The results released today just show London's anti-Russian position once again; the narrowness and lack of desire among the British to find the real reason for the death of Litvinenko.' Dmitry Peskov, Putin's press spokesman, was mocking. He dismissed the inquiry as a 'quasi-investigation'. And ridiculed the judge's use of 'probably', calling the report an example of 'subtle English humour'.

The Foreign Office summoned Russia's ambassador, Alexander Yakovenko, for the dressing-down usual in such cases. Emerging afterwards, the ambassador defiantly accused his British partners of a 'gross provocation' that would hurt bilateral ties. The inquiry had 'whitewashed' the incompetence of Britain's spy agencies, he told Russian TV. Sergei Lavrov, Russia's foreign minister, talked of groundless accusations and unanswered questions. It was 'a farce'.

The Russian blogosphere hummed with alternative explanations, many of them peddled by salaried Kremlin internet trolls working out of a glassy office in St Petersburg. Their argument: the inquiry was clearly a sham, since some of its sessions were held in secret. Oh, and Litvinenko was actually killed by MI6 and Alex Goldfarb.

Russia's state of denial put one in mind of King Leontes in *The Winter's Tale*, after the oracle proclaims his wife Hermione chaste and him a 'jealous tyrant'. Leontes declares: 'There is no truth at all i' the oracle … this is mere falsehood.'

As might have been predicted, the Kremlin's reaction was the old cocktail of bluster, evasion and conspiracy theory. For anyone who bothered to look, however, the truth was just a mouse click away. The report was published on the inquiry's website. Owen's conclusions and final statement were translated into Russian.

It was, all in all, a model document. Owen's argument was easy to follow; his prose clear and candid. There were arresting passages. For example: 'It is, to put it mildly, unusual when inquiring into a death to have available lengthy transcripts of interviews with the deceased, conducted shortly before his death.' Or: 'It is apparent that Mr Litvinenko was not mourned long in Russia, at least not by the government.' There were outings for Latinate words: sometimes a fact would 'fortify' his reasoning; Litvinenko faced 'posthumous opprobrium'.

Beyond this, one got the sense of a strong judicial personality working calmly through the evidence. It was evidence, Owen made clear, that led him to the view that Kovtun and Lugovoi were murderers. When the evidence was inconclusive he found in Russia's favour: he couldn't conclude, on the facts available, that Moscow had deliberately frustrated Scotland Yard's inquiries. The Met had 'painstakingly pieced together' the last weeks of Litvinenko's life, using conventional methods as well as 'unprecedented sources', like alpha radiation.

Much hinged on what precisely happened in London. The judge accepted that Lugovoi and Kovtun's refusal to give oral evidence to the inquiry didn't necessarily mean they killed Litvinenko. But he took a dim view of the contradictory accounts they'd given over the years. He dismissed these versions – one of which had Litvinenko grabbing the Pine Bar teapot, and gulping down two cups of tea – as having 'serious deficiencies'. They were consistent with 'a deliberate attempt to mislead'.

Owen found that one or both men had lied about important details. In an interview with the German tabloid *Bild*, Lugovoi claimed the Pine Bar was fitted out with surveillance equipment ('he was lying'). Lugovoi said that Litvinenko had repeatedly rung him ('it's plain from the telephone schedule that Mr Lugovoi and Mr Kovtun were wrong about this'). The judge dismissed too Kovtun's 'elaborate' explanation as to why he called C2, the cook, in London. Kovtun claimed he wanted to offer C2 a job at a Moscow fish restaurant ('a tissue of lies'; 'fabricated').

By contrast, Owen found the testimony given by D3, Kovtun's Hamburg restaurant manager friend, to be credible: 'Mr Kovtun's boast that he was planning to poison Mr Litvinenko with "*a very expensive poison*" may have appeared outlandish to D3, but there is a wealth of independent evidence before me that shows that that is exactly what he was planning to do.' He went on: 'Making unwise comments is something Mr Kovtun appears to have done from time to time.'

Again and again, the report returned to the polonium trail. The forensic evidence was 'highly compelling', the judge found. In part six, under the question 'Who administered the poison?', he ruled that the two Russians had indeed handled Po-210 in three of their London hotel rooms. They had even got into a 'routine' connected with the 'preparation and/or disposal' of the poison. In the Millennium and Best Western hotels, the 'natural inference' was that they had tipped it 'down the sink'.

Sometimes Owen made no finding, especially if the subject was on the margin of his inquiry. If the judge didn't know something he said so. One intriguing example: when Litvinenko arrived at the Millennium Hotel, Lugovoi made a six-minute call to Vladimir Voronoff. Voronoff was an ex-Soviet 'diplomat' who was based in the early 1990s at the Soviet embassy in London. He is now a British citizen. His testimony to the inquiry was evasive. Why the call? 'It is unexplained,' Owen wrote.

The other central part was nine – 'Who directed the killing?' Owen ruled out many of the fantastical theories supplied by Moscow: Berezovsky, the mafia, Chechens and the UK's own spy agencies. There were 'several reasons', however, why the Kremlin might want him dead, not least the 'undoubted personal dimension' to Litvinenko and Putin's antagonism. A core theme was Litvinenko's claim that the FSB carried out the 1999 apartment bombings ('an area of particular sensitivity for the Putin administration'). The judge said he was satisfied that by 2006, Putin, the FSB, and those around, 'had motives for taking action'.

But what had prompted them to act? Owen diverged from Emmerson's view: that there was a causative link between Litvinenko's scandalous Ivanov report and his subsequent murder. 'The difficulty is in the timing,' the judge noted. Litvinenko gave Lugovoi his report in late September 2006; it was only a matter of days afterwards that Lugovoi and Kovtun made arrangements for their first trip to London. Still, Owen conceded that the Ivanov dossier 'may have provided extra motivation and impetus to a plan that had already been conceived'.

It was more likely, in his view, that the plot to assassinate Litvinenko was cooked up earlier, possibly much earlier. Lugovoi had first flown to London to meet with Litvinenko as far back as October 2004. Owen: 'I regard it is entirely possible that Mr Lugovoi was already at that stage involved in a plan to target Mr Litvinenko, perhaps with a view to killing him.' There was 'no evidence at all' that either Kovtun or Lugovoi had 'any personal reason' for murder. Someone else had directed the 'protracted and costly operation'.

From the High Court, the protagonists minus Sir Robert headed across Holborn to Gray's Inn Road and the offices of Matrix Chambers, Emmerson's law firm. Here, Marina and Anatoly gave a small press conference. Marina thanked her son for his 'extraordinary support'. She said she found the government's non-response to

Owen's report unpersuasive. Yes, Russia played a role in international relations. But this was no reason to ignore the judge's 'very important message', she said.

Emmerson pointed out that David Cameron had always taken a tough line on terrorism, promising that he had 'zero tolerance' for this modern scourge. It appeared, the QC suggested, that Cameron was only tough on terrorism done by non-state actors.

'It would be surprising if the prime minister, who prides himself in keeping London safe from terrorism, could sit on his hands in the face of a judicial finding of state-sponsored terrorism. I don't think the British people think this is the right outcome.' As it was, he risked looking cowardly. 'It would be the abdication of his responsibility to do the thing which is the first function of a state: to keep its citizens safe.'

Others, including Bill Browder, said the UK government was making an error that might later haunt it. In a letter to the prime minister, Browder argued: 'Had this attack been perpetrated by Isis or al-Qaida there would be bombing runs, huge intelligence operations and pledges to never let it happen again.' Cameron's analysis was wrong: 'Putin and others like him look for weakness wherever they can find it.' The government's inaction, he wrote, would embolden Putin and 'surely lead to more killings on British soil'.

In the wake of Owen's report there was recognition that neither of Litvinenko's killers would face a jail cell in the near future. 'It would only be possible after the final fall of Vladimir Putin. It's inconceivable he could send

them for trial after he sent them to commit a murder,'
Emmerson said. And what about Putin? Might he
stand trial in the international court? The short answer,
according to Emmerson, was no.

The lawyer had a word of caution, though. 'History
shows us that political sands shift. People who seem
invincible suddenly find themselves on the receiving end
of an indictment. Mr Putin is not in a position to sit
comfortably.'

In the meantime, Marina was going to sue the Russian
government in London. Inevitably, Moscow would claim
state immunity. Nevertheless, Emmerson thought, there
was a reasonable chance of success. She would also revive
a 2007 claim made against the Kremlin in the European
Court of Human Rights in Strasbourg. To anyone who
had been following the case, it was obvious that Marina
was broke. She had, for some years, been living on a
pittance. She was entitled to compensation from Russia,
Emmerson said. He added that MI6 hadn't made her an
ex gratia payment.

Afterwards, I met Marina in a side-room. We kissed
on the cheek. Through high windows came a delicate
winter light; you could see trees, a moving car, city life.
It had been an overwhelming morning. Minutes earlier,
Anatoly had shifted uncomfortably when asked what he
remembered of his father. 'It isn't easy. It's still difficult
for him,' she told me, adding that he was months away
from his final summer exams.

Had she expected that Owen's report would be so
bold? 'We looked at it and thought: "Yes!" It surprised

us.' Not because she disagreed with his conclusions, but because few people were willing to accuse Putin so directly. 'It was a very strong message,' she said. Marina added the classified intelligence material – which she hadn't seen – was decisive, adding: 'One day we will know the details.'

The report marked another victory, over sceptics who doubted that she could beat Britain's political establishment, which had fought her most of the way. 'We have achieved a tremendous amount. So many people said: "You'll never get an inquiry. It won't happen." Then they didn't believe Sir Robert would deliver his report. Now we have hard facts. I feel very emotional.'

She acknowledged that Sasha's murder would invariably be seen as a 'political moment' and another low in the UK's eternally vexed relations with Moscow. But, she said: 'For me it's personal. I was able to get through all these long years because it was my personal case. It was my husband who was killed. It was my thirst to know who killed him and who was responsible.'

I wondered if she could envisage ever going back to Russia. 'I very much miss my mother, who is now alone,' she replied. In the summer of 2015, shortly after the inquiry wound up, her father died. 'I couldn't go to the funeral. I realised you had to pay the "price". Unfortunately, the price is I cannot go to Russia.' The current political reality, she said, meant that she didn't 'feel safe there'. The danger wasn't only from the state: it was possible a 'patriot' might take matters into his own hands.

She said her conflict was never with her fellow Russians – or her Moscow friends, whom she misses. Rather it was with the regime. 'I wish Russia to be a successful place, a happy country,' she said. She saw herself as a real patriot, in contrast to the phoney ones inside the Kremlin who typically have secret property in the west and offshore bank accounts. 'I want my son one day to go back to Russia, to do something in Russia, to be proud of Russia,' she said.

Sir Robert's report had brought to an end an almost ten-year saga of international intrigue and Cold War-style recrimination. At the end of it: vindication. Marina quoted from what Litvinenko had said in his dying declaration: that Putin might snuff out one man but not 'the howls of protest from around the world'. 'I believe what my husband Sasha said. You can of course silence one person. But you can't silence the world.'

A Note on Sources

The Litvinenko inquiry website, www.litvinenkoinquiry. org, is an invaluable source of information about the Litvinenko case, much of it used in this book. For more than eight years, details of Scotland Yard's murder investigation remained secret. Now the evidence is publicly available: witness statements, including Litvinenko's; a forensic report into every location contaminated by polonium; testimony by expert scientists; police interviews with the two killers in Moscow. The website features transcripts of all thirty-four days of hearings at the High Court, and the evidence of sixty-two witnesses.

This was one of the UK's most extensive murder inquiries. Many details are remarkable. The Met's modelling department mapped radiation readings onto graphic 3D reconstructions of key locations. We can see for the first time the object used to murder Litvinenko. (The actual photo reveals an ordinary white ceramic teapot. The graphic version is a lurid purple; purple is the colour code used to illustrate deadly levels of alpha radiation.)

There is CCTV footage of Litvinenko arriving at the Millennium Hotel; it freezes the moment before he was poisoned. Plus phone logs that confirm Dmitry Kovtun, one of history's more inept murderers, was looking for a cook to administer what he called 'a very expensive

poison'. We get some of the official record: confidential e-grams from Britain's ambassador in Moscow; a
brush-off from the Home Office to Litvinenko's solicitor, in the wake of death threats from Moscow. And
Litvinenko's own writings and interviews.

The evidence we are missing belongs to the UK
government. This was presented in secret to Sir Robert
Owen. It informed his final report, but wasn't made
public. I asked one former MI6 officer when the agency's files on Litvinenko might be released. He replied:
'Never.' He added: 'We haven't declassified anything
since the beginning of the service in 1909.' These documents might compromise serving agents, he said.

Still, we live in an era of large data leaks: Edward
Snowden, WikiLeaks, the banking secrets of the rich
and powerful. I'm confident that the files will eventually
find their way into daylight. (If anyone wants to hasten
this process, please send me what you can in a brown
envelope.) Inside Russia there are likely to be few written
documents: state murder is a clandestine business;
Stalin's instruction to assassinate Trotsky was delivered
orally. But when Putin's reign in Russia ends, new details
may emerge, including from inside the FSB itself.

Most of the quotations in this book come from two
primary sources: my conversations with those involved,
and their public evidence before the inquiry. I'm grateful
to the following who agreed to be interviewed: Marina
and Anatoly Litvinenko; Alex Goldfarb; Ben Emmerson;
Yuli Dubov; Nikolai Glushkov; Viktor Suvorov; Vladimir
Bukovsky; Akhmed Zakayev; Olga Kryshtanovskaya;

Professor Norman Dombey; Bill Browder; and others. One or two of my interlocutors didn't want to be named.

In Moscow, I interviewed Andrei Lugovoi twice, in 2008 and 2010, and Dmitry Kovtun in 2008. In Italy, I interviewed Litvinenko's father and siblings. Before their deaths I met Boris Nemtsov, in Sochi, and Boris Berezovsky, in London.

I give a fuller account of the harassment my family and I faced in Moscow in my 2011 book *Mafia State: How One Reporter Became an Enemy of the Brutal New Russia* (published in the US in 2012 as *Expelled*). Some details are retold here when they are relevant to Litvinenko's story. Others are new: the fact that I inadvertently flew to Moscow on Lugovoi's polonium plane, sitting a few rows away from his contaminated seat.

I'm grateful to my colleagues at the *Guardian* – especially Kath Viner, Paul Johnson and Jamie Wilson – for allowing me to combine book writing with international reporting. And to Laura Hassan and my wonderful publisher Guardian Faber. Most of all, thanks to my wife Phoebe Taplin, my first and best reader.

Acknowledgements and Photo Credits

The author would like to thank:

Fiona Bacon, Louis Blom-Cooper, Robert Booth, Irina Borogan, Oliver Bullough, Barbara Caspar, Paula Chertok, Lindsay Davies, Lizzy Davies, Martin Dewhirst, Norman Dombey, Ben Emmerson, Michael Fleischer, David Godwin, Alex Goldfarb, Felicity Harding, John Harding, Laura Hassan, Henning Hoff, David Leigh, Anatoly Litvinenko, Marina Litvinenko, Robin Milner-Gulland, Peter Neyroud, Richard Norton-Taylor, Robert Service, Alex Shprintsen, Andrei Soldatov, Adam Straw, Phoebe Taplin, Andrei Terekhov, Elena Tsirlina, Cyril Tuschi, Federico Varese, Shaun Walker, Jamie Wilson.

Index

(the initials AL refer to Alexander Litvinenko)